Dedicated to

*My husband, Hendrik, my pillar of strength & stability.
And my two children, Noah & Sarah, my heart
outside of my body.*

GW00480792

Second Edition | September 2021

A letter from Caitlyn
the author

For as long as I can remember I have found solace in the ocean, in breathing in the salty air, hearing the roar of waves crashing, watching as the sets roll in and feeling the sand between my toes. It was during one of the toughest seasons of my life, when facing a physical condition that had me feeling hopeless, that God reminded me that He is living water, He calms the seas. He empowers us to walk out on the water, and He leads us beside quiet streams.

A close friend challenged me amidst my hardship to return to a place where I hear God's voice the clearest, and so we spent a weekend at our beach house to recoup and reconnect with God. I was hopeless, depressed, in physical pain and living under grey skies, but that's often where God meets us. His grace is found exactly where we are. God began to speak to me about suffering. He reminded me that my faith does not exclude me from suffering but that my hope is eternal. He spoke to me of Him being living water and that nothing on Earth would ever fill me like He can. I knew this deep down but I suppose life had caused me to forget. And then He laid a desire on my heart to write this devotional; a letter of love about our King. He is enough for you. For me. His grace is that good, His love that deep. Nothing can separate us from His love, which is found in Jesus. He is the happiness and the peace that our soul thirsts for.

May this devotional be a source of hope and encouragement to you on your faith journey. May it draw you closer to Jesus, and may it reignite a flame within you that burns to see God's will done on earth.

All my love,

Caitlyn x

Instagram | @caitlyndebeer

Foreword One

"The one who believes in me, as the Scripture has said,
will have streams of living water flow from deep within him."
- *John 7:38*

Water: the essential component for nourishment and life.

In the scriptures, God is described as the stream of living water, the source of life and salvation to those who come to Him. As you read this daily devotional, may you thirst for the One who is the source of all life. As you turn to the scriptures, may God quench the deep thirst of your soul by pouring His Spirit into your heart. And may you find that living water runs deep, flows within and nourishes you for life.

I trust that Caitlyn's devotional will act as a conduit between you, the power of the scriptures and the Living God; the source of all life.

Caitlin Barnes

*Co-Lead Pastor at West Point Church
& Founder of Anvil and the Altar*

Foreword Two

Reading the title of Caitlyn's book, *Walk out on the Water*, my heart stopped. These were words I have become so familiar with this year.

2020 turned out to be the challenge none of us expected. It was also the year that I moved, with my family, to a small Channel Island called Jersey. 01.01.2020 - we landed on the island, expecting a year of adventure, hope and excitement. Nothing could be further from the truth.

At every turn we were challenged. One night I woke from a panicked dream - terrified about how we would survive in this foreign land with the unexpected challenges COVID delivered. In my half-sleep, I saw myself stepping out of a fishing boat to walk on water but as I took that first step I began to sink. Then, I clearly heard Jesus say to me, "Look up." A simple instruction to look full in His wonderful face, to trust Him alone. This image had been my encouragement every time I have faltered since.

So, when on a flight back to Jersey in October, Caitlyn's book launch invite landed on my lap, I knew it was our Lord reaching out to me again. I cannot say that looking up in faith is easy. I am often full of doubt and dread, but I do know that the only way that I can 'walk out on the water' is through faith.

I have found when dipping through this wonderful daily devotional, that Caitlyn shares simple, clear messages of hope, faith, comfort and love. I know that for the journey of walking in faith - out on the water - this book will go a long way to encouraging me daily in my walk with God. May it be so for you, too.

Meg Fawre

OT & Author of Sense-series

Foreword Three

As women, and even more so as moms, we live our lives on empty... We give all of ourselves to the ones we love, and those that rely on us, easily running dry, trying our best to pour from an empty cup. A cup we try our best to fill with mom hacks, cleaning schedules, meal plans, daily routines, wellness habits and whatever current fad catches our attention.

Yet, the only thing of value we could ever fill our cup with is the living water that is Christ. Water that never runs dry. Water that will quench our thirst with mere drops. And water that is always available to all of us.

May this devotional bring you closer to the never-ending well that is Christ's love. May your cup overflow and may this book awaken a new desire for God's life-giving water and His will for our lives.

The day is today, the year is now. It's your moment to draw near to God, inviting Him into every season and area of your life.

Mari-Louise Candiotes

South African Parenting Blogger
& Founder of Just A Mamma

JANUARY

living waters

"Whoever believes in Me, as Scripture
has said, rivers of living water will
flow from within them"
- John 7:38

"Now, no shrub had yet appeared on the earth and no plant had yet sprung up, for the Lord God had not sent rain on the Earth and there was no one to work the ground, but streams came up from the Earth and watered the whole surface of the ground."
- *Genesis 2:5-6*

This is the first page of this devotional but also the first page of your book called 'my year'. The pages ahead are blank, full of opportunity, promise and hope. The year awaits much like an open body of water, ready for you to dive in – to explore, discover wonders, find joy, be refreshed, perhaps struggle through waves but moreover to float with arms stretched wide and eyes fixed to the sky.

An ocean swim on the first day of the year is a non-negotiable for me. I love the therapeutic feeling of diving into the sea and allowing the water to wash over me. It's almost as if the past year is washed away and I am alert and ready for what the New Year will hold. In the beginning of the Bible, God transforms a bleak, uninhabited wilderness into a garden through a stream that waters the ground.

May you allow this analogy to unfold for you in your own way, especially today. Find freedom today in knowing that Jesus is the living water that flows through your blood. He waters your heart, your soul and your spirit and prepares you for a life of abundance.

As you dive into this New Year with plans and dreams, bring yourself before Jesus and let Him refill you with His living water.

———

Jesus, I fix my eyes on You today. Come and quench my thirst and fill me with deep contentment as I enter this New Year. Amen

Foundations over resolutions

"Because I am righteous, I will see You. When I awake, I will see You face to face and be satisfied."
- Psalm 17:15

New Year's resolutions are often the centre point of every conversation at this time of year. If you're anything like me though, you probably spend the first part of the year resenting yourself for giving in to chocolate, working long hours or remaining critical. Then by March you start each week with a "On a Monday I'm...". By June you throw in the towel and decide that this 'change' is clearly not for this current year and that you will try again next year. It is only in the second half of the year that you actually start loving yourself again. And by 'love' I don't mean just giving in to your 'grumpy inner child' who got you to eat everything in sight for the first half of the year. But actually, by August, you find you're kinder to yourself and actually enjoying life a little more.

Self-compassion is God's idea. God isn't into us chasing our tails in an attempt to find inner peace – He is peace, and He lives in us.

Just as the man who built his house upon the sand learnt that when storms rage, foundations are key; so too, we need to ensure that that on which we are building, is steadfast. Chasing goals can feel empowering but reaching them will never provide the true peace we long for. That space is only for Jesus to fill.

———

Father help me to build on powerful foundations this year, rather than believing in the notion that achieving goals will bring me peace. Amen

Fill your love tank

"As the Father has loved Me, so have I loved you. Now remain in My love."
- John 15:9

There is a lagoon on the beach that we call home. For some seasons it remains closed off from the sea. But then the summer rains come and eventually its borders break and what starts as a trickle towards the ocean, turns into a mighty constant flow. If this lagoon were to remain open year-round, the life on its banks and in its stream would suffer.

Our year ahead can be compared to this lagoon. If we live this year running from ourselves and pouring into the lives of others at our own expense, we will eventually run dry. The effect of pouring from an empty cup is devastating on our physical, mental and spiritual selves, on our closest relationships and on our circle of influence. But as we keep boundaries in place and allow Jesus to fill our love and energy tanks, so eventually our borders will break open naturally and our love will overflow into the world.

Let us be encouraged early in the New Year, to ensure that our love and energy tanks are full, before we begin allowing them to overflow.

Jesus, help me to take this year slowly, allowing You to fill me up, before I move into the World as Your hands and feet. Amen

Creative juices

"I will instruct you and teach you in the way you should go; I will counsel you with My loving eye on you."
- Psalm 32:8

Whilst the temptation is always there to believe that a new year equates to a whole new you; it's unrealistic and sets us up for failure. Instead, let's approach this new year with wisdom and intent.

Walt Disney described his team as 'imagineers' and I believe that there is an imagineer in each of us. God is creative by nature; we need to merely open our window or look in the mirror to know the depth of our creative God. And God has placed creativity within you, too. It may be visible, or it could be hiding within, waiting to be shared with the World.

A lovely way to approach a new year is to ask God to confirm your values for the year ahead. I love creating a picture vision board for each new year and I build this around the key values in my life that year. Our future lies in the hands of our Heavenly Father, but He also loves to teach and guide us as we walk along life's path.

Enjoy being creative with a vision board this week. Perhaps a written word, a paragraph, an image or a collage of images. Allow God to inspire this project and do it in a way that feels right for you.

Father, thank You for Your hand in teaching and guiding me into this year. Amen

5ᵗʰ January

Potential over problems

"You are their glorious strength.
It pleases You to make us strong."
- Psalm 89:17

It is not uncommon to enter a new year with a list of problems or glitches that we hope to solve. Habits we want to break, friendships we want to adjust or careers we want to change; but as individual as our lives are, we too are part of a greater mission.

God is at work already; He doesn't wait for a new year to begin a new project. We have the privilege of joining forces with our Father, as we seek out potential in the year to come rather than mere problem solving. God is doing things in and around you, and He longs for you to be a part of His mission. Open your heart and eyes to what He is doing and join the greatest mission of all, this year.

Ask God what He is already doing and how you can join His mission this year. Let's be builders of something remarkable, not just demolishers of internal walls.

———

Father show me where and with what You're at work, so that I can join Your mission and take my eyes off myself for a minute and keep the big picture as my guide. Amen

Walking in the light

> "When Jesus spoke again to the people, He said, 'I am the light of the world. Whoever follows me will never walk in darkness but will have the light of life.'"
> - John 8:12

There is little that compares to the beauty of a sunrise or sunset. It is in the light that we feel most free. It is in the light that we flourish; safe and secure. Light is a beautiful phenomenon that is spoken of so often in the Bible.

We are encouraged as followers of Jesus to the walk in the light. I love the action included here. We are not to sit in the light, but to walk, meaning to take action, to move. Our faith and journey with Jesus move us, it never leaves us the same.

What does it look like for you, to walk in the light this year? For me, it's less about following rules and more about the state of my heart and mind. When my heart and mind are aligned with Jesus, I find it easy to let go of selfish ambition that so easily leads to darkness, or secrets, or stagnating.

Be encouraged today. Jesus is the light of the world and will fill your heart and mind with light as you seek Him out, every day.

Father lead me into the light, as I set my heart and mind on following You. Amen

7th January

A great waterfall

"His voice was like the roar of rushing waters, and the land was radiant with His glory."
- Ezekiel 43:2

Too often we are told of the quiet voice of God, but this can cause us to perceive God as only meek and mild. Yes, and amen to quieting ourselves in order to hear God speak but this is no discreet God that we are waiting on. Rarely is His voice audible, but there is enormous power behind God's voice, no matter the way He speaks to us.

In other translations of today's scripture, God's voice is referred to as a great waterfall. I think what I love most about Ezekiel's reference to God's voice as a great waterfall or rushing waters, is the power I immediately parallel between the two. God's voice may be a quiet whisper, but it does not lack in clarity, depth or life. Yes, we serve a God who is merciful and kind, but He is also powerful. A God who holds the world in His hands and has the power to turn off the 'lights' when He sees fit.

May we humbled today by the might of the God we serve. As we seek Him out in our daily lives, may we be reminded of His grandeur and His holiness.

God, open my ears today to hear the words of life that You are whispering over me. Amen

8th January

Remove your blinkers

*"Dear friends, now we are children of God…
we know that when Christ appears, we shall
be like Him, for we shall see Him as He is."*
- 1 John 3:2-3

Many of us live within our own prisons; walls created by negative thinking, small mindedness and sometimes even just settling for what is comfortable. When we practice curiosity with faith, we broaden those boundaries – it allows us to push past the clouds and helps us to see the view of from the summit. Curiosity is to discover the potential for your life, with your hope firmly grounded in Jesus and thus not limited by an earthly perspective.

Practicing curiosity with faith is like removing our blinkers, the boxes that we fit into, that say 'do this' or 'don't ever try that.' It gives us courage to take steps that we previously may have cowered away from. It adds an element of excitement to experiences that could otherwise seem daunting. Living out curiosity with faith challenges us to live free, to live bold, to live true to who we are. To explore, to discover, and to be vulnerable in our pursuit of Jesus, life and what we find of interest.

As you walk by faith, you will continually become more curious. And as you begin to seek out God in everything, He will meet you there with His goodness and you will begin to see His hand at work, everywhere.

Father, as You draw me to Yourself, stoke the fire of curiosity within me to seek You out in all that I do and to see You in everything. Amen

Character over sacrifice

"The Lord is more pleased when
we do what is right and just than
when we offer Him sacrifices."
- Proverbs 21:3

I learnt a valuable lesson in a trail race a few years back.

I was running this race with my husband and a close friend of mine. It was my first long run since having kids, so I was taking strain. At about 20kms in, we hit a fork in the path. It was poorly marked, and we had no idea which way was the correct route. We chose to go left down a steep hill rather than right onto a single track. As we hit the bottom of this hill, we realized that we'd overtaken the female leaders who had taken the 400m roundabout route on single track. We had a decision to make. We could keep going and explain at the end that we took a shortcut, we could claim our newfound leader positions and put foot, or we could backtrack up the hill and do the extra 400m. We chose the latter, which wasn't appealing after 20kms of a hilly trail race, but we knew we'd done the right thing.

Life often offers us short cuts; easier ways to get successful or make money fast. This year will no doubt have moments when you're faced with opportunity for short-cuts. But jumping the gun rarely builds character. God is far more into character building than He is into short cuts or even sacrifices.

Father give me strength and endurance to run the race marked out for me and to not be tempted into taking shortcuts that don't serve me, or You. Amen

Rivers of living water

"Whoever believes in Me, as Scripture has said, rivers of living water will flow from within them"
- John 7:38

The ocean has forever been a place of solace for me; a place of safety, always refreshing and refuelling. The seas may roar, the storms may roll in, the waves may crash but then there are the moments between sets, when the sea is still, the horizon present and all is well.

Life in many ways is like this too. Struggles we will face, waves of emotion will wash over us, but as we take it all before Jesus, He will refuel, He will refresh, He promises to quench your deep thirst and reminds you of the abundance of life in and with Him. I love today's scripture and how we are reminded that whilst Jesus is living water, He too promises that as we believe in Him, living water will flow within us.

God is the only true source of living water and He is calling you to walk beside quiet waters with Him this year. Ask Him today what this means for you personally as you begin this year.

Lord, help me to personally internalize this message that living water is within me. I love you Jesus. Amen

You in the crowd

> "'You aren't one of this man's disciples too, are you?' she asked Peter. He replied, 'I am not.' It was cold, and the servants and officials stood around a fire they had made to keep warm. Peter also was standing with them, warming himself."
> - John 18:17-18

Isn't it amazing how memories are often connected to emotions? This takes place due to the way that memories are stored in our brains, often together with other characteristics of a situation. When I read today's scripture, I am immediately transported back to my Primary School years, when we spent many an evening having bonfires on the beach. Living in a small town, our bonfires often consisted of a range of children and teens, and being at a susceptible age to peer pressure, I remember always wanting to fit in with the older crowd.

In today's scripture we read how Peter denies knowing Jesus. But what was recently suggested to me is that perhaps it was Peter's desire to fit in, that caused him to change his position or character that day. He denied Jesus as it meant that he would thus not stand out in the crowd around him. How often do we do this even as adults too?

Let's approach this year with the conviction of who we are, and a challenge in our hearts to remain the same person, regardless of who we are surrounded by.

Jesus, You are the same today, yesterday and tomorrow. Help me, this year, to find comfort in knowing my identity in You and bravery to not feel pressure to conform to fit in and compromise who I am. Amen

Understanding God

"Oh, the depth of the riches of the wisdom and knowledge of God!"
- Romans 11:33

A wise man once said that the goal of communication is not agreement but rather understanding. Our communication with God should be the same. As we seek to communicate with God, we should make it our goal to understand God better. We are made in His image. As we seek to understand Him better, we also understand ourselves better. It's a win-win. Don't limit your understanding and experience of God to just a book, or a place or Christmas day. Dig in deeper because the diamonds that He wants you to find are not on the surface.

Jesus is the living water that runs through our blood. He is the model that we get to follow of how to live our lives. God is our Father, our King and our Creator. The Holy Spirit is our inner guide, our conviction and our helper. But together they are one. Three but one. Understanding the Trinity and the role that each part plays in our lives is part of understanding and communicating with God.

Understanding the trinity can provide us with access to the greatest force on earth, and the truest form of love.

Father, You are love and I was made in Your image. Help me to understand Your character more that I may too understand myself better. Amen

Walk towards Jesus

"He has shown you…what is good. And what does the Lord require of you? To act justly and to love mercy and to walk humbly with your God."
- *Micah 6:8*

Walk away, but also be sure to walk towards something.

Walking away is a powerful way to reinforce personal boundaries, but it can also lead to a hardened heart, resentment or even deeper sadness. To walk towards something is empowering. It is to take action, but in a direction that you intentionally choose.

This month and year ahead let us…
Walk away from fear, from judgmental people, from arguments and from gossip. Walk away from things that are toxic to your mind and cause your soul to be discouraged. Walk towards the one who is eager to love you. Walk towards the one who is the author of love, your creator but not your puppet master. Walk towards the one who longs to inspire your brilliant mind with new ideas and fresh perspective. Walk towards the one who understands your intricacies, your quirks and requires no explanation for your personality. Walk towards the one who put dreams in your heart before you were even born, and longs to bring those to fulfilment. Walk towards Jesus.

May the year ahead be one of walking away from that which no longer serves you but mostly walking towards the One who holds your heart.

———

Father draw me closer to You, that I may know You and in turn know me. Amen

Water is life

"He said to me, 'This water flows toward the eastern region…where it enters the Dead Sea. When it empties into the sea, the salty water there becomes fresh. Swarms of living creatures will live wherever the river flows. There will be large numbers of fish, because this water flows there and makes the saltwater fresh; so, where the river flows everything will live.'"
- Ezekiel 47:8-9

Where the river flows, everything will live. Where Jesus is present, everything is alive. Us too. Jesus is living water. He is life. We all know the concept of referring to someone social as being 'the life of the party'. Where there is life, there is fullness. The chase for success in the world has proven again and again to leave us dissatisfied. Jesus is the only one who can breathe life into us, a fullness of life that sustains. Jesus can make us feel most alive within ourselves - the very thing that many of us have craved from the moment we were born.

When we commit our lives to Jesus, we are filled with living water and we carry His Holiness and His righteousness. As we are filled by Him, we then become a source of life for others. But we need to constantly come back to the river, to Jesus, to be refilled, so that our cup will overflow into the lives of others and we won't feel burnt out by pouring from an empty cup.

I encourage you to read the full chapter found in Ezekiel 47. Know that as you are made new in Christ, you are filled with His presence and living water. You are alive!

Jesus, fill me up afresh today. Allow me to feel most alive so that wherever I go I bring life. Amen

15th January

Dare to dream

"Commit to the Lord whatever you do, and He will establish your plans."
- Proverbs 16:3

Whilst I'm a stickler for rules, I'm also hugely competitive, so I rarely turn down a dare. My husband often tells the story of us walking through a market in Chiang Mai, Thailand, and him betting me R5 that I wouldn't eat a fried cockroach. It's safe to say that I walked away R5 richer.

While this story is more on the amusing side, I want to encourage you this year to dare to dream again. I have a friend who does the most remarkable motivational talk on daring to dream. She challenges us to see beyond what seems possible, imagine it in our minds eye and then begin to take small steps towards this one-day big dream. She tells of how she did this when growing up in a rural town in KZN, dreaming of sailing the world. She is now a ship captain and Africa's first Female dredge master, who has indeed sailed the world.

It takes deep courage to dream. Dreaming can be risky. But dreaming can also open your eyes to a potential future you may never have walked towards.

I encourage you today to take just one step forward in pursuing a dream on your heart right now.

———

Father, please ignite the dreams on my heart that are on Your heart too and give me the courage to dare to dream a little more. Amen

Return to Him

"'Now return to me, and I will return to you,' says the Lord of Heaven's armies."
- Malachi 3:7

I remember a time in my life when the presence of God felt distant, and I believed that my only way back to God was through Church or good works. This false belief only drew me further away from God as the road back felt too heavy and hard to journey.

All this changed one day when my heart suddenly shifted whilst having a conversation with a friend over an idea that I was wrestling with. God met me in my disbelief; His presence was real and tangible right there at our dining room table. There was no church. No fancy prayer. I had done nothing to deserve it. But there He was. That moment changed me. I realised that God doesn't want me to try harder or for my theology to be perfectly sound – He just wants me. And once I returned to Him, He then had access to my heart. The very heart He has since moulded and changing into something more beautiful than I had seen possible.

God is calling you to Himself today too. Wherever you're at right now, know that He is there and requires only that You call out His name.

––––––––

Father meet me in my messy world today. I give you my heart, change it to glorify You. Amen

The big picture

"And we know that in all things God works for the good of those who love Him, who have been called according to His purpose."
- Romans 8:28a

I was fortunate to be raised by parents who are big picture kind of people. I am grateful for the lessons they taught me in not getting anxious over things outside of one's control. As we keep the big picture in mind, the smaller more trivial things of our lives pale in comparison. This is not to say that the detail of life is unimportant, not at all. Every part of our lives is important to Jesus, but in order to remain stable, and less anxious, we can adopt a mindset of keeping the big picture, the big picture.

A big picture mindset empowers us to look at every situation that we face as if we have zoomed out and are looking from afar. It is with this perspective that we often make wiser decisions and are able to release the hold that anxiety has on many of us.

Be encouraged today to begin including the words 'zoom out' to your internal dialogue, especially when dealing with situations that usually cause you anxiety.

Father, guide me on a path to greater peace this year. Help me to keep in mind that which really does matter and to lay the remainder of my burdens at the Cross. Amen

Choose joy

"And this is my prayer: that Your love may abound more and more in knowledge and depth of insight."
- *Philippians 1:9*

Whether your January has started out on a positive note or a not so positive one, happiness remains a choice that you have access to.

We often assume that joy will return when a tough season of life passes, but the truth is that it's rarely that simple. Happiness isn't for a select few. Happiness isn't luck. Or chance. Or karma. There's no magic wand that we can wave that will suddenly land happiness in our lap. Happiness, or joy, is a choice. We choose every morning how we will frame our reality. The eyes that will see and then perceive that which lies before us.

Joy comes in the morning but not because things are different then. No. After a good night's rest, or perhaps a restless one, we get a new chance to choose joy again. To choose happiness or stability or hope, despite our circumstances.

Let's begin today by living with authenticity, letting go of our chase for happiness and rather choosing joy as we embrace the mundane and the hope that we have in Jesus.

Jesus, You are my source of joy. You sustain my joy despite my circumstances. Help me to live with this in mind, today. Amen

The Lord is peace

"But the Lord said to him, 'Peace! Do not be afraid. You are not going to die.' So, Gideon built an altar to the Lord there and called it The Lord Is Peace."
- Judges 6:23-24

An angel appeared to Gideon to show him God's plan for deliverance for his people. Gideon then goes on to build an altar and calls God, 'Jehovah Shalom'. Jehovah Shalom meaning 'The Lord is peace'.

Peace is a phenomenon that many of us seek out day in and day out. Peace as we often know it in the world, is fleeting; it comes and goes much like any other emotion. It lasts only as long as our minds are at rest, only to be stolen a minute later by anxiety, shock, anger, doubt or disappointment. But the peace of God is different to this. God's peace surpasses understanding. God's peace is present even while we face uncomfortable emotions. God's peace is deeper; it stands against anything that challenges it. Peace is a gift, one we can accept right now and be wrapped in.

Find comfort and rest as you open your mind to be receptive to God's peace. May it wash over you and give you hope, despite your circumstances throughout this year.

Jesus, wash me in Your peace. Help me to be soaked in peace, that I may no longer be swayed by emotions but rather steady in my knowledge of You and what that means for me. Amen

An anchor

"We have this hope as an anchor for the soul, firm and secure."
- *Hebrews 6:19*

We often enter a new year with high hopes. We expect a year that will differ from the last, mostly in pain. We hope for less pain, for more joy. But unfortunately, life rarely goes as planned. Maturity in Christ is not a life free of pain but rather includes less striving for an easier life, and more acceptance of the hope that we have in Jesus, our future secured.

Whilst struggling with chronic pain and experiencing real hopelessness, God spoke to me about suffering. He reminded me that my faith does not exclude me from suffering but that my hope is eternal and that is my gift. He spoke to me of Him being living water and that nothing on earth would ever fill me like He can. I knew this deep down but comparing my present condition to others caused me to forget.

Be encouraged that your year may or may not be easy. The year may not go as planned. But you have access to a Great God, who loves you deeply, and has gone before you on the path that you are yet to walk. You are in safe hands.

Father God help me to trust You with my future and to walk by faith, whether through storms or fields of flowers. Amen

Mircales everyday

"By faith in the name of Jesus, this man whom you see and know, was made strong. It is Jesus' name and the faith that comes through Him that has completely healed him, as you can all see."
- Acts 3:16

One of my greatest faith tests and joys was a trip I did to Heidi Baker's mission base in Pemba, Mozambique. It was there that I saw my first physical miracles, and then more. I sobbed day in and day out, humbled to my core by the power of God. I'd never known faith to that degree. The power of God to make blind eyes see, lame children walk and deaf ears open.

Einstein said that there are two ways to look at life. One, as if nothing is a miracle or, as if everything is a miracle. Faith is our challenge to embrace life as a set of miracles; to expect goodness and hope and peace despite our circumstances. What a beautiful way to live, to not allow our circumstances, or suffering, or disappointments to stand in the way of the power of God.

Let's be encouraged to trust God despite what we face, and to expect miracles anew every day.

Father, make me aware of Your unfolding miracles every day. Amen

God is with us

> "'Because He will save His people from their sins.' All this took place to fulfil what the Lord had said through the prophet: 'The virgin will conceive and give birth to a son, and they will call Him Immanuel'(which means God with us)."
> - Matthew 1:22-23

God thought of us when He named and brought Jesus into the world. He told Joseph that his son would be called Immanuel – God is with us. How remarkable is this? The name that God chooses to give to His Son, before He is even born, is one that describes Him as God being with us (you and me).

Scripture is full of names that hold huge significance. In the scriptures, God is rarely just called God or Father but more often called names that suggest His character. As mentioned, today's scripture refers to Jesus as 'Immanuel' - God is with us. That is who Jesus is. He is God, with us. Let that sink in for a moment. God sent His son to Earth, to die a sinner's death, so that we could be with Him and He with us. That was who He was born to be. To be with you.

Ask God today to make this concept more tangible to you that you may know in the depths of your being, that He is with you! Always!

Jesus, thank You that You are Immanuel - You are God with us. Amen

23rd January

God nudges

"How beautiful are the feet of those who bring good news, who proclaim peace, who bring good tidings, who proclaim salvation, who say to Zion, 'Your God reigns!'"
- Isaiah 52:7

I was recently so encouraged when I heard of a powerful experience that a friend of mine's dad had.

He was sitting on a flight, overwhelmed by a business struggle that he was facing, but showing no outward expression of this inward wrestle, when suddenly he got a tap on the shoulder and handed a note from a stranger. The woman had written how God had told her to encourage him that God was with him in his struggle and that he was not alone. Naturally he was overcome with emotion. As I am, merely writing this. This woman's obedience to listen to God and be His hands here on Earth, gave this man the courage to walk the hard road ahead with unwavering hope.

Sometimes we'll be on the receiving end of such nudges, but other times we're called to literally be God's hand, nudging and encouraging others.

Ask God how He can use you today, to love on others as He loves you.

Jesus, thank You that I am Your daughter and I do hear Your voice. Speak to me, I am listening. Amen

Your best foot forward

> "You will be a crown of splendour in the Lord's hand, a royal diadem in the hand of your God. No longer will they call you Deserted or name your land Desolate… as a bridegroom rejoices over his bride, so will your God rejoice over you."
> *- Isaiah 62:3-4*

At the start of a new year, we all want to put our best foot forward.

The fear of man, or fear of rejection, is considered to be one of the greatest fears of mankind. If we crave acceptance from others it points to our inability to accept ourselves. The hold that acceptance or lack-there-of has on many of us, can be crippling. For some this is founded in physical appearance, others in the size of their home, others their Instagram following, others their career success, others their generosity scale or still others their kid's wardrobe or manners.

Worrying about what others think of us is not all bad. It's important that we take pride in who we are and how we present ourselves in the world, but not at the expense of our identity. You are NOT what you wear. You are NOT what you eat. You are NOT the size of your home. You are NOT the mom raising perfect children. These may be some characteristics that you possess but it is not who you are. You are a child of God.

Let this sink in for today - YOU are a child of God. Our highest reward on Earth is to please God. It is then, and only then, that our hearts will be at peace and our minds at rest.

Father help me to continuously assess this year where my identity lies. Help me to let go of comparison and to keep renewing my mind in the truth of who I am, in You. Amen

Let it be

"When anxiety was great within me,
Your consolation brought me joy."
- Psalm 94:19

Perhaps, like me, you read the heading for today and immediately begin singing the words to the song 'Let it be' by The Beatles. What an anthem to sing over our lives today, as we head into the final week of a rather long first month of the year.

It takes wisdom to truly let things be. Without wisdom or knowledge of God and His power in our lives, it is almost impossible to simply let things be. Control is an illusion but one that we all cling to for the false sense of security and safety that it masquerades as.

You get to choose right now to release your grip on control and the shackles it locks you into, and rather to lay everything before God and LET IT BE. This is a lifelong lesson that I don't think any of us will ever be proficient in, but we can, right now, choose to begin this letting go.

Begin today by bringing everything that is occupying space in your mind before God. Tell Him everything. Cry if you need to. And then trust Him to hold it all.

———

Father help me to trust You so deeply that my heart and mind begin to find freedom despite my circumstances. Amen

Open my heart

"One of those listening was a woman from the city of Thyatira named Lydia, a dealer in purple cloth. She was a worshiper of God. The Lord opened her heart to respond to Paul's message. When she and the members of her household were baptized, she invited us to her home. 'If you consider me a believer in the Lord,' she said, 'come and stay at my house.'"
- Acts 16:14-15

Lydia's story is a beautiful one to read and meditate on. Lydia had a family, was a businesswoman and was one of the first converts to Christianity. Knowing that Lydia dealt in purple cloth reveals that she was likely a wealthy woman and yet in today's scripture, she happily opens her home to strangers.

What speaks to me most though in this scripture is not her hospitality, or wealth or faith even. Rather it is that the scripture reads 'The Lord opened her heart to receive Paul's message'. How powerful is this? Her conversion to Christianity, and later her outpouring of hospitality and love into the lives of others, was not done in her own strength. It was God who did this. The scripture tells us that 'He opened her heart'. And He can do this in us too. Our outpouring of love into this world is less about us trying harder, and more about God filling us and opening our hearts.

Let us submit our hearts to God today and ask Him to do in us what He needs to do, for us to be His hands and feet in our circles of influence.

Father, open my heart. Let me see what You see. May my life be an overflow of what You are doing in me. Amen

Water sustains

"He makes springs pour water into the ravines; it flows between the mountains."
- Psalm 104:10

Water sustains, it is one of the few elements that we cannot live without.

The purposes of water are endless. Water is life. Water is used for economic growth. Water divides, but water also unites. Water is a means of transport. Water is a natural essential resource. A lack of water is the source of crisis.

In so many ways, water can be compared to relationships. Relationships feed our souls but also have the ability to create crisis, they unite us but also divide. Connection is known to improve mental health, thus making relationships essential. As with water, the healthier the source of water, the better quality the water; so too with relationships. In order to ensure that relationships are healthy and of high quality, they need to be built from a healthy source. They need to be built on trust, honesty, authenticity, respect and love.

God waits outside the noise. Claim your silence today and reconnect with God as you bring all of your relationships before Him.

Father, help me to reassess my relationships from Your standpoint. May I be changed by You, and be a source of joy, love and truth in my relationships and to keep this standard for those feeding into me too. Amen

Your place of safety

"The Lord is my rock, my fortress, and my Saviour; my God is my rock, in whom I find protection. He is my shield, the power that saves me, and my place of safety."
- Psalm 18:2

Know where your help comes from!

It's easy so early in the year to begin with a 'I can do it' mentality. And gracious, I know that you can. But it is so much more powerful when we live and build from a place of safety. There is less striving when we let go of our need to impress or make our mark, and rather slow down and move from a place of stability.

I personally know all too well, the internal pull towards wanting to prove something to the world, or even ourselves, but this often leaves us empty and merely jumping from one goal to the next. Instead, let us seek out stability. Let us build healthy foundations, happy homes, and then build a life from there. That is not to say that we kick goals to the side path, no, goals are fabulously empowering; but let's set them from our safe place, alongside Jesus – not 7 steps ahead of Him.

Let this sink in today: Jesus is the one who requires least of us. Yet He has the most power in giving us the stability and ability to build lives that we love, accomplish more than we ever thought possible and glorify Him in the process.

Jesus, I come back to You today. Help me to slow things down, to look to You first, and to build from there. I love you. Amen

Let love lead

> "In Your unfailing love You will lead the people You have redeemed. In Your strength You will guide them to Your holy dwelling."
> - *Exodus 15:13*

God's unfailing love is our guide. Love was the driving force of Jesus' behaviour and love should and can play a lead role in our lives (and year too). Let's let love be our guide.

Let love lead you on days when life makes no sense at all, when you're forced to make difficult decisions. Let love lead you on quieter days when all is well with your soul. Let love lead when anxiety fills your mind and money pressures have the potential to rob from your peace. Let love lead when you're exhausted and let love lead when you're on mountain tops. To let love lead is to be guided by grace. It is to practice patience, self-compassion, giving and forgiveness. It is firstly opening ourselves to the acceptance of love from God, and then loving ourselves and in turn pouring love into others.

Find comfort today in knowing that God first loves you, and you get to dwell in His love. Then it is from this standpoint, from a love tank that is fill to the brim, that you can let love lead you in your thoughts, speech and behaviour.

Father, take me deeper in my understanding and acceptance of Your love, so that I can let love lead me as I go about my life. Amen

Copycat

"And no wonder, for Satan himself masquerades as an angel of light. It is not surprising, then, if his servants also masquerade as servants of righteousness"
- 2 Corinthians 11:14-15

When we travelled through South East Asia it was interesting to notice how many counterfeit items we could purchase on the streets. Items like Lacoste T-shirts, Tag Heuer watches and Louis Vuitton handbags. All counterfeit items are copies of something that is valuable. Nobody ever copies something that isn't of value. Nobody is ever going to copy a R1 coin or a toothpick. Why is that? I'd like to think it's because it would require too much work for something that holds little worth. We obviously know that if we were to purchase that branded fake handbag or watch or T-shirt, while it might look and feel like the genuine item, it doesn't have the same value as the real one.

Having faith in God without Jesus is much the same. It may look and feel the same but there is no eternal hope, no grace, no redemption, and it thus has no true value. We are all created in the image of God, but we are not God. We could create a lie believing that we are, but it will be merely a copy of the real thing and it will hold no value and in turn offer no long-term benefit.

The pull in today's society towards edifying the self, seeing ourselves as God, is merely the perfect illustration of the worth of our faith in Jesus. The World only ever copies that which has worth. Our faith is worth far more than perhaps we give it credit for.

Jesus, remind me today of the power of the Cross in my life. Your sacrifice gives me access to God Himself and an eternal promise of a life with You. Amen

31ˢᵗ January

Let go of fear

"He said to me: 'It is done. I am the Alpha and the Omega, the Beginning and the End. To the thirsty I will give water without cost from the spring of the water of life.'"
- *Revelation 21:6*

In the words of my 4-year-old: "Mom why are elephants scared of tiny little mice? I think it's because they learnt it from their moms and them from their moms, but they actually don't know why they're scared."

This recent conversation brought on a serious aha moment for me.

What if all of our fears are there merely because we've never questioned them? What if everything that causes us anxiety is in fact founded in a lie? What if God really is the elephant, and He lives in us, and the world and its problems but a mouse?

This idea is one I'm taking with me into this year and I hope you will too. That we will begin to challenge that which we fear, and which holds us back, and that we'll be catapulted into a life of faith over fear.

Ask God today to show you how big He is compared to that which you are facing. May you find comfort in knowing that the God of all creation lives in you!

Father God, help me to gain perspective on the magnitude of You and what that means for my problems today. Amen

FEBRUARY

identity

"He will quiet you with His love."
- *Zephaniah 3:17*

1st February

You are His love

> "Yet to all who did receive Him, to those who believed in His name, He gave the right to become children of God."
> - John 1:12

Jesus is crazy about you. He knit you together in your mother's womb. His intention in your creation was as detailed as it comes. He wanted you to be you: your looks, character, strengths and weaknesses; He designed it all.

And God longs, yes longs, to lead you beside quiet waters as He affirms and re-affirms His deep love for you and your identity as His daughter.

He could have designed you as a puppet subject to the moves of His hand, but instead He gave you the power to choose; to choose Him, to choose eternal life and life in abundance. What a privilege to choose Him and, in turn, to discover who you were created to be.

Today marks the beginning of an exciting quest as we are led along streams of quiet waters; where our identity is made clear to us, away from the noise and roars of the world.

———

Jesus, lead me beside quiet waters and empower me with the truth of my adoption as Your daughter. Amen

You are complete

"For we are God's handiwork, created in Christ Jesus to do good works, which God prepared in advance for us to do."
- *Ephesians 2:10*

The word "captivated" is defined as "to attract and hold the attention or interest of, as by beauty or excellence; enchant."

There is a deep desire in the heart of every woman to be accepted and loved. We crave it before we can even say the words, and I don't think I'd be wrong to say that we take this to our deathbeds. Truth be told, many of us were taught to rely on somewhat fickle self-esteem boosters from a young age. To rely on attraction from the opposite sex, or the rush of acceptance, that achievement provides for us. In the words of Paul, "You are complete in Him."

Just for today, repeat the words, "I am complete in Him" every time that your brain tells you otherwise. Because Darling, YOU are.

Jesus, help me to find my identity, my belong, in You. Amen

Jesus is the only answer

"We love because He first loved us."
- 1 John 4:19

For me the innate desire to be accepted was highlighted through my school years. I think it's safe to say, that while my few long-lasting relationships brought great joy (and sorrows), they were ultimately there to reaffirm my beauty and in that, my acceptance. I was accepted. Or was I ????

You see, while I thought that being loved by a man would fulfill me, I missed the very essence of what love even is. Even amidst some healthy relationships, I felt this deep longing for more. Love from a guy just wasn't enough. And so it became the argument we often had; the thoughts in my head that I would throw out, sometimes even controlling or manipulating, all with the single purpose of my "guy" saying it again, "I love you ". But my relationships were not the only thing that I leant on, there was performance too. Doing well in something meant affirmation, which meant acceptance. And that's all my little heart desired.

If this is you today, you are not alone, Beautiful. This is the challenge that every woman will face in this lifetime and the only answer to our hearts' deepest cry, is Jesus.

———

Jesus, help me to go deeper with You. Show me Your face that I may know that I belong with You, that You are my security blanket. Thank You for Your unconditional love for me. Amen

Perfect love

"Perfect love drives out fear."
- 1 John 4:18

You were created with enormous intention; with unique talents and giftings that God specifically placed within you.

Choosing love over fear is no easy task. But every day, we get to make that choice as we look AT ourselves and INTO ourselves. 1 John speaks of "perfect love" casting off all fear; not some fear, all fear. If you think back over your life, how often has fear stopped you in your tracks, especially from living out your God-given talents, dreams or desires?

Fear plays a huge role in society and in our lives everyday; but God speaks into this space. He says that His "perfect love" will expel all that is holding us back.

Start today by asking God to fill you up with His perfect love so that your cup will overflow into the world, perhaps in the form of your giftings, as a product of God's love for you.

Jesus, thank You for making me so intricately, and loving me so deeply. Help me to accept and be washed by Your love daily, so that fear can be eradicated from my life once and for all. Amen

5th February

New creation

"Therefore, if anyone is in Christ, the new creation has come: The old has gone, the new is here!"
- 2 Corinthians 5:17

For a long time I struggled to grasp my newness in Christ.

I couldn't understand how one minute I was full of sin and the very next, blameless. That was until the day I got married, and for the first time, my true nature in Christ and the extreme change God had made in me, couldn't have been clearer. I walked down the aisle of my garden wedding as a Keal (my maiden name), and I walked out of the service merely one hour later, as a De Beer. My entire name had changed in an instant. Did I feel like a De Beer? No, I felt exactly the same, but it was in the months to come that on repeating my new name (identity) that it started to feel more natural.

As you spend time with Jesus, ask Him to remind you that He sees you as blameless, a new creation. Your past is part of your story, but Jesus is the author of your new chapter to eternity.

Jesus, thank You that I get to leave my past behind me, and by Your grace and goodness, embrace all that is new within me. Help me to grow in my likeness to You. Amen

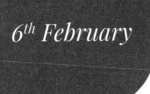

Who told you that?

"He answered, 'I heard you in the garden, and I was afraid because I was naked; so I hid.' And He said, 'Who told you that you were naked? Have you eaten from the tree that I commanded you not to eat from?'"
- Genesis 3:10-11

For as long as I've actively walked a journey of re-establishing my identity in Christ, this scripture has been a light unto my feet. Adam and Eve have just eaten the fruit from the forbidden tree and God speaks out to Adam audibly and asks where he is. Adam replies by saying that he has hidden, as he is naked. His nakedness is not a new state for him, but one he is suddenly aware of and ashamed of. God replies with 'who told you that?' Wow! Just because we know something, does not make it true. Adam had always been naked, but only after sin entered the world, did he see it as a problem and found a need to hide.

God is clear in pointing out that this fact did not come from Him. Self-loathing, self-doubt or body shaming is not of God. We are not born hating our bodies, but as we listen to the voice of the world, our beliefs become altered.

Today, you have the power to begin asking yourself, 'Who told me that?' Take every thought captive that does not come from the Word of God, from the only Truth that exists, and ask God to replace it with His truth about you.

Jesus, thank You that whilst the world's voice is loud, it is not the truth. You and Your Word are the only truth I need to believe and stand on. Amen

Truth over lies

"After fasting forty days and forty nights, He was hungry. The tempter came to Him and said, 'If you are the Son of God, tell these stones to become bread.' Jesus answered, 'It is written: Man shall not live on bread alone, but on every word that comes from the mouth of God.'"

- Matthew 4:2-4

Just because you are a new creation in Christ, does not exempt you from the lies of Satan. Just as we read yesterday how God asked Adam, "Who told you that?", the Holy Spirit asks us the same thing every time we bow down to a belief system or thought that differs from the Word of God.

Even Jesus, whilst without sin, was tempted by Satan, sometimes for days on end, but the strategy that we see Him use again and again in response to Satan's lies are the very Words of God. We need to KNOW the Word of God to ACCESS and PROCLAIM it in times of temptation. We need to know what God says about us, in order to fight thoughts and beliefs that differ from His truth.

Today, let's spend some time in God's Word, reading in Matthew 4 about the temptations that Jesus faced and overcame by declaring truth over lies.

Jesus, help me to soak up Your truth so that I can fight every lie that is launched at me. Amen

8ᵗʰ February

Boast only of Him

"For it is by grace you have been saved, through faith – and this is not from yourselves, it is the gift of God - not by works, so that no one can boast."

- Ephesians 2:8-9

I've found in my experience that many of us fall into one of two extremes when it comes to our view of salvation. There are some who are deeply convicted of their fallen nature and need for saving; they tend to be reliant on God and not on their own strength. And then there are those who have, by upbringing or nature, been formed to think rather highly of themselves. Whilst they may understand that they are sinful by nature, they find it harder to grasp their salvation.

A beautiful way that I love to see salvation is to know that as I am, whether I believe that to be magnificent or lousy, I am unable to enter the Kingdom of Heaven. It is only by accepting Jesus, and His dying on the Cross, that I gain access to fullness of life and all eternity. It's less about what I think of myself, and more about the truth we read in the Bible. Jesus believes in you as you are!

Ask God today to confirm in your heart, in as tangible a way as possible, that it is through Jesus that you have life for all eternity.

———

Jesus, thank You for the gift of salvation and that despite my own efforts, You alone save me. Amen

He delights in you

"He will take great delight in you; in His love He will no longer rebuke you, but will rejoice over you with singing."
- Zephaniah 3:17

It is not uncommon to wrestle for years with the notion of finding your identity in Christ and not in things of this world. I'll never forget an encounter with my husband in our early years of marriage, when I approached him, saying I was having a 'fat day' (*Girls, you'll know what I'm talking about*). After proclaiming to my husband that I felt 'fat', he replied with a simple "Love, when last did you spend time with Jesus?"

My immediate reaction was shock, then bitterness, and then the tears came. His words could not have hit a deeper chord within me. He nailed it. While I hoped, even longed, to hear these words from him, he wasn't going to give them. Not because he doesn't think I'm beautiful. He does. But rather because he too has come to this realization that his praise will never fulfill his wife's need for love. That void was made for one man only. The creator. My creator. Your creator. God. Jesus.

Take your longing for acceptance and approval from the world, and bring it before God. Allow Him to speak these words over you: I love you. Enough to die for you. You were chosen. Created with utmost purpose and intention. You are mine!

Jesus, I am Yours. Help me to learn to live within Your love. Amen

Slow down, Darling

"The Lord will fight for you, and you have only to be still."
- *Exodus 14:14*

'Hustle harder. Don't stop when you're tired, stop when you're dead. Do more. Be more.' The lingo of today is all go-go-go and yet many of us sit shattered in our hurried lives.

We're constantly anxious, our cortisol levels are through the roof and whist we boldly reply to 'how are you?' questions with 'busy', deep down our bodies and minds despise this word. In the words of a recent client of mine: "I feel as if the hamster wheel I'm on has become SO comfy that I haven't realized it isn't even turning any longer. I'm stuck in 'busy mode' but actually accomplishing so little".

Slowing down takes intention, but more than that, it takes bravery. As we spend time alone, we have the opportunity to settle the battle within: to quiet the voices in our head, to bring them under submission of our High King; the Creator of peace.

Take a moment today to quiet yourself and ask God to begin to show you where 'the rush' is robbing from you more than it's adding to your life.

———

Jesus, show me more of what "slow" looks like in this day and age. Teach me to be okay with my own space, with my own silence. Amen

"Do not let your hearts be troubled. You believe in God; believe also in me. My Father's house has many rooms; if that were not so, would I have told you that I am going there to prepare a place for you? And if I go and prepare a place for you, I will come back and take you to be with me that you also may be where I am. You know the way to the place where I am going.
- John 14:1-4

I love walking alongside women who are on a journey towards self-discovery. I assume it's mainly because not only do I get it; the ugliness, at times, of figuring out who you are, what you want and why you're here. But I think I love it more because in the depths of my soul, I know that you belong. That I belong!!

You may not have found your space or place just yet, but it is there. You were created to belong!! To belong is to be safe, protected and cherished. A desire to belong is not self-serving, it's not selfish or peer-pressured or fake; it's real and innate and alive within all of us. You were created to sit at the right hand of your Father.

This week, when you experience lonely days, know that you are not alone. Please never let this lie take root in your heart. Be intentional. Be kind to yourself. You are not alone; your home awaits you and you can find peace right here, with Jesus in your heart.

Jesus, thank You for the choice I get to make each day to find my home in You. Amen

Self-talk

*"Above all else, guard your heart,
for everything you do flows from it."*
- Proverbs 4:23

Imagine spending 70% of your day with one person. If this person were to criticize you most of the day, what effect would this have on your self-worth? I once heard a loose statistic that as women we can spend as much as 70% of our day in our own heads, and I can totally relate to this. All day long we are determining, by the thoughts we entertain, our level of self-confidence and identity.

Many of us have forgotten what it is to speak kindly to ourselves. Whilst Jesus never sinned, he lived a life that could easily have led to self-doubt. One such example is that we often see Jesus retreat when feeling sad. Many of us may do the same, but due to the thoughts we entertain, this isolation may lead to guilt for taking time out or over-thinking our behaviour, producing self-doubt.

Today, I urge you to challenge yourself to speak (in your head) in a way that would be appropriate speech, and words, to a young daughter. Choosing encouraging, uplifting self-talk over self-doubt and criticism, will set you up for a self-assured mind.

Jesus, thank You that everyday I get to choose what thoughts to entertain and what to write off as harmful. Empower me to live as You did, with self-assurance and a peaceful mind. Amen

13th February

A gentle & quiet spirit

"Rather, it should be that of your inner self, the unfading beauty of a gentle and quiet spirit, which is of great worth in God's sight."
- 1 Peter 3:4

I was always a confident, extroverted girl, and now woman, and so, for many years, I avoided scriptures that encouraged gentleness or those with a quiet-nature. I believed that these simply weren't for me and were for quieter souls, which I was not. As the years have gone by and especially since I've become a mother, I've realized that life isn't one big race to the end; that burnout is real and that hardwiring is simply the repetitiveness of a thought or behaviour, not just personality. You can be both confident and gentle. You can be a typical go-getter and learn the art of quietening one's soul.

I love that Peter points this out in scripture, that both gentleness and a quiet spirit are precious in God's sight. I understand this now, as it's often in these states that we are most humble, and most open to hearing and acting on the Lord's instruction.

I encourage you not to fight your personality or nature by writing off certain God-given characteristics. Ask God to highlight these for you, and to make them more accessible to you, however He sees fit.

Jesus, thank You that You have given me the ability and maturity to change in ways I may never have thought possible. Highlight for me what it is that You are currently doing in me. Help me to press into You, as You teach me ways that honour You, and that truly are Your nature, and thus my nature. Amen

Mary & Martha

> "'Martha, Martha,' the Lord answered, 'you are worried and upset about many things, but few things are needed - or indeed only one. Mary has chosen what is better, and it will not be taken away from her.'"
> - Luke 10:41-42

Mary and Martha are sisters, and their story is a well-known one.

Jesus had come to dinner at the sisters' home, and whilst Martha prepared the food and setting, Mary sat at Jesus' feet. What I love about this scripture is that, when Martha calls out Mary's behaviour in front of Jesus, He merely praises Mary for being present with Him, while speaking to Martha in an endearing manner.

In another scripture, we read a different story about a man called Lazarus, who happened to be Martha and Mary's brother. The scripture reads, "Now Jesus loved Martha and her sister and Lazarus" (John 11). I love how on this occasion Jesus refers to Martha and her sister, Mary (without reference to her name). It is also Martha who runs out to meet Jesus on His arrival, and Lazarus is then raised from the dead.

Today let each of us ask of ourselves, which of these two sisters we relate to most? Jesus admits to loving both sisters, despite their obviously different personalities.

Jesus, thank You that despite my personality, I can bring You great joy by living out who You created me to be, in everyday life and as a worshipper. Amen

You are braver

"For the Spirit God gave us does not make us timid, but gives us power, love and self-discipline."
- *2 Timothy 1:7*

You are braver than you think and stronger than you know.

It is true. God, the bravest of them all, created you in His image. He made you brave. Whatever it is that you are facing today or this week, know that God has gone before you. You are His daughter and He cares deeply for you. Your true nature, you at your core, are the daughter of God. How crazy to think of ourselves as a princess? But truly that is who you are.

Lift up your head, Darling, roll back those shoulders and straighten your crown. You are who He says you are! You are His, and that is the foundation on which you stand.

Where is God calling you to be brave today? Remember that we are not brave because of who we are, but because of who He is. Rely on Him as you wave your bravery flag.

Jesus, thank You that in You, I am brave. I am who You say I am. Amen

God chose you to be you

"So God created mankind in His own image, in the image of God He created them; male and female He created them."
- Genesis 1:27

One of my earliest memories is of me at age six, colouring in a welcome home sign with my younger brother. The sign was for my parents after they'd been away for two weeks. I don't remember missing my parents or any other facts from their time away, apart from this one: My brother kept colouring out of the lines and this eventually drove me to tears, as I couldn't understand why he couldn't in my words 'just try harder'.

This story makes me giggle now, as I love how personality traits really are evident from such a young age. My ambition, energy and often perfectionism, have at times made me question my like-ability. As I've grown older and searched the scriptures, I am reminded again and again that we are each made in the likeness of our Father. God is not frightened off by your ability to multi-task, or your impulsive nature or that you're a deep thinker or not a thinker at all.

God chose you to be you. Ask Him today to remind you of how deeply He loves the complexity of your heart, mind and body. And bring these into submission at the Cross, that He may refine you into all He has designed you to be.

Jesus, thank You that You adore me. Thank you that You understand the intricacy of me, something that no one else may ever understand: You get and You love. Amen

Woman at the well

"Jesus answered, 'Everyone who drinks this water will be thirsty again, but whoever drinks the water I give them will never thirst...' The woman said to him, 'Sir, give me this water so that I won't get thirsty and have to keep coming here to draw water.'"
- John 4:13-15

The very first person to whom Jesus chose to reveal His true nature as the Messiah, was the woman at the well. She was a Samaritan woman and having had five husbands, she was a woman that no Jewish man would usually converse with. This woman arrived at the well that day, thirsty, alone and with little hope; but she left the well, after her encounter with Jesus, changed and with living water – access to a life force that would never run dry. Jesus never discounts anyone based on his or her sin. He merely calls us to Him, in repentance, to drink of His goodness. Nothing will scare away our big God: not your mistakes today or those yet to be made. His blood sanctifies you and His living water never runs dry.

Approach Jesus today with a deep conviction that your sin is indeed covered by His blood.

Jesus, thank You that You are living water and the source of all things good, will never run dry. Amen

Your flavour

"I praise You because I am fearfully and wonderfully made; Your works are wonderful, I know that full well."
- *Psalm 139:14*

God made you in His image – you are perfectly formed with deep intentionality. He gives you permission, everyday, to be yourself. Whatever that means, as messy as it is, you are allowed to be you. You were never meant to be anyone else. And you will always, and I mean always, fail when you're trying to replicate someone else's life, schedule, body, parenting style or even faith.

It is so natural to imagine that life would be easier if we were to be someone else, if we had her home, hair, bank balance or faith. But the truth is that God meant for you to be yourself. You add a flavour to this world that wouldn't exist without you. Let that sink in for a minute. You are meant to be YOU.

Today, every time a thought surfaces that makes you doubt your purpose on this earth, address it quickly with the higher truth, found again and again in the Bible, that God made you with full intentionality.

Jesus, thank You that I am meant to be alive. Thank you that I add a flavour to this world that You believed that the world needed. Amen

Power to choose

"Finally, brothers and sisters, whatever is true, whatever is noble, whatever is right, whatever is pure, whatever is lovely, whatever is admirable - if anything is excellent or praiseworthy - think about such things."
- *Phillippians 4:8*

A scary reality for many of us as we explore who we are as a woman in Christ, is: what if we don't like ourselves? My simple answer is: Then you don't know yourself, or your God, well enough yet. The world's voice is louder than ever, and yet still your own voice remains the most influential on who you are and believe to be.

By the grace of God, you have been cleansed and made new, but this doesn't mean that every thought of the flesh has now escaped you. The temptation to conform to the thoughts and ideas of the world, or past beliefs about who you are, or were, will forever remain prominent in your mind. But you have the power to choose what you allow in and ultimately what you allow your brain to fester on, especially regarding your identity.

Scripture is the most beautiful place to begin when you actively choose to renew your mind and see yourself as God sees you, your mind as He designed it. Search the Bible or an online app on the topic of identity in Christ and speak these truths over yourself.

Jesus, show me more of what "slow" looks like in this day and age. Teach me to be okay with my own space, with my own silence. Amen

Delight in the Lord

"Delight yourself in the Lord: and He will give you the desires of your heart."
- Psalm 37:4

In 2007 I hit a rough patch and in my attempt to rebuild myself, I wrote in the middle of a page 'What makes me come alive?' and daily I took note of moments that felt entirely 'me'. I initially filled the page, my spider diagram, with the obvious; I love running, sea swims, and my family. But then came the tougher bit, finding that which the world perhaps didn't yet know about me but things that ultimately filled my tank.

Everyday I journeyed with my page and every time I had a 'me' moment, I jotted it down. Quickly my page became filled with 'me moments'. Things like eating croissants, swinging on swings, hearing children laugh and watching movies. In time this page became a canvas that now consists of habits that fill up much of my time, my days and even make up my career.

I encourage you to begin your 'what makes me come alive?' sheet this week and watch as God reminds you of who He made you to be.

Jesus, thank You that You designed me with desires and talents that bring You joy. Help me to see these this week so that I may bring You joy, by Your grace, as I embrace a life as truly 'me'. Amen

21st February

Freedom fulfilled

"She is more precious than rubies."
- Proverbs 3:15

Yesterday, we spoke of a life that makes you come alive.

One person feels most alive whilst re-packing their cupboards, another in a Zumba class and another whilst punching numbers into a calculator. As you'll know all too well, when you're in the midst of a moment of doing something that you know you were created to do, it's hard not to like yourself, to not know that THIS is who God made you to be.

This activity does not end at you alone, though. As you get to know yourself, your talents, interests, longings and dreams, you too will be set free from comparison. As you live out your desires, as God's child, and celebrate your uniqueness, you do not merely stop comparing, but also give others permission to do the same.

I encourage you today to take a moment to point out in a friend or loved one, something that you've noticed they are really good at or find joy in, and bring it to their attention.

———

Jesus, thank You that as You fill my cup, I recognize what is in it and take stock of it, that my cup will overflow. Amen

Connect with yourself

"The one who gets wisdom loves life; the one who cherishes understanding will soon prosper."
- Proverbs 19:8

In the jungle of 'busy' that we live within, many of us have forgotten, or perhaps have never learnt, the art of quiet, of reflection and of connection with oneself.

After struggling with a nasty injury for the past 8 months, I've learnt the importance and beautiful gift of connection with my own body. For years I disregarded my physical body. I ran it into the ground, ate what I wanted and rarely practiced self-care. It took a year of being crippled with chronic pain, for me to wake up and realize that my body mattered, and my mind needed to learn this too. Daily, I challenge myself to connect with my body now in a way that once felt foreign. There is much in life that we fear or dread from a distance but when up close, it's less scary. May your body be one of these things? Connect with it and watch as those busy, negative thoughts around the state or shape of your body, start to dissipate in light of its brilliance and intricate design: God makes no mistakes.

One beautiful way to do this is to have a bath or lie on your bed and massage your tummy, roll the skin across your tummy (yes we should all have skin to roll) and simply acknowledge what feels tight and then breathe deeply into that spot.

———

Jesus, I give myself full permission to acknowledge my body, to connect with my body and to choose to not speak unkindly to my body today. Thank You that daily You whisper affirming truths over me and that You love me just the way I am. Amen

Nourish to flourish

"Do you not know that your bodies are temples of the Holy Spirit, who is in you, whom you have received from God?"
- 1 Corinthians 6:19

We all know that without water, plants wither and it's much the same with humans. We need to nourish to truly flourish; in our physical bodies, in our minds, souls and spirits. We are whole beings and each part of us affects the other parts. We cannot have healthy emotions but be treating our bodies with hatred; the one will eventually affect the other.

Our bodies are referred to in scripture as temples. What a beautiful analogy. Let that sink in for a moment. Your body is a temple and it is home to the greatest of Kings.

For today, take one action that will nourish all 4 parts of you: body, mind, soul & spirit. For me today I'll be drinking an extra 2 glasses of water, protecting my mind by not engaging with content on social media that makes me feel lesser than, eat a slower dinner at the table with my family & dedicate an extra 5 minutes to prayer in my quiet time.

Jesus, thank You for this temple. Empower me today to honour my whole being and, in turn, honour You, my Creator. Amen

Renew your mind

"Do not conform to the pattern of this world, but be transformed by the renewing of your mind."
- Romans 12:2

In many University Psychology subjects that I have lectured over the years, we touch on Ernest Hemingway's Iceberg Theory. This theory suggests that the Titanic was sunk by what was not visible above the water level, not the visible bit that the ship and her crew could see. And this couldn't be truer of us as women too.

It's not your busy schedule, bad eating habits, flabby love handles, loud laugh or inability to find time for exercise that is sinking you – no my friend, it's your beliefs, fed into thoughts, that do so.

You have the power today to begin a process of self-awareness. Start by simply noticing the thought patterns that lead you down a road of self-hatred. Once you're aware of these, it is so much easier to begin challenging them with truth that only God can inspire.

Jesus, teach me to renew my mind, to take hold of thoughts that rob from me and to replace them with truths that You whisper over me everyday. Amen

Comparison

"Each one should test their own actions. Then they can take pride in themselves alone, without comparing themselves to someone else, for each one should carry their own load."
- Galatians 6:4-5

"She is the epitome of perfection. She is gorgeous as is her little princess. She dresses beautifully, always on trend and her hi-lights never seem to reach touching-up-stage. Her home is a sanctuary for her beautiful family, it is decorated as if created for a magazine and her money never seems to run out."

You know her, I'm sure. She may not be one person, but there are bits of her we find in many of those we admire from afar. Perfection. Idealism. It is so easy to get caught up in comparison. We compare, as we long for someone else's story to become our own. BUT, in actively creating our own story, in pressing into God and asking for direction for our own life, we combat the need to look at another's.

Today may you focus on creating a life, home environment, headspace, spirit and routine that you love and may this empower you to turn your back on comparison.

Jesus, thank You that by Your grace all things are possible. Help me today to celebrate who You created me to be, and allow others to do the same. Amen

Live as woman of God

"His divine power has given us everything we need for a godly life through our knowledge of Him who called us by His own glory and goodness."
- 2 Peter 1:3

Oh the absolute relief we can experience as children of God, in knowing that nothing in our power can earn us or make us worthy of God's love. It is by His goodness and His own glory, that we are empowered to live beautiful, full lives as women of God. I love that by God's grace, every time we get caught up in acts of works, in attempts to earn our right to eternity, He humbles us and reminds us of how small we really are.

Gracious, I can think of a number of such occasions when my pride has got the better of me, and then just like that, I am nothing, and I am reminded in my weakness, that He is my strength.

May we allow God to be strong when we are weak, but also to be open to His readiness to be our source of strength in our human frailty.

Jesus, thank You that it is Your goodness and Your glory that allow for me to have everything that I need to live as a woman of God. Amen

He is the potter

"Yet You, Lord, are our Father. We are the clay, You are the potter; we are all the work of Your hand."
- Isaiah 64:8

Just as a potter moulds his handiwork, so God longs to mould us. The potter only has access to that which is before him, and God has given us the freedom to choose as to whether we allow Him in, giving Him access to our being, open to His moulding. I love the fact that God thought of each of us long before we were created, He knows who we are at our greatest and He longs to see us live that out.

As we open ourselves to our potter, He takes pride in chipping away that which is no longer serving a purpose, and adds further beauty and refinement, moulding us into the person we were designed to be.

Today, allow Him to mould you as you bring your heart before Him. Be open to God's prompting to refine you in ways that may not feel comfortable but ones He knows, without a doubt, will only serve you better.

———

Jesus, thank You that You want to continue working on me, that I'm not a finished work but rather a work in progress, that You take huge pride in. Amen

Your days are written

"Your eyes saw my unformed body; all the days ordained for me were written in Your book before one of them came to be."
- Psalm 139:16

As we come to the end of this chapter and month, it is my deep prayer that you are more aware now than ever before, that God created you with enormous intent. He recorded your days in the book of life, and He knew you before you were born. You were no mistake and your life remains no mistake. You are deeply, truly loved by God who created love itself. You are a mighty tree, planted with intent, and God is your gardener. Continue to water that tree as you renew your mind, finding your identity in Christ, and allow Him to do the growing.

May He lead you beside quiet streams and may you drink of His goodness, today and always.

Jesus, thank You that you know me at my most vulnerable and You choose me. Amen

MARCH

streams of compassion

"He who believeth in me, out of his
heart will flow living waters."
- John 7:38

Connection

"As soon as Jesus was baptized, He went up out of the water. At that moment heaven was opened, and He saw the Spirit of God descending like a dove and alighting on Him. And a voice from heaven said, 'This is my Son, whom I love; with Him I am well pleased.'"
- Matthew 3:16-17

Connection is at the heart of God. He reveals this through the Trinity. Instead of functioning alone, we know that Jesus sits on the throne with God and the Holy Spirit. God operates with others to bring about His will on earth and in eternity. This is big. God could have made Jesus's identity merely the Messiah, but professed Him to be the Son of God.

I love that just as we consider water to cleanse us or refresh us or refuel us, God uses this powerful moment of baptism in water, to tell the world that Jesus is His son. Humans are made for connection too, it's in our DNA. We function best when connected to others, as we are made in the image of God. Jesus goes as far as calling believers, the body of Christ – again connection being the key element to our purpose on earth. God calls us firstly to Himself, but then instructs us to love others; this is our true purpose on earth: God first, people second.

Today, begin by recognizing God, Jesus and the Holy Spirit as one connected force that lives within you. Ask God to ignite a deeper desire for connection, in your heart, as He models.

———

Jesus, thank You that at the heart of God is love. You are love and You desire love from me, and of me. Amen

The treasure of friends

"If either of them falls down,
one can help the other up."
- Ecclesiastes 4:10

Friendship or community can provide us with safety, love and protection. I once heard a quote that read "I've heard it takes a village to raise ones kids. Is there a number I need to call? I don't think they've found me yet".

Whilst this sure made me giggle and nod, I too know that deep friendship and community, come with intentionality. We need to invest in those around us whom we believe God has brought into our lives for a reason. Whether it's a listening ear, a good laugh, a bed to sleep in, a shoulder to cry on or coffee shared, friendship provides us with a range of foundations for growth, support, joy and love to abound.

May we bring our awareness today to the power of friendship in each of our lives and how full our lives are due to the relationships we have.

Jesus, thank You for my friends and those who I can rely on for laughs, tears shared and joy celebrated. Amen

3rd *March*

Sowing & reaping

"A man reaps what he sows."
- Galatians 6:7

As we sow, so we reap. A time in my life that will be marked forever in my memory was when, due to a chronic condition, I was homebound, riddled with pain and numerous physical complications. Whilst one would usually rely on friends to step in and help, and of course, many did just that, what humbled me most was the community around me who suddenly appeared when I needed them most. It was less about how I defined these relationships beforehand and more about how over months we'd shared laughs in the street, the odd evening get-together or conversations at school pick-up. Suddenly when life didn't make sense to me, when I could have felt more alone than ever before, the little interactions I'd sowed into became the harvest I reaped; meals, flowers and helping hands with my kids from neighbours.

For today, ask yourself where and what you are sowing into in this season of life, and in what ways you are reaping too?

Jesus, awaken me to see the opportunities for me to sow more intentionally into people and situations and thank You for the numerous ways in which I reap. Amen

4th March

Friendship was God's idea

"And now these three remain: faith, hope and love. But the greatest of these is love."
- 1 Corinthians 13:13

God created friendship. We merely need to read snippets from the Gospels and again and again, we see that at the core of Jesus's life were His friendships. Jesus's disciples shared in both His joy and His sorrows; they were there in His greatest moments, they witnessed His successes as well as His hardships. Jesus experienced betrayal but also the joy of sitting around a table with His closest friends sharing a meal. In the world we live in today, busy-ness marks many of our lives and friendships can be pushed to the side for the sake of work, success or money.

Today, let's reflect on the joys that past friendships have brought us, and perhaps even message or call a friend whom you haven't chatted to for a while and relight the flame of friendship.

Jesus, thank You for modeling true friendship and thank You for the years of friendship that have marked my life; the ups and the downs. Amen

Deep connections

"The pleasantness of a friend springs from their heartfelt advice."
- Proverbs 27:9

I have a friend, who I've known almost my entire life, and who I can truly say understands me in a way that few others do. We don't see each other often, but when we do, tears are always shed, some happy, some sad.

In a society obsessed with digital connectivity, deep and meaningful friendships that are tangible are becoming ever so scarce. While this may seem okay, we know that stats show us that seclusion can be incredibly dangerous for the psyche of humankind. As we move into this new month, perhaps with the presence of predicted mid-year exhaustion, may we be intentional in keeping our soul connections alive.

There is something incredibly beautiful about recognizing a true soul connection, an understanding between two people that feels deeper, more real, and vulnerable than time or space.

My encouragement today is to nurture those connections. Begin by recognizing those friendships, or a friendship that can truly be deemed a soul connection. And reconnect as often as your soul needs filling. The impact of a true soul-filled conversation will leave you far more connected than simply scrolling on an online platform ever will.

Dear Jesus. Thank You for creating friendship. I acknowledge today that no one will fill me like You do, but thank You Lord for earthly bonds that provide us with refreshing here on earth too. Amen

Mentor or mentee

"And the things you have heard me say in the presence of many witnesses entrust to reliable people who will also be qualified to teach others."
- 2 Timothy 2:2

I love reading of the friendship between Timothy and Paul. Paul was Timothy's mentor and yet their friendship was bound by deep trust and mutual respect. The beauty of a friendship such as this one is that whilst Paul initially refers to Timothy as "my true son in the faith," (1 Timothy 1:2), he later refers to him as his "fellow worker" (Romans 16:21). More often than not, a mentor relationship may begin as one person leading or encouraging another, but in time, might develop into something more mutual. In the same breath, nearing the end of Paul's life, he encourages Timothy to go out and impart wisdom to others; the mentee becomes the new mentor.

Do you have someone whom you look up to for wisdom, or encouragement, or someone who you can ask for prayer from and know that they will indeed be praying for you? And is there someone who perhaps relies on you as his or her mentor or encourager?

Jesus, thank You that as You lead us, so we get the privilege to impart into others' lives and to be touched by others' lives and faith. Amen

The body of Christ

"Now you are the body of Christ,
and each one of you is a part of it."
- 1 Corinthians 12:27

The body of God has many parts, yet human nature is so quick to judge others who are different before we celebrate their uniqueness. What a boring world we'd live in if we were all gifted with the same traits, thoughts, looks and behaviours. Instead, our creative God planted elements of Himself in each of us. He celebrates our differences because He formed us in His likeness.

This does not mean that you need to get on with, or even like everyone you interact with, but it does mean that we can let go of wanting them to conform to standards or behaviours that feel right for us.

One fun way that we can let go of judging others is to turn our judgment into prayer. Every time you're tempted to judge someone, pray for him or her instead.

Jesus, thank You that each of us was made uniquely according to Your perfect will. Amen

8th March

Let Him bear the weight

"Jesus said, 'Come to me, all you who are weary and burdened, and I will give you rest. Take my yoke upon you and learn from me, for I am gentle and humble in heart, and you will find rest for your souls.'"
- Matthew 11:28-29

Relationships can, at times, feel awfully heavy and even burdensome. Some relationships can rob more than they add, leaving us depleted, dry and running on empty. We may even go as far as asking God where He is amidst these tough relationships?

This scripture reminds us that God is there, in the hardness of life and that restoration is possible, even when relationships have led us to deep hurt. Jesus Himself knew what it felt like to be on the receiving end of raw brutality and yet still He was without sin.

May we model the behaviour of Jesus and lay our heavy burdens on our Father instead of hardening our hearts or turning to resentment.

———

Jesus, thank You that right now, in this moment, I can hand over the relationship/s that are heavy on my heart. Thank You that You will bear this weight for me and provide me with a peace that only comes from You. Amen

Forgiveness in love

"Whoever would foster love covers over an offence, but whoever repeats the matter separates close friends."
- *Proverbs 17:9*

Relationships have the power to both add great joy and initiate great sorrow. It is likely that each one of us will experience both of these extremes in the relationships we find ourselves in, within our lifetime. Proverbs reminds us that love is at the heart of forgiveness. To forgive is not to disregard hurt. Jesus models that in His lifetime, He too experienced hurt, but He always forgave. Forgiveness is less about the deed done and more about the peace of God that follows letting go of something heavy on your heart.

Use this moment now to take note of someone in your life that perhaps you are struggling to forgive. Remember that we cannot forgive in our own power but by God's grace, given to us.

Jesus, help me today to forgive just as You have forgiven me. Amen

Bear with each other

"Therefore bear with each other and forgive one another if any of you has a grievance against someone. Forgive as the Lord forgave you."
- Colossians 3:13

In my personal experience, resentment is by far, one of the toughest emotions to bear. As resentment builds, especially within a relationship with a loved one, so does distance. To forgive is to be freed of resentment and anger. It is not to accept the behaviour of another, or to pretend that something hurtful did not take place or even to return to that relationship. Forgiveness has the power to tackle limiting beliefs like 'I am worthless' or 'I am a victim'; as it is redemptive in nature.

A beautiful practice that I adopted a few years ago is to address my pain, and to be honest with myself about what I feel. This is the first step in forgiving, as we cannot forgive what we have not yet acknowledged.

Today, take a moment to bring your pain or hurt before God. Allow the emotion to surface as you face your pain, and let God be your comforter, remembering that forgiving another is less about what they did and more about modeling what Jesus taught us.

Jesus, today I bring You my past hurts. Help me to practice forgiveness just as You have taught me. Amen

Vulnerability & comfort

"Therefore encourage one another and build each other up, just as in fact you are doing."
- 1 Thessalonians 5:11

We have all been made so uniquely.

To some, vulnerability comes easily and for others it's more of a challenge to open up. One of the beautiful lessons I've learnt about vulnerability has been that in my sharing, especially in the low seasons of life, I have found comfort and safety in the arms of others. It is only as we share that we discover how normal we in fact are, and that even within our hardship, or success, others will always relate, or at the very least, empathize or celebrate with us.

My encouragement today is to take note of friendships or relationships that you have and ask yourself whether you feel that you have been open enough with those closest to you. Have you allowed for them to offer comfort when needed or to celebrate with you when appropriate?

Jesus, thank You for the people that I have in my life and the freedom that You give me to open myself in vulnerability. Amen

Pray for your friends

"After Job had prayed for his friends, the Lord restored his fortunes and gave him twice as much as he had before."
- Job 42:10

What a beautiful scripture today's verse is.

I know first hand how easy it is to utter in kindness to a friend that you will be praying for them, and then to totally forget that the conversation ever took place. Job, we know, was no saint, and yet here in this scripture, we read that he prayed for his friends, and God honoured that by offering to him restoration. How many of us crave restoration, but rather than turning our prayers to others, we desperately beg for God's favour in our own lives?

May today's scripture encourage us all to pray for our friends, and to know that our good Father will honour this act of kindness.

Jesus, today I want to lift up my friends to You. Thank You that You love them so deeply and I ask today that You will make Yourself known to them as they go about their daily lives. Amen

Honourable in speech

"Be devoted to each other in love. Honour one another above yourselves."
- Romans 12:10

As women, it is so easy to enter friendships that quickly become marked by habitual gossip.

It takes merely the mention of another friend to fuel the fire and the habit of talking about others builds faster than we often realize. It's important to note that there is a difference between pouring out your heart to a close friend who holds your hand, prays with you and walks a tough road with you, be it relational or not, and mere spreading of information about others, for the sake of the thrill it gives both the provider of information and the receiver.

As women of God, may we daily ask for God's grace to direct our conversations and to keep us above reproach, honourable in our speech and loving, above all else.

Dear Jesus, Thank You that Your grace is sufficient in our weakness. Please empower us to take note of conversations that are dishonouring of others and give us the grace to admit our fault, to accept Your forgiveness and to walk above reproach. Amen

A bitter pill to swallow

"Get rid of all bitterness, rage and anger, brawling and slander, along with every form of malice."
- Ephesians 4:31

There will come a time in life when someone will let you down.

Whatever the catalyst, it has the potential to leave you bitter or sarcastic. There is no denying, that relationships can, and will, be incredibly tough sometimes, and it's not fair. But the truth is that it is our reaction to such circumstances that will have the greatest impact on our lives going forward.

I was recently in a room with a few rather bitter ladies. I listened to their chatter, which was saturated with sarcasm, dread and negativity. What started as bitterness over an interaction with one person, had catapulted her into a state of bitterness. Bitterness may feel like revenge but it's not. Instead of outwardly hurting the person who may have wronged you, you internalize this hurt and inwardly prolong the fight.

Today, instead of allowing bitterness to fester within, breeding negativity and a life you never envisioned for yourself; ask God to shine His light into the situation. It is only God who can empower us to forgive and to move past and beyond that which was holding us back.

Jesus, thank You that I can find refuge in You. You know my hurts, and today I bring them before You. Help me to stop letting them define me; so that instead I may embrace Your perfect peace. Amen

Walk with the wise

"Walk with the wise and become wise,
for a companion of fools suffers harm."
- *Proverbs 13:20*

I remember a time in my past when my friendship group consisted of people very different from me. Whilst I loved the excitement and 'crazy' that they brought to my rather controlled world, I too, quickly realized that I was changing by the day. My language, behaviour and thoughts, even, began to look very different from what felt 'truly me'. I began to forsake my usual hobbies and what brought me joy for what brought them joy. This was entirely my own doing, but the wake up call wasn't an easy one to face; I learnt my lesson fast, it wasn't one easily forgotten.

We all know too well the saying "you are who you surround yourself with". This is true and will forever remain true.

A lovely way to challenge our thoughts on this concept, is to begin by exploring who YOU are. And then to question whether those who you consider companions are supporting who you want to be, and believe, are.

Dear Jesus, You know me better than anyone else does. Help me to discover more of who You made me to be, so that I can surround myself with like-minded people, and honour You as I live out my life. Amen

No greater friend

"Greater love has no one than this: to lay down one's life for one's friends."
- John 15:13

There is no greater friend than Jesus. Close friends know your secrets, your strengths and your weaknesses and love you just the same. Many of us will openly confess to being willing to lay down our lives for a close friend, but when push comes to shove, would we do it? Would we sacrifice our life, perhaps a life we in fact loved, for the sake of another? Would we do that to our loved ones; would we willingly leave them behind?

Jesus took it upon himself to lay down his life so that you may have life, and life in abundance. Abundant life and friendship with Jesus includes intimacy, vulnerability, trust, loyalty, obedience... and the list goes on.

"Will you be my friend?" He asks, daily. *You are but to reach out. He is waiting!!*

Dear Jesus. Thank You that Your love knows no end. That Your friendship goes beyond mistakes, pleasure or fun; that You understand every inch of my being and still You choose to love me. Amen

Let it go

"Do nothing out of selfish ambition or vain conceit. Rather, in humility value others above yourselves."
- Phillippians 2:3

We are all born with a certain set of basic needs. Then, through a mixture of upbringing, personality and choices, we start to form agreements with certain thoughts or ideas, and those become the belief systems that we live by. The thing is, those are YOUR belief systems, and may not be mine.

As soon as we start to see a person's behavior, speech and ideas as separate from ours (i.e. according to their belief system), we free ourselves from taking things personally. To take something personally is to admit that we all have the same belief system, agreements and thoughts – which is impossible.

Today, ask God to teach you to start to see people's behaviour and words from whence they come, and not to take them on as your own. By reflecting on why a certain person may have felt the need to behave or act in such a way, you may be able to free yourself from self-judgment and make it 'their focus and not yours'.

Jesus, empower me today to see each set of actions or words spoken by others, as mere expressions of their personal agreements. Help me to find my identity in You and not in something as fleeting as others' opinions of me. Amen

True kindness

"Be kind and compassionate
to one another."
- *Ephesians 4:32*

Has an act of kindness by another, perhaps a friend or even a stranger, ever left you speechless? I can think of numerous occasions when small gestures done by others have humbled me to my core and when larger gestures of kindness have even brought me to tears.

One such occasion was when, in my University days, after a really tough break-up, I returned to my room in a home I shared with 7 close friends, only to find the words 'I love you' cut out of newspaper and stuck across my entire bedroom wall. It was a close friend who had done this for me and of course it brought on many tears. She held me up when I couldn't find the strength to hold myself up. She was and remains a true friend.

Kindness is a gift we get to offer to others, and one that we can receive with humility and joy. Today, let's partake in a joint act of kindness – choose one way in which you can pass love on to another today.

Jesus, You model for us true kindness. Help us each day to remain humble enough to live lives that impact others, just as You have impacted our lives, with Your kindness. Amen

David & Jonathan

"After David had finished talking with Saul, Jonathan became one in spirit with David, and he loved him as himself."
- 1 Samuel 18:1

There are many friendships in the Bible, but that of David and Jonathan may be the closest bond we see in the scriptures.

Logically, their friendship should not have taken place; they should have been enemies as Jonathan's dad was King, the position that God had ready for David to step into. Jonathan risked his life when telling David of his father's plans to destroy him. The two were bonded and even felt the freedom to be emotional in front of each other. Their friendship was marked by deep loyalty and vulnerability; two traits that we can all strive to bring into our close friendships.

Trust God to show you which friendships in your life may allow for you to practice greater loyalty or deeper vulnerability.

Jesus, thank You that just as You blessed David with Jonathan, You have also blessed me with friendships. Amen

A match made in Heaven

"You shall speak to him and put words in his mouth; I will help both of you speak and will teach you what to do. He will speak to the people for you, and it will be as if He were your mouth and as if you were God to him."
- Exodus 4:15-16

Not all friendships are made for sleepovers and giggles; God too can add friendships that go beyond social benefits and become more like partnerships. Moses and Aaron's friendship, in the Bible, is a perfect example of this. Scriptures show that Moses and Aaron's personalities complemented each other perfectly, their strengths filled in for each other's weaknesses and this made them more effective together than they ever could have been alone. Have you ever had a friendship like this, a partnership that just worked? It's amazing how God can bring two or even more together, with different strengths and gifting, making them unstoppable when partnered.

Are you a team player or do you prefer to work alone? God can bring partnerships into our lives in the most unlikely of places – let's be open to His workings in our lives.

Jesus, open my eyes to the partnerships that You have for me in my life, whether personal or work related. Amen

Jealousy & disappointment

"For where jealousy and selfish ambition exist, there will be disorder."
- James 3:16

A season of my life that I found incredibly tough was when my husband and I were desperately trying to fall pregnant and this took significantly longer than we anticipated. I will never forget the deep disappointment on hearing of the news that a close friend had fallen pregnant. I couldn't possibly understand why God had given her something that she wasn't even desperate for, and yet there I sat, longing for what she had.

Was my disappointment warranted? I believe yes, but it was an emotion I needed to take before God and surrender at the Cross. This was not the last time I experienced this jealousy and disappointment and I'm sure you can recall your own experience of going through this or something similar, too.

May we give ourselves time and space to process our emotions in the presence of God, and learn to celebrate with our friends when they experience things that perhaps we long for too.

Jesus, thank You for Your sufficient grace, even when I turn to jealousy and wrestle with longing. Help me to bring my tough emotions to Your throne. You are my safe place and Your timing is always perfect. Amen

22nd March

Nothing to prove

If I think back over my life thus far, I can most certainly point out relationships that had me living in a state of constant seeking-of-approval. Certain people, perhaps those we admire or feel are more successful than we are, can drive us to act out of character.

To seek approval is often to engage in behaviour or to utter words or even attend events that do not feel authentic to our true nature. Seeking approval can go as far as driving us to do things that we would later regret. I sure have a few of those moments that spring to mind when I allow my thoughts to go there.

May we be encouraged today that God identifies us as His daughters —this is our true identity. We have nothing to prove in this world.
We are deeply, fully loved by the King of Kings.

Jesus, renew my mind today in the knowledge of the deep love and true identity I have as Your daughter. Thank You that no-ones approval can affect my true identity, which, by the power of Your blood, is pure and blameless. Amen

Carry their burdens

"Carry each other's burdens, and in this way, you will fulfill the law of Christ."
- Galatians 6:2

I love hearing stories of how friends have stepped up and carried another's burdens when life felt too heavy to bear alone. I will never forget when my mum had cancer for the second time and was due to do radiation half-an-hour's drive from our home, everyday for 30 days. My mum's friends rallied around her and created a schedule of who would take her down to the oncology unit each day. She was capable of driving herself, and being the strong woman that she is, she would happily have done so, but her friends simply wouldn't allow it.

How beautiful it is to have friends who know, perhaps even better than you do yourself, when to take the load off your shoulders.

May you be encouraged to build into the friendships that feel safe and set apart.

Jesus, thank You for the beautiful friends that I have and help me to continue to build into the friendships that You bring into my path. Amen

Live true to yourself

"Why do you look at the speck of sawdust in your brother's eye and pay no attention to the plank in your own eye?"
- Matthew 7:3

Have you ever listened to a sermon or a podcast and thought 'I wish ____ was here to hear this?' You are not alone in thinking this. It is so common for us to project onto others what we feel would be right for them, or could change their life. Rarely do we humble ourselves to the point of receiving a message in season, for ourselves.

I once read an article written by a woman who worked for Hospice for many years and who got the privilege of spending the final few hours with those passing on to a better place. She spoke of listening to their greatest life regrets. One of the main regrets that she mentioned was people wishing they had lived true to themselves and not lived up to the expectations of others. The truth is though, that it is often easier to focus on what others think, and what we likewise think of others, than it is to truly bring ourselves before God, and allow Him to work in us.

Today, ask God to open your eyes to the work He is doing in you, and to prevent you from analyzing the lives of others.

Jesus, thank You that You meet me today exactly where I am. Amen

Stand on the side of 'good'

"Hate what is evil; cling to what is good.
Be devoted to one another in love.
Honour one another above yourselves."
- Romans 12:9-10

Confrontation has, for as long as I can remember, not come naturally to me. I would rather settle for peace then to confront. For years I thought my peace-making ability was honourable, but as I've grown up, I've come to realize that there is both a place for peace and a place for confrontation.

Confrontation, especially if in support of God's truth, isn't just an option, it is encouraged. I love how Paul encourages in his letter to the Romans (in some translations) to 'stand on the side of good'. What a beautiful way to put it. This may be easy when it is the favoured opinion, but far tougher to 'stand on the side of good' when it requires challenging the status quo or walking away from a harmful conversation.

As you approach the day or week ahead, ask yourself how you can better go about standing on the side of good. Lean in and allow God to lead you on this path of truth.

Jesus, thank You that You are good, and that You empower me every day to love with genuine affection. Amen

Power of the inner circle

"The Lord God said, 'It is not good for the man to be alone. I will make a helper suitable for him.'"
- Genesis 2:18

I so clearly remember sitting in a small leadership meeting at high school and our headmaster saying to us, "Girls, you will need to choose your inner-circle wisely next year."

I have always been an open book, but one thing that I have realised as I've grown up, is that when you spread yourself thin, you not only allow everyone to see you for who you really are, but you give them access to your dreams, your desires and your future. God tells us that it is not good for man to be alone, so He created a companion for him. How beautiful. He did not create 10 but 1. This doesn't limit us in having a bigger circle of friends, but it is a reminder of the power of a close-knit inner circle.

Ask God to reveal to you today who you can trust to hold your dreams with care, to encourage you and not break you down. Ask Him to show you those who will continuously push you in the direction of your dreams, with words of encouragement, sometimes the hard truth and always from a place of love.

Jesus, thank You for the friendships or friend in my life that make(s) up my inner circle. Teach me to trust and allow others in, to be Your hands and feet on this earth. Amen

Cheerful company

"Anxiety weighs down the heart,
but a kind word cheers it up."
- *Proverbs 12:25*

There is little that hits the spot quite like a conversation or catch up with a positive friend. I have been reminded many times over the years, just how powerful my daily interactions are on both my mood and energy levels. I am fueled after spending time with positive people, who uplift, speak life and are down-to-earth in nature. I believe it isn't just important, but essential, that we're cognisant of who we are surrounding ourselves with, and what affect they have on who we are as people.

Life is so busy and often rushed, that it's important that we protect our energy and are intentional with what information we allow into our minds.

Everything that comes in to your mind, will find a place to rest. This week, may you be aware of the relationships that leave you fueled and those that leave you empty.

Jesus, thank You that I get energised in Your presence. Help me to manage how I choose to spend that energy. Amen

Seek first His Kingdom

"But seek first His kingdom and His righteousness, and all these things will be given to you as well."
- Matthew 6:33

Healthy relationships add enjoyment to our lives.

I recently did a trip on my own; I was so excited about the time-out that I didn't anticipate the loneliness that would come with it. I was reminded of the degree to which shared joy often equates to more joy. This is true mostly for relationships that are healthy; where neither party feels used, resentful or bitter. A beautiful way to build a healthy relationship is to begin by putting God first in that relationship. As the scripture says, we are encouraged to seek first His Kingdom, and then all things will be added to us. As we seek to know Jesus intimately, we cannot but be transformed into His likeness and it is the very characteristics of Jesus that make for a great starting point in building into healthy relationships.

Today is as good as any day to begin a journey of building healthy relationships. Be empowered today, knowing that the process begins with seeking God first, and this is totally within your reach.

Jesus, thank You that as I seek You, so You will add to my life abundantly. Amen

Glass balls

"All you need to say is
simply 'Yes' or 'No'."
- Matthew 5:37

Setting boundaries is hard work.

Whether you are a people-pleaser, workaholic or socialite, we are all faced with the need to set boundaries, all the time.

I'll never forget a day when I was desperately trying to do and be everything until it all caught up with me. I was juggling way too many balls and I simply didn't have the tools to know which to drop and when. We arrived at the beach on a public holiday and I literally couldn't get out of the car as I was crying so much. My lack of setting boundaries did not just affect me, but had overflowed into my family. My husband felt the burden, my daughter felt the burden and no doubt, my son in my womb felt the burden too.

Today, as you throw the balls, that you are so familiar with juggling, into the air, ask God to empower you with knowledge and humility to know which ball is truly made of glass and which is actually a bouncing ball and can be picked up at a later stage.

Jesus, thank You that You carry my burdens. Teach me today to lay them at Your Cross so that I can wisely discern how to set healthy boundaries. Amen

30ᵗʰ March

Jesus set boundaries

"Yet the news about Him spread all the more, so that crowds of people came to hear Him and to be healed of their sicknesses. But Jesus often withdrew to lonely places and prayed."
- Luke 5:15-16

Personal boundaries have been defined by some to be as important as the boundary lines of your own property – they define your distinctiveness. In order to say "no", we need to be able to handle difficult emotions.

Boundary-setting unleashes emotions and sometimes, ugly ones. People may get angry, upset or even hurt with your "no" but we need to know our value. Jesus was the perfect model of healthy boundaries. He knew when to rest, He kept open and honest relationships with those closest to Him and He never professed to experience guilt when He acted on what He felt that He needed to do in any one moment. Jesus communicated when He needed time alone and He prioritized His time with God above all else. He valued it as essential to His lifestyle.

Today, ask God to reveal to you more of the character of Jesus, so that as you understand Him more, you can begin to model His standard to avoid burnout.

Jesus, thank You that You are always the perfect model. Help me to set boundaries just as You did, and to feel the freedom to stick to them with conviction and humility. Amen

A friend of God

"And the scripture was fulfilled that says, 'Abraham believed God, and it was credited to him as righteousness,' and he was called God's friend."
- James 2:23

Oh, but to be called a friend of God. We only need to read snippets of the Old Testament to know of what we deserve as sinners, and yet, by the blood of Jesus, God has washed us clean and calls us His friends.

There is no greater privilege on earth than to be known by God, personally, but he takes it further and calls us friend. You are His daughter, His friend, His beloved and He longs for nothing more than to be in an intimate relationship with you. He longs to plant ideas in your head, to reaffirm your worth, to direct your path and to promise you everlasting life, in Him.

Today may you answer His call to be His friend. When the greatest of them all asks for your hand to dance, it would be crazy to turn Him down.

Jesus, I take Your hand today – lead me on life's path in the way that only You can do. Amen

APRIL

is your soul thirsty?

"The Lord is my shepherd; I shall not be in want. He makes me lie down in green pastures, He leads me beside quiet waters, He restores my soul."
- *Psalm 23:1-2*

Waves of emotions

"The Lord is my shepherd; I shall not be in want. He makes me lie down in green pastures, He leads me beside quiet waters, He restores my soul."
- Psalm 23:1-2

Waking to a crying child or buzzing alarm clock, then preparing lunch boxes and somewhere in between, showering, putting on your make-up and rushing out of the door, you remember that you haven't eaten breakfast. It's often not before 7pm when you collapse onto the couch, exhausted, that your mind wonders to your personal wellbeing. I hear you.

Emotions are those fleeting feelings that come in waves, some raging, some calm, but they're there whether we suppress them, explode because of them or flow with them.

Feelings are natural. God made you a feeler. He's not angry or confused about the fact that you face a range of emotions every day. It's not just okay – He expects you to acknowledge both the easy and uncomfortable emotions that you feel, to learn to manage them with grace and wisdom.

To begin our journey in the waves of emotions as women, I encourage you today to merely bring your awareness to your feelings. What is it you're feeling right now?

———————

Jesus, thank You that You have created me to feel, and that You are not afraid of my big feelings. Amen

Jesus wept

"Jesus wept."
- John 11:35

Today's scripture is the shortest of all the scriptures we find in the Bible and yet it is powerful beyond words.

When I was going through intense therapy in my late teens, I so clearly remember saying to my psychologist, after not being allowed to exercise for weeks, that if I couldn't go for at the very least a walk, that I would indeed CRACK!! She replied with, "Caitlyn that's why you are here. I doubt you've ever allowed yourself to get to cracking point and you'll probably find as soon as you do, that cracking isn't so scary after all." Crack I did.

I cried for seven days straight, but I exited that week fully transformed. Emotions are normal, we were created as emotional beings and yet from a young age many of us are taught that uncomfortable emotions are wrong, that feelings are fickle and should be escaped. This is not the way of God; this is not what Jesus modeled.

Remember today, that God made you in His image, thus an emotional being. You are mind, soul and body. Let that notion be your truth for today.

Jesus, thank You that just as You modeled, I have permission to be an emotional woman. Amen

Think, feel, act

"My soul is downcast within me… Deep calls to deep in the roar of Your waterfalls; all Your waves and breakers have swept over me."
- *Psalm 42:6-7*

In Cognitive Behavioural Therapy we learn that emotions always follow thoughts, and lead to behaviour. You may wake up feeling stable, then look in the mirror and be triggered by a negative thought, this in-turn ignites frustration which is then vented on your family. David shares in the Psalms how his life was being threatened by Saul and thus his soul was downcast.

Thought first, then emotion.

I am fortunate to work in the space of emotions every day, and watch as women are transformed as they connect with their emotions. We cannot change what we do not know, and yet God meets us exactly where we are at today. The most powerful way to begin working with your emotions as a woman of God is to acknowledge your feelings as they surface and validate them for yourself.

For today, make it your mission to bring your awareness to what you are feeling, a few times, throughout the day. Once you can connect with those recurring emotions, take them before God.

Jesus, thank You that You are a feeler. You do not despise my feelings and You are not threatened by my uncomfortable feelings. Help me to acknowledge what I am feeling today and to bring all my feelings before You. Amen

Your thought life

> "We demolish arguments and every pretension that sets itself up against the knowledge of God, and we take captive every thought to make it obedient to Christ."
> - 2 Corinthians 10:5

Emotions are good and a gift from God. Emotions empower us to act on conviction, to make changes, to pursue big dreams and to speak up for the truth. The expression of emotion also brings with it freedom. As we express or acknowledge an emotion, we are free from its hold on us. It is often the suppression of emotion that leads to depression. Many of us have a small vocabulary when it comes to emotion and so we're taught to pool our emotions into one. I have had a 'bad' day, I am 'exhausted', I'm 'no-where' or the worst of the lot, 'I feel fat'. Of course few of these are feelings at all.

Once we become familiar with the uncomfortable feelings that we experience often and perhaps that trigger responses that we aren't proud of, we can begin to connect the thoughts that precede these feelings. Thoughts like, 'I will never be accepted' may lead to 'disappointment', which may lead to 'emotional eating'.

God is bigger than your feelings and He empowers you today to take hold of thoughts that rob from your wellbeing and feed emotional rollercoasters.

Jesus, meet me in the space of my thoughts today. Help me to stop when an uncomfortable feeling triggers an unhelpful response, and to go back to the thought that fed that emotion, and bring it before You. Amen

Powerful presence

"When Jesus heard what had happened, He withdrew by boat privately to a solitary place."
- Matthew 14:13

I love how Jesus modeled leaving the crowds, to be alone and connect with Himself and God.

An illustration that resonates with me with regard to living in the present moment is: If one were to drop a penny in a quiet room, surely we'd all turn to see where the noise had come from? So it is with us. We need quiet, in order to hear the noise within and to take note of where it is coming from.

A habit I've adopted is to practice something I call a PENNY drop moment, at least 5 times a day. I usually do this every time I make coffee, but I know for some it would work to do it while sitting on the toilet perhaps. The purpose of this activity is merely to become aware of what's going on internally for you. The activity includes a quick self-check-in on the following things: P is for Posture, E is for Energy Levels, N is for Nourishment, the next N is for Notice Thoughts and Y is for Yield.

As you begin to practice PENNY drop moments today, ask God to reveal where He is within the noise. It is often through self-awareness that we realize our deep need for God in our thought life.

Jesus, empower me today to take note of my presence in this world and to invite You in to my thinking space. Amen

Vast range of emotions

"'I have had enough, Lord,' he said. 'Take my life; I am no better than my ancestors.'"
- 1 Kings 19:4

Have you ever had a moment when you were simply overwhelmed by the magnitude of your emotions?

I once had a friend proclaim that she thought she'd gone mad, as she was convinced that she felt a whole range of emotions at one time. This is completely normal and to be expected. We can, and do, daily, experience more than one emotion at one time. I can feel exhausted because my kids were up in the night, excited for my morning coffee, anxious for a social gathering later that day and utterly in love with my two children as they cuddle me in bed. Elijah is a beautiful example of this in the Bible. The scripture above speaks of his deep despair, but we read just prior to this emotional outburst before God, that Elijah had just conquered an amazing spiritual victory. He moved from an absolute high to the lowest of lows in merely one day.

Whatever it is you are feeling in this very moment, know that God is with you. He does not think you are extreme or over-sensitive – He meets you right where you are.

Jesus, thank You that my ups-and-downs are both normal and expected. Help me to turn to You when experiencing both extremes or the in-betweens. Amen

A gentle whisper

"Then a great and powerful wind tore the mountains apart.. but the Lord was not in the wind. After the wind there was an earthquake, but the Lord was not in the earthquake. After the earthquake came a fire, but the Lord was not in the fire. And after the fire came a gentle whisper."
- 1 Kings 19:11-12

Today we continue to look at the life of Elijah.

After we read yesterday of his deep despair as he cries out to God, an angel is said to then have appeared and offered him food and drink which fueled his next 40-day journey. Then, the Lord came to him and called him from the cave he was in. God met Elijah exactly where he was at, but not in the way that Elijah had expected. The elements were all around him and yet God was not in the powerful wind, or earthquake or fire, instead He revealed himself as a gentle whisper.

Today, may you quiet yourself before God and ask Him to reveal to you His glory, in your life, in ways that only He can. He knows you intimately and whilst He may not meet you in the way you hoped He would, His ways are always perfect and His plans for you are always good.

Jesus, I repent today for when I've tried to play God and predict how You would move in my life. Take the wheel, Jesus. I am listening. Amen

8th April

Jesus was emotional

"He looked around at them in anger and, deeply distressed at their stubborn hearts."
- Mark 3:5

There are countless accounts in the gospels where Jesus displays or admits to feeling emotion. We know that Jesus felt many positive emotions, like empathy, compassion, joy and peace; but we also know that Jesus admitted to experiencing many uncomfortable emotions too: exhaustion from ministry and pressures, sorrow over loss, frustration with his disciples and their lack of faith at times and anger. Whilst Jesus experienced all of these emotions and acted on them, He remained without sin. What this means for us as followers of Christ, is that it is not the feeling of an uncomfortable emotion that is a sin, but rather our response to that emotion that can lead to sin.

What a beautiful lesson to take into your day, knowing that just like Jesus, you have every right to feel the range of emotions that surface for you on a daily basis. Be empowered as you ask God to teach your heart to know the correct response to each emotion that you face.

Jesus, thank You that You too know the depth to which I feel things. Help me to honour You with what I do with those feelings. Amen

Cracked cisterns

"My people have committed two sins: They have forsaken me, the spring of living water, and have dug their own cisterns, broken cisterns that cannot hold water."
- Jeremiah 2:13

It is almost expected in the society that we live in today, to find our identity in things of this world. Fashion, body shape or size, success, home décor, travel schedules, bank balances and the likes, are some of the elements in which many of us find value, and on which we build our identity.

Today's scripture speaks of cisterns that cannot hold water. A cistern was considered a water reservoir in Bible times; in todays' times a cistern could be compared to a jojo tank, collecting rainwater for a specific use. If the tank or cistern was built cracked, it could not be used. God has a specific purpose for your life; He designed you with great intention and He longs for you to bring your cracks before Him, to mend as He prepares you for all that He has for you.

Today I encourage you to see yourself as a cistern, a vessel ready to be filled, and used for a specific purpose. Ask God to come today and begin to heal your cracks.

———

Jesus, I surrender my life before You now. In many ways I feel broken, but You are the ultimate Healer and I acknowledge right now that only You can heal the hurts or cracks within my soul. Amen

Fire escapes

"Remain in me, as I also remain in you. No branch can bear fruit by itself; it must remain in the vine. Neither can you bear fruit unless you remain in me."
- John 15:4

A coping mechanism is a term that we are all familiar with, but one that we rarely take cognisance of, until we're knee-deep in trouble.

When I was going through a rough patch in my teens, I realized that in many ways I only had one coping mechanism for dealing with uncomfortable emotions. I've since learnt that many others are the same. When experiencing one or more uncomfortable emotions, some women binge on food, others exercise, some talk, others numb by scrolling on their phones and others drink.

But by only having one coping mechanism, we set ourselves up for either addiction or find ourselves at a loss when our one option fails us. I learnt that feelings pass, as they should, and that by sitting with the feeling, acknowledging it and then choosing what to do with it, has been when I have found my greatest coping mechanisms.

Jesus modeled crying when sad, throwing over tables when angry and retreating when exhausted. We too, have the power within us, to find effective coping mechanisms for our own uncomfortable emotions.

Jesus, thank You for Your strength and wisdom as I learn to manage my emotions in constructive, powerful, God-honouring ways. Amen

Your feelings matter

"But do not forget this one thing, dear friends: with the Lord a day is like a thousand years, and a thousand years are like a day. The Lord is not slow in keeping His promise, as some understand slowness. Instead He is patient with you."
- 2 Peter 3:8-9

You may wake to news that sends you into a panic or perhaps you go to bed in that state. Know that every feeling that you feel is valid. You have every right to feel what has surfaced for you. Whilst we all differ in the depth of our feelings, we are all emotional beings by nature. It is in our wiring and it is not a weakness.

Just as God is patient with us, we need to practice patience with ourselves: patience to sit with our feelings, patience to practice kindness to ourselves and patience to wait on God amidst what we are feeling and patience to not react but thoughtfully process our feelings.

Practice patience today as you flow with your feelings. Let feelings come in, recognize them, and then let them pass. Feelings don't have to rob from your stability or joy but rather are merely a part of being human.

Jesus, I acknowledge today that no one feels exactly the way that I do. Help me to understand that my feelings matter, but grant me patience as I learn to manage my feelings better. Amen

Rest & reset in Jesus

"The Lord will guide you always; He will satisfy your needs in a sun-scorched land and will strengthen your frame. You will be like a well-watered garden, like a spring whose waters never fail."
- Isaiah 58:11

How often do we as women feel heavily burdened and run-down? All too often, we allow our cups to run on empty and, in the process, affect those around us with emotional outbursts.

I love it when scripture speaks of gardens and water and here in today's scripture, our hardships or day-to-day chores are compared to sun-scorched land. That metaphor, I know, will resonate with many of us women. But we are reminded here that Jesus is our strength. After suggesting that we turn to Jesus for strength, the scripture goes on to describe us as a well-watered garden. Just this notion helps me breathe easy. We have access to life as a well-watered garden.

Be encouraged today: you were not created to burn out or live on empty. Jesus is your source, and as He fills you, so you will become a spring and be empowered to continue the works that lie ahead of you.

Jesus, remind me to turn to You for strength. May my cup never run dry, because I bring it before You daily to refill. I love you. Amen

Clinging to control

"Do not worry about your life, what you will eat; or about your body, what you will wear. For life is more than food, and the body more than clothes. Consider the ravens: they do not sow or reap; they have no storeroom or barn; yet God feeds them. And how much more valuable you are than birds!"
- Luke 12:22-24

Are you a control freak? It's a statement that causes us to put our backs up. Our desire for control is almost always fueled by our fear of things being out of control. I have always been organized by nature, although I don't deny a fair share of nurture may have contributed to this too. Over the years, I can recall many last minute plans or rain on planned outdoor-event days that caught me off guard and at times, even brought with them a spring of tears.

But I am grateful for these lessons, as true control is a myth. God is the only one in control and as long as we believe that we have it all in our control, we will be disappointed. The art of letting go is as swift and freeing as the words sound exiting your mouth.

A beautiful way to begin the process of letting go is firstly admitting your desire for control and accepting this with no judgment. Then, bring it before your heavenly Father and ask Him to make your heart teachable as you practice mentally separating that which you can and can't control, and letting Him handle what only He can.

Jesus, I may find comfort in control, but You created me and You know that about me. Thank You that I can approach You with full confidence that I am loved deeply. Please make my heart open to the lessons of control and teach me how to give over that which only You can control. Amen

Surrender at the throne

"Praise be to the Lord, to God our
Saviour, who daily bears our burdens."
- Psalm 68:19

It is often when we feel most out of control that we turn to dysfunctional habits to trick our minds into believing that we really are, still, in control.

Control is an illusion though. Food and exercise are two forms of abuse that women know all too well. Whether we restrict or reward with either behaviour, neither is fair on our mental or physical wellbeing. What if, just for today, you let go of your ropes on control? I encourage you to embrace the thought that perhaps all along, control had never been yours for gripping so tightly to. It takes great courage to lay our lives at the foot of the Cross and it isn't a once off activity.

Daily, we get to participate in this act of surrender. God has got you. You can let go.

Today repeat these words to yourself: I was never in control and thus my behaviour now has nothing to do with control & everything to do with learning to surrender and hand my journey over to God.

Jesus, I surrender, again today, my need to control everything, at Your Cross. Amen

Vulnerable before God

"When anxiety was great within me, Your consolation brought joy to my soul."
- Psalm 94:19

Early motherhood remains one the hardest seasons of my life.

For my first year of having two kids under the age of two, I approached life with an 'I am okay' mentality. That was until one day when I got home from work and simply couldn't get out of the car and 'mom'. As the tears rolled down my cheeks, Jesus whispered a beautiful truth into my longing, and very tired heart. He said that I was a good mom, that I had handled this so well but that now it was okay to get others to help me. He never meant for me to 'mom' alone. The last truth that He placed on my heart was a deep knowing that by sacrificing my sanity, I was in fact hindering my babies, not helping them. You may not be a mother, or in the throes of chaos, but wherever you find yourself today, know that you can bring it all to the Cross of Jesus.

Jesus is your safe haven. It is often when we approach Jesus in our most raw, vulnerable states that we hear from God in the most tangible ways.

———

Jesus, thank You that expressing my emotions in Your presence is the safest place to do so. Amen

Shared sorrow

"When Job's three friends heard about all the troubles that had come upon him, they set out from their homes and met together by agreement to go and sympathize with him and comfort him."
- Job 2:11

Whilst I am yet to experience deep loss, I have walked a road of suffering and know first-hand the power of both comforters and those who sympathize with you, in your time of suffering.

To empathize is to have gone through a similar situation and to understand another's pain. At times empathy can be incredibly helpful, but in today's reading we read that Job's friends set out to sympathize with him. They did not confess to understand his pain, but they were there to comfort him with their presence and perhaps words. It is tough when in a dark place to ask for help, or reach out for comfort, but we can trust that God will bring the right people across our paths at the right time.

All we need to do is to be obedient to God when we are led to comfort others.

Today, open your heart to Jesus, the ultimate comforter, and let Him direct you to those who desire to comfort you or to those whom He is calling you to offer comfort.

———

Jesus, You are my true comforter – teach me to rely on others when I need them and also to listen when You are prompting me to do the same for others. Amen

In your anger

"In your anger do not sin:
Do not let the sun go down
while you are still angry."
- *Ephesians 4:26*

God is not horrified or surprised that you get angry. The world may have told you a different story for a long time. They may have made you believe that strong, uncomfortable emotions are wrong, but scripture is clear in pointing out that both Jesus, and we, are guaranteed to experience these emotions.

I love how Paul, in today's scripture taken from Ephesians, says 'in your anger', not 'if you are ever angry' or 'don't get angry'. God says 'in your anger'. He gets it. He knows the thoughts and behaviours that drive your anger, but He too, knows that by His grace, you have been made righteous and what's more, cleansed of all need for retaliation.

Today, as you speak to God, ask Him for His guidance in teaching you how to manage your anger constructively and then through trial and error, practice these new coping mechanisms.

Jesus, thank You for Your understanding and Your acceptance of me, always. Help me to manage my behaviour in a way that honours You. Amen

Guilt-cleansed

"Let us draw near to God with a sincere heart and with the full assurance that faith brings, having our hearts sprinkled to cleanse us from a guilty conscience and having our bodies washed with pure water."
- Hebrews 10:22

Guilt has been defined as 'the sense that you're not living up to the expectations that you have about who you should be or what you should be doing. Or the kind of person that society suggests you should be.'

Daily, we are bombarded with messages of who we should be, what we should be doing & more so, who we are not. May we be reminded today that the expectations set by others, the very ones we compare against, causing us to experience guilt, may not be in line with our God-given design. In order to stop feeling guilty, we need to stand firm in our identity in Christ!

Today, do what you can, with where you are at and with what you have access to, and then simply let go of expectations that fall outside of your realm.

Jesus, thank You that You cleanse me of a guilty conscience, that I am blameless before You. Help me to receive Your grace every day, to begin again, and to let go of striving to be something that the world suggests I should be. Amen

Cycles of shame

"Those who look to Him for help will be radiant with joy; no shadow of shame will darken their faces."
- Psalm 34:5

There is a cycle that we speak of often in the Psychology world where guilt is considered feeling bad about behaviour, shame is internalized, as 'I am bad'. Shame often produces cycles linked to destructive behaviour.

An example I often use with clients is this one: In Grade One, a young girl may have experienced bullying on the playground. She retreated to the tuck shop and bought some chips. Her brain processed this transition as helpful, as she was feeling out of sorts and now the chips helped her feel happier. Unintentionally, a habit developed where every time this girl experienced something uncomfortable, she ate. Her friends then began teasing her about gaining weight. And so the shame cycle began. An uncomfortable emotion drove her to eat which made her feel she was a bad person, and so she did it in secret.

Shame is one of the scariest emotions to acknowledge, so be gentle with yourself as you acknowledge the shame that you experience. From here, take it before God and begin to build positive habits where previous habits brought on shame cycles.

———

Jesus, thank You that as I look to You for help that I will be radiant with joy and that no shadow of shame will darken my face. Amen

Allow more joy in

"Nehemiah said, 'Go and enjoy choice food and sweet drinks, and send some to those who have nothing prepared. This day is holy to our Lord. Do not grieve, for the joy of the Lord is your strength.'"
- Nehemiah 8:10

As women we're often so hard on ourselves, yet Jesus models again and again the power of being present within our own lives and being gentle with ourselves. After receiving sad news, Jesus would retreat to a place of solitude, not run to the crowds to numb his pain. And too, when joyful, He'd do what filled His tank. I know for me, when, unexpectedly, a good song comes on the radio, it's as if I've been lit up from within. I smile, inwardly. There is so much good in the world, amidst the bad; may we find those moments of JOY and revel in them.

Allow for more joy in your life. Recognize that which brings joy and don't be afraid to go a little wild when an unexpected moment of joy presents itself.

———

Jesus, thank You that You created joy. You love a joyful heart. Help me not to be a joy seeker but to allow for joy to surface when a moment allows or it and not to limit my enjoyment of that which is to be enjoyed. Amen

He cares for you

"Cast all your anxieties on Him, because He cares for you."
- 1 Peter 5:7

At school level, a simple request from a teacher for me to come and see her would send me into anxious-Annie mode.

At University the workload or a potential all-night-in-town got me munching on my nails. Then, hitting the working world meant night-upon-night of restless sleep knowing the mountain of work that I would face in the morning. For years I let anxiety be my guide – it ruled and I listened. Stress, and often anxiety, is guaranteed in the world that we live in today: what we can be in control of is the way that we manage our own anxiety levels.

Jesus models removing Himself from society when life felt heavy, and re-connecting with His Father. There is no greater model than this: quiet connection.

Today, turn down the noise of the world, breathe slowly, and take your anxiety before Jesus. An evening bath, a good stretching session, worship music or prayer are a few ways which can calm your nervous system and reconnect you with your Father.

Jesus, You are peace. Help me to connect with You, fully present, every time that the world begins to feel too heavy to bear. Amen

Do not be anxious

"Do not be anxious about anything, but in every situation, by prayer and petition, with thanksgiving, present your requests to God."
- Phillippians 4:6

It is often certainty that we desperately seek as humankind. We want answers, we want stability and we want control.

In the world we find ourselves in today, children of younger and younger ages are experiencing the deep burden of anxiety. The world can feel so heavy, our responsibility so big and our coping mechanisms so limited. Paul writes in Philippians that we should not be anxious about anything, and I find great comfort in this. He does not say that God will remove all of our problems or pressures, or that we will live easy lives; no, instead He provides us with a coping mechanism, perhaps the greatest of them all, prayer and thanksgiving.

There is no greater freedom from anxiety, than taking the pressure off your own shoulders and placing it onto Jesus's shoulders. This may feel unnatural, but a simple reminder that control is but an illusion can help to bring us back to the Cross, on a daily basis.

Jesus, thank You that You willingly take the load off my shoulders and place it on Your own. Amen

What's inside your heart?

"For the mouth speaks
what the heart is full of."
- Matthew 12:34

What comes in will come out.

As we continue to process the topic of emotions, we cannot ignore the fact that what we take in through our eyes, ears and experiences, will likely form the basis from which our hearts and minds operate. These days many of us spend hours on end scrolling through Instagram or watching series, not always aware of what we are allowing into our brains. We believe somewhere deep down that these resources will numb us from the world and that our brains won't take in the messages they are providing us with. We couldn't be more wrong! Our brains simply can't just turn off. It is our responsibility to be wise in what we choose to watch, see or experience, as it will shape our worldview, our feelings and us.

I encourage you to begin a process of filtering that information that you receive through screens and experiences. Choose wisely to allow in that which adds to your lives, that which serves you (and your relationships), and creates a safe headspace.

———

Jesus, convict me of what I am taking in each day without realizing it, and help me to be wiser as I choose what I allow into my subconscious and in turn my heart. Amen

Walls of protection

"By faith the walls of Jericho fell."
- Hebrews 11:30

For as long as I can remember, I have built walls around me, much like you, perhaps.

Walls that protect me from others, but sometimes even from myself. These walls weren't predestined, or chosen with huge intention; they just sort of happened. In life our hearts sometimes get bruised, feelings hurt, and our immediate response is to self-protect. It's our way of saying, "I'm going to do everything in my power to avoid going through that again."
Much like the Bible stories when walls literally crumbled, in my late teens, my self-protecting walls got shaky, and eventually fell to the ground. While it was one of the saddest, and hardest times of my life, it was also the very moment that, for the first time in years, I learnt to fly again.

Today, as you bring yourself before God, ask Him to begin to prepare your heart as you look to the walls around you, and ask yourself – "Are these still serving me or are they boxing me in?"

————————————

Jesus, thank You that by Your strength I can overcome anything. Help me to let down my guard with You, so that I too can be freed from the walls holding me back in my life. Amen

25th April

Vulnerability

"No temptation has overtaken you except what is common to mankind. And God is faithful; He will not let you be tempted beyond what you can bear. But when you are tempted, He will also provide a way out."
- *1 Corinthians 10:13*

In the words of Brene Brown, the guru of vulnerability, 'Vulnerability is the only bridge to build connection'.

I have personally always worn my heart on my sleeve, happy to share all that goes on within me, with the world. I always loved that my vulnerability allowed others the permission to be vulnerable too.

More recently though, I have realized that it is often only in having overcome a struggle that I share it openly, not whilst in it. I have since begun a process of embracing deeper vulnerability, not strength, real brokenness too. Connection is certainty deepened by vulnerability. I know that I feel closest to those who have openly shared both their struggles and strengths, and with whom I have shared mutual vulnerability. Our vulnerability before the Lord is much the same. The more we open ourselves to Him, the deeper we are bonded.

I encourage you to explore Brene Brown's work on this topic and to take your deep questions, struggles and shame before God and allow Him to enter that space within you.

Jesus, teach me to journey deeper with You as I reveal more of my rawness. Amen

A love that changes us

"Where can I flee from Your presence? If I go up to the heavens, You are there; if I make my bed in the depths, You are there. If I rise on the wings of the dawn, if I settle on the far side of the sea, even there Your hand will guide me; Your right hand will hold me fast."
- Psalm 139:7-10

I love this scripture and how its descriptiveness merely highlights the depth of the love that God has for us.

There is nowhere that we can escape to, to hide from the love of God. He is with us in the valleys and He is with us on the mountaintops. He is with us as we wrestle with emotion that leaves us burdened and bleak and He is with us as we experience the flow of joy and peace that follows a happy experience. There is no denying that that kind of love changes a woman's life.

May you know today, with whatever waves of emotions that you ride, that He is there, amidst it all, holding your hand.

———————

Jesus, thank You for Your constant presence in my life. I am never alone for You are my rock. Amen

Burnout averted

"A time to weep and a time to laugh,
a time to mourn and a time to dance."
- Ecclesiastes 3:4

I remember a day, whilst living in Korea, when I hit a "wobbly".
I got home after a long day and so desperately wanted to cry, but
'Caitlyn in work-mode' doesn't cry and so instead of collapsing on
my bed, I did what most people would do *(right?)*, I opened my
laptop and continued working for a while.

After suddenly seeing the time, I quickly changed into more casual
attire and walked to where I was meeting my husband for dinner.
Upon seeing him, brave little me, let it all out and with puffy tear-
stained cheeks, I announced, 'I need a holiday from my mind.'

My husband asked what I would tell a client who came to me with
this very problem. The first thing I knew that I'd ask the person, is
'What do you do for fun?' Tears began forming in the corners of my
eyes again, as I choked out the answer to my question. I'd forgotten
how to have fun.

*If, in the craziness of life, you've forgotten about things like 'having fun',
now is your moment. Fun looks different to all of us, so ask yourself today
what it is that would give you the break you need right now, and go for it.*

———————

Jesus, thank You that I don't need permission to have fun; You have wired
me in a way that certain things bring me joy and refueling. Help me to
find those things again. Amen

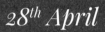

A special blessing

"Therefore, with minds that are alert and fully sober, set your hope on the grace to be brought to you when Jesus Christ is revealed at His coming."
- 1 Peter 1:13

It is almost always easier, in this world, to give in to pleasures of the world, than it is to practice self-control. In a world that encourages us to act on impulse and what feels right in the now, we can be quick to do everything but practice self-control.

I feel that God is not trying to punish us by encouraging us to practice self-control, but rather remind us that a life of the 'flesh', a life lived on impulse, can lead to far more brokenness than one submitted to the authority of Jesus.

One such example that I can think of, and mentored many a mum through (in the midst of exhaustion in early motherhood), is finding pleasure and consoling outside of marriage. Whilst this may feel like true freedom, we know that with clear thinking and exercising self-control, we reap the rewards that come with a long, faithful marriage and the friendship that comes with that.

There is no quick fix for developing a life of self-control; hence Peter's encouragement to exercise self-control. This week, and day, let's be intentional about exercising this self-control muscle, knowing that with time, our brains will learn to adopt this exercise as habitual.

———

Jesus, thank You that You meet me exactly where I am. Thank You that Your grace is sufficient for me, right now. Forgive me for the times when self-control has felt distant and help me to practice self-control. Amen

Do you remember?

"Because of the Lord's great love we are not consumed, for His compassions never fail. They are new every morning; great is Your faithfulness."
- Lamentations 3:22 – 23

I had the privilege of attending a Korean wedding in Korea a few years back. We found ourselves a seat in one of the pews behind a young family. Throughout the service, two young kids repeatedly looked at us and burst into hysterical laughter. Then, suddenly both kids surfaced from behind their pew pushing the corners of their eyes in – in an attempt to replicate our 'odd' western eyes. We had a good chuckle as the kids' very embarrassed parents apologised profusely.

What I learnt from that moment was that while Western kids see Asian eyes as different, they too see Western eyes in the same light. By seeing the same thing repeatedly, or by repeating a certain behaviour in time, our brains deem this as normal, regardless of whether it is accurate or not.

Often we take strides forward in our faith and are creating positive lifestyle changes, but then experience sets us back. This is merely our brain remembering old habits. Repetition is where our brains learn new positive coping mechanisms, and eventually these become our go-to's.

Today, take a moment to pause and do a quick internal reflection of where you're at, what you're feeling and what can change immediately, and then do just that.

Jesus, thank You that You have sanctified me and that Your compassion for me is new every morning. Amen

God will heal your wounds

"'You intended to harm me, but God intended it for good to accomplish what is now being done, the saving of many lives. So then, don't be afraid. I will provide for you and your children.' And he reassured them and spoke kindly to them."
- *Genesis 50:20-21*

The story of Joseph has always been one of my favourites. Joseph was the 11th son of Jacob and was referred to as his father's favourite son. Joseph's brothers hated him but instead of having him killed, they opted to sell him off as a slave, to the Ishmaelites. You may know the story of how Joseph eventually becomes second-in-command in Egypt, the very place he was a slave, and even has the power to later provide for his brothers.

But what struck me recently as I read the child-friendly version of this story to my children, was how long it took before Joseph began to step into his calling. His brothers' evil intentions, did, for a good few years, appear to have succeeded, until one day that all changed and Joseph's true calling was made apparent.

If you have been hurt, disappointed or shamed by others, know that God has the power to use even your deepest hurts to bring you back onto the path that He has for you.

Jesus, thank You that You will use that which was intended to harm me, and felt like it had, for good. Amen

MAY

saturated in Him

"But blessed is the one who trusts in the Lord, whose confidence is in Him. They will be like a tree planted by the water that sends out its roots by the stream."
- Jeremiah 17:7-8

God the gardener

"Jesus said to them, 'My Father
is always at His work to this very
day, and I too am working.'"
- John 5:17

In the Psalms, the heart or spirit is often referred to as a pasture where the shepherd walks. Our hearts can be seen as a garden, and God the gardener. God desires to tend to our hearts, much like a gardener would their garden.

I love this idea and the image it brings to mind. For each of us this idea will elicit a different image in our minds. Allow your mind to go there now. Picture a garden (your heart) as you see it and then imagine God walking around it. I like to see my heart as an expansive green field, and God walking through the lush grass. Nevertheless, amidst any garden or field, there are weeds to tend to, seeds to be planted and plants to nourish. God is the one who does this all, but only as we allow Him access to our hearts, our gardens.

Enjoy picturing your heart today as a garden and ask God to speak to you about this picture and how He sees your beautiful heart.

———

Lord, You are the gardener. Thank You that You tend to my heart with gentleness and kindness. Amen

Deep roots

"But blessed is the one who trusts in the Lord, whose confidence is in Him. They will be like a tree planted by the water that sends out its roots by the stream."
- *Jeremiah 17:7-8*

An element of faith that I love and find comfort in is that whilst it remains our duty and privilege to water our faith, to engage in behaviour and habits that grow our faith, God is the true gardener. Not all trees, even with adequate water, grow deep roots. There are elements of gardening that remain out of our human control. Faith is the same. We get to engage in prayer, worship, reading of the Bible and sharing our faith but God, the true gardener, is the One who ensures that our roots grow deep and that His water truly quenches our thirst. As we trust in Him, He allows our roots to grow deep.

Begin today by submitting your faith and life back at the feet of Jesus. Ask God to forgive you for when you've tried to earn your seat in Heaven and acknowledge Him as the true Gardener.

Jesus, take the wheel. I love spending time in Your presence but I too, apologize for when I've tried too hard to do things in my own strength. You are God. Amen

Water your garden

"Remain in me, as I also remain in you. No branch can bear fruit by itself; it must remain in the vine. Neither can you bear fruit unless you remain in me."
- John 15:4

I have recently become invested in my garden at home.

One of my favourite pasttimes, especially in winter, was watering my garden. I've always loved the smell of wet soil, but more than that it felt therapeutic to give water to my plants on our dry winter days. I could literally envision the water being soaked up by my flowers, much like I gulp down a cold Coke after a long run. Our faith is comparable. Our spirits will remain dry until such time as we water them. Spiritual food can be considered prayer, time in the presence of God, stillness in our lives to listen to His quiet voice, friendship with other believers and of course time in the word of God. As we water our gardens, our faith, like fruit, will begin to grow.

This week as you consider your faith, see each act of faith as a watering of your very own garden, a quenching of your spirit's thirst.

Jesus, thank You for the opportunity to grow my faith by actively taking steps to water what has been planted. Amen

Weeds grow in gardens

"A farmer went out to sow his seed... other seed fell among thorns, which grew up and choked the plants. Still other seed fell on good soil, where it produced a crop - a hundred, sixty or thirty times what was sown."
- Matthew 13:7-8

I've always loved the rain. The smell of rain transports me back to a happy, free childhood. Where we live, we get our rains in spring and therefore spring is one of my favourite seasons.

I love pottering around my garden before the pre-spring rains, planting new flowers and preparing old flowerbeds. But as spring arrives and I watch my garden be watered by the Heavens, I know too, that weeds will be growing. In no time at all - I'll need my gardener's help in weeding our blooming garden.

As we water and grow our faith, we need to remain humble and fully reliant on Jesus. By doing this we prevent ourselves from getting caught up by weeds - like worries of the world, or anxiety over comparison, or anything else that can grow up alongside our faith and choke it.

I have personally watched the choking effect of weeds that have disguised themselves as blossoms, grow in my life, and I know that it is only by God's grace that we get to start again. Be encouraged today to take your faith before God, with humility and trust.

Father meet me where I am at today, water and grow my faith but help me to remain humble as You pull out weeds along the way too. Amen

Childlike faith

"Therefore, whoever takes the lowly position of this child is the greatest in the Kingdom of Heaven."
- Matthew 18:4

One of the favourite parts of my day is putting my kids to bed at night and hearing their prayers. They thank God for the simplest things, and the greatest things too.

My daughter is a constant source of inspiration as her prayers are always real and vulnerable. Just the other day she thanked God for both a lovely day and for full healing of Mommy's pelvis. Her ability to shift from being thankful for something like the weather and then to trust God with my healing, reminded me of the power of child-life faith. It is the humility of children that drives them to trust and believe with such conviction. They have no fear or pride in admitting that God is King, and that everything good in our lives is from Him. What a beautiful way to approach both life and God.

May our hearts be open today to praise God for who He is, our provider, protector and great King.

Jesus, we praise You for You are good and Your mercies endure forever. Amen

God's handiwork

"Open my eyes that I may see wonderful things in Your law."
- Psalm 119:18

God has a way with words. He is the ultimate author, and the Bible is His handiwork. Whilst it can be incredibly daunting to begin reading the Bible, the Bible holds answers to the longings of your heart.

Many ask where to begin when reading the Bible, and my simple encouragement is to begin with the life of Jesus. Read it like a storybook but ask God to highlight things for you as you read. Then, the books that follow the gospels are full of life lessons, particularly appropriate for this day and age. Do not fear that you won't understand the Bible or that you'll be reading it out of context. God is bigger than our fears. Ask Him to speak, and He will. His Word is there to provide life as you discover more of His character, and of course who you are, through the books of the Bible.

A fun way to explore the Bible is to merely set 5–10 minutes of reading every morning or perhaps a morning over the weekend. This way the task at hand will feel less daunting.

———

Jesus, as I open up Your scriptures, speak to me in a way that only You can. Make it personal. Breathe living water into my being that I may know in the depths of me, that You are tangible, alive and within me. Amen

Worship Him in song

"Speaking to one another with psalms, hymns, and songs from the Spirit. Sing and make music from your heart to the Lord."
- *Ephesians 5:19*

Whilst I can't quite imagine making music to the Lord *(I leave that to our church worship team)*, I do know that music, Christian inspired music especially - moves me in a way that little else can. I have had many of my greatest moments with Jesus in worship sessions alongside others, on runs with worship music blaring in my ears and on my bed with Spotify playing my latest Christian music. I love how others have been gifted with an ability to write music, or be inspired by scripture to put together powerful praise songs, that we then get to take part in.

Praising God may feel strange for some, but singing along to a popular song is familiar for many of us.

I encourage you to do some research around worship music. Find or create a playlist that speaks to your spirit and find time in each day, perhaps early morning, or on the drive to work or on the school run, to let this music speak to your spirit and your spirit to Jesus.

Jesus, may You find pleasure in my praise. Amen

8th May

God is good

"Give thanks to the Lord, for He is good; His love endures forever."
- 1 Chronicles 16:34

Many of us live lives that are so rich and full but instead of relishing in life's goodness, we are blinded by uncomfortable moments or negative experiences. Much like when mist rolls into a mountainous area and disguises what was so beautiful to the human eye just minutes before; it's often as if the mist has rolled in and blurred our vision of what is good in our lives. Gratitude or thanksgiving through prayer is a beautiful habit that teaches our brains to recognize good, amidst hardship. It wipes clear the lens through which we see the world and gives us the pleasure of praising God for what we do have, rather than merely asking for what we do not.

A beautiful neurologically proven way to establish any new habit is to reinforce something enough times that our brains hardwire it and in-turn it becomes habit, a new normal if you will. Much like the process of driving a car and how at first it felt so tough, but through repetition it eventually became as natural as breathing.

Creating a gratitude journal or thanking God every day for just three things you're grateful for, is a powerful way of challenging your current thinking and establishing this new habit.

Jesus, thank You for the joys I experience every day. Thank You for Your helping hand when times are tough. Teach me to be more thankful and to shift my focus to the wonders that I do experience every day. Amen

9th May

Open my eyes & ears

"He changes times and seasons; He deposes kings and raises up others. He gives wisdom to the wise and knowledge to the discerning."
- Daniel 2:21

Whilst I'd lived in the same town for years, it took a visitor from another province to open my eyes to the beautiful changing colours of the trees in my very street, mid-Autumn. It blew my mind how I drove this street every day and yet had never noticed the array of colours and beauty in the change around me.

How often does this happen in life too? There is potential for a change of season in our lives but we're so stuck in our routines or comforts that we don't notice the changing of the seasons. We miss the fresh ideas, or seasons ending or new passions in bloom.

Take note of the season you're in right now and ask God to bring awareness to any shifts He has you moving towards or into.

Lord God help me to notice what You are doing in my life right now; where I'm heading, what doors are opening, and which others are closing. Amen

Sit at His feet

> "'Martha, Martha,' the Lord answered, 'you are worried and upset about many things, but few things are needed – or indeed only one. Mary has chosen what is better, and it will not taken away from her.'"
>
> - Luke 10:41-42

The story of Mary and Martha is one many of us know well.

I'm more of a Martha by nature. I find comfort in the busyness of life; but fortunately for me, my husband, whilst an A-type personality as well, brings a great calm to my chaos. He is not scared of slowing down. I'll never forget how long it took me to not feel guilty watching a series on a Saturday afternoon on the couch. He taught me this. That rest was essential if I wanted to flourish. Jesus does not reject Martha based on her desire to be more of a doer and less of a be-er; he merely points out that Mary chose better. Regardless of our personality, we get to choose whether to fill our lives with distractions or embrace the calm of Jesus.

Be encouraged today that You are not criticized for being either a Martha or Mary in character but rather that the power to choose to rest in Jesus, is in your hands.

Father today, show me how to apply this lesson to my life. To accept that sometimes the dishes or my workload can wait, and me spending time in Your presence is far more beneficial. Amen

How to pray

"Our Father in heaven, hallowed be Your name, Your kingdom come, Your will be done, on earth as it is in Heaven. Give us today our daily bread. And forgive us our debts, as we also have forgiven our debtors. And lead us not into temptation but deliver us from the evil one."
- Matthew 6:9-13

We have access to God all day; it is the privilege of having the Holy Spirit live within us. I personally find such freedom in knowing that I can call on God in any moment, or situation, or place, and He is there with me. The Christian faith is clear that there is no rule or instruction on where we should pray; but Jesus does model how we should pray. Jesus shares His model for prayer, after one of His disciples asked Him how he should pray.

The prayer that Jesus models is first praising God, secondly asking Him to meet our needs and thirdly asking Him for forgiveness and protection.

Prayer is a particularly special way of connecting with God, and how empowering to have a perfect model as to how you could engage in, or further develop your personal prayer life.

Jesus, teach me to pray as You prayed. To thank and praise You, to bring my needs before You, to ask for forgiveness daily and to trust You with my protection. You are my redeemer. Amen

Learn to listen

"But the Advocate, the Holy Spirit, whom the Father will send in my name, will teach you all things and will remind you of everything I have said to you."
- John 14:26

There are many ways in which we hear God's voice, and none of these are more wrong or more right. God wants a personal and intimate relationship with us, and longs to speak to each of us in a way that will be meaningful to us. God can speak to us through the Bible, through other people or through our own minds (discernment or promptings from the Holy Spirit). God is speaking and does speak to you.

If you struggle to hear His voice, do not be discouraged, this is not abnormal. We often doubt our thoughts, as we are unsure if the Holy Spirit or merely our own minds planted them. A lovely way to test this is to ask God to either ignite this thought/idea further or to take it away; this way you can trust Him with confirming His voice.

Remember that the more time you spend in God's presence, much like with a friend, the more familiar you get with hearing their voice.

Lord, what are You speaking to me about at the moment? Open my spiritual ears that I may hear You. Amen

Step out in faith

> "By faith Noah, when warned about things not yet seen, in holy fear built an ark to save his family. By his faith he condemned the world and became heir of the righteousness that is in keeping with faith."
> - Hebrews 11:7

Walking in faith can at times feel totally opposed to the ways of the world. Where certainty is sought after, the self-worshipped and instant gratification a must; it is no wonder that believing in something unseen conflicts with many of our realities.

But it is by faith that we are called to walk. Faith is believing in things unseen but knowing that peace and discernment is our guide. Whilst we cannot see God, we certainly can know and experience God and this begins by us opening our hearts to Him. He is waiting with His hand outstretched. I've often found great comfort in knowing that each time I've asked God to reveal Himself to me, He always has. Faith is putting ourselves out there and trusting Him.

May you find comfort in knowing that whilst faith is risky, it's reward is eternal.

Father reveal more of Yourself to me as I place my faith and trust in You. Amen

Faith foundations

"Their work will be shown for what it is because the day will bring it to light. It will be revealed with fire, and the fire will test the quality of each person's work."
- 1 Corinthians 3:13

We all know the story of the man who built his house upon the sand and how it fell to the ground in the first storm it faced. Gracious, even the childhood story of the 3 little pigs teaches us this notion. The foundation on which we build is paramount to how we build; but how and with what we choose to build is just as important. We need to be wise about how we see the concept of truth, in a world that believes in many truths. Truth or what we consider to be true is our foundation.

Once our foundation is established, it is then our responsibility to be wise with what practices we use to build our faith and lives; to ensure that our faith will stand the test of time.

How solid would you describe your foundation to be? Can you think of any habits or practices that you'd like to add to the building of your faith?

Jesus, You are the only foundation on which I hope to build my life. Give me wisdom as I live my life with authentic, deep faith in You. Amen

Fountain of life

"You give them drink from Your river of delights. For with You is the fountain of life; in Your light we see light."
- Psalm 36:8-9

As a woman, you may, like me, love a spa experience. I have been to a few beautiful spas in my life. I love how spas often house serenity and offer tranquillity. I recently noticed how often water is used as a calming agent in such places; a pond, fountain, pool or mere bowl of water; all symbolizing stillness.

The scriptures speak often of water in this same light. Water brings calmness, life and is sustaining in nature. Today's scripture focuses on fountains specifically. An element I love about fountains is that they are perpetual; their water keeps on coming. As they empty, so they refill. What a beautiful picture of what faith can look like too. As we empty, so we can refill. Jesus is the fountain of life.

Take some time today to acknowledge Jesus as your fountain of sustenance; your tranquillity.

Jesus, You are the fountain of life, You sustain me. Take me deeper in my knowledge of this concept. Amen

The Word is life

"Keep this Book of the Law always on your lips; meditate on it day and night, so that you may be careful to do everything written in it. Then you will be prosperous and successful."
- Joshua 1:8

Do you consider the Bible an essential element of your faith?

Journeying with the Word of God has sure been a ride for me. There are seasons of life when I devour the scriptures and others when my Bible has grown dusty and forgotten. But I am reminded every time I draw close to God, that reading and meditating on scriptures is a beautiful way to water our spirit. The Word of God is food for the spirit and provides us with a mighty tool for fighting for truth. The Bible is a manual of love, inspired by God, to bring us freedom, hope and guidance. It is our gift from God, on how we should and can live on earth. The Bible has the power to transform us, as we meditate on it and soak it up, so the Bible begins to change us and create a new standard of living and truth in our hearts and minds.

How do you approach reading your Bible? Do you feel this is an area of faith you'd love to sow into? Take this longing before God, He will draw you nearer.

Father, Your word is truth and You know how I could do with more truth in my life. Draw me to Your word and guide me as I read and meditate on truth. Amen

The Word is alive

"For the word of God is alive and active. Sharper than any double-edged sword, it penetrates even to dividing soul and spirit, joints and marrow; it judges the thoughts and attitudes of the heart."
- *Hebrews 4:12*

Have you ever found an interesting sea creature? I remember a day when we found the strangest worm-like sea creature in a tidal pool. It was arm-length; slug-like with antennas and spikes on its back. We watched this beautiful creature in absolute awe for well over an hour.

I have found my experience of the Word of God to be somewhat similar to this encounter we had with the sea creature. We ventured out for the day to a spot we know so well, but instead discovered something incredible, something fresh, something that caught our attention and pulled us in. The Word of God does this too. We can read the same passage of scripture over and over, but each time find something new, something appropriate and applicable for the season we're in. The Word of God is alive, and time spent devouring it, changes us.

Be encouraged today knowing that God has the power to reveal new things to you every time you open the Bible. Allow Him to speak into your life through the Word, as you simply open it up and ask for His guidance.

Father, draw me to Your Word, that I may make new discoveries of Your goodness, Your character and my purpose in this season. Amen

Wrestling with God

"Consider the ravens: They do not sow or reap; they have no storeroom or barn; yet God feeds them. And how much more valuable you are than birds!"
- Luke 12:24

Have you ever questioned your faith or wrestled with God on a matter?

I had the privilege of living in Asia for a year. That year happened to fall after I'd hit Church-burnout and so whilst I had a remarkable year, for the first time in my life, I questioned the existence of Jesus. It took a year of wrestling with God, but I remember a moment that utterly changed me. I was grappling with tolerance versus Christianity.

I was sitting on a tiny verandah in a small non-touristy Vietnamese town, really taking my deepest life questions before God. I looked across the narrow street and directly opposite me was a Buddhist man sitting contemplating life, I suppose. And on the verandah above him, a woman lighting an offering to her Hindu statues. And just as I saw this, out of the corner of my eye, I saw two birds on one of the many power lines across this street. And just like that the scripture hit me – "See how I look after the birds, too I will look after you."

Wrestling with God is acceptable; many mighty characters of the Bible did so often. But the privilege of having one mighty God to wrestle with is in fact more significant than the wrestling itself.

Father, You are the one true God. Thank You that You are not threatened by my big life questions. Amen

The in-betweens

> "I am the Lord your God, who brought you up out of Egypt. Open wide your mouth and I will fill it."
> - Psalm 81:10

Do you ever have days when you feel like you're running on empty and desperately need your tank filled up, but you have no idea how to fit your own needs into your busy schedule?

I experience these days often, amidst the juggle of work, home, kids, friendships and other responsibilities. How do we find time for quiet, for reflection, for refilling, when we feel that there simply is NO time available? The simple answer is that we make time; we squeeze the quiet out of in-betweens.

In-betweens for me sometimes look like 5 minutes amidst the chaos of young kids, with a cup of tea on the patio while the kids jump on the trampoline. Other times it's squeezing in 3 minutes of quiet by closing my eyes and remaining in my car when I arrive early for a meeting. And other times it's asking my husband to take over kid duty or dinner duty once he's home and retreating to my bath for 30 minutes of quiet.

Whilst it's not always possible to find an hour of quiet, take hold of the in-between moments, when you can create space for stillness and refilling.

Jesus, help me to capitalize on moments when a mere few minutes of prayer or praise is possible. Refill my cup, Jesus. Amen

The spirit comes in truth

"But very truly I tell you, it is for your good that I am going away. Unless I go away, the Advocate will not come to you; but if I go, I will send Him to you."
- John 16:7

The Holy Spirit is our inner guide.

Just as Jesus modelled behaviour and faith for His disciples and the people that lived in those times, so the Holy Spirit's job is to guide us. The beauty of the Holy Spirit is that by accepting Jesus as our Saviour, the Holy Spirit comes and resides within us. The idea that Jesus lives in you, is not just an idea, it is truth. He does.

I love how Jesus refers in today's scripture to the Holy Spirit telling us about the future. He can do this. He can help us be guided in truth and know which steps to take or which direction to head in.

Quiet yourself today, acknowledge Jesus as your Saviour and ask the Holy Spirit to make Himself known to you.

Holy Spirit, You live within me but I don't always know when it is You speaking to me or directing me. Help me to practice listening to You that I may know Your voice and trust Your guidance. Amen

We can stand firm

"May the Lord direct your hearts into God's love and Christ's perseverance."
- 2 Thessalonians 3:5

Did you also have the habit as a child of simply being able to smell an item of clothing left at your house, to know whom it belonged to? I've always found it interesting how some people have such distinct smells. My daughter recently received clothes from a friend's daughter who'd outgrown them, and every time she wears them, I'm transported back to this friend of mines' home.

We need to create these memory connections with our encounters with God too. We need to hold tight and truly recognize moments when God speaks to us and it feels undeniably real. As we recognize these moments and solidify them as memories, we allow similar moments later in life to transport us back to these times. And our trust in God is restored.

Ask God to bring to your memory today moments when His presence has felt so tangible in your life.

———

Lord, thank You that by remembering the peace and joy that Your presence or voice has brought to me before, I can find longing to return back to You for answers. Amen

Flow in your habitat

"Surely the righteous will never be shaken; they will be remembered forever. They will have no fear of bad news; their hearts are steadfast, trusting in the Lord."
- Psalm 112:6-7

Isn't it noteworthy how apples don't simply grow in the wilderness nor do avocados grow in icy climates? No, instead every type of tree requires a specific habitat and climate for it to bear fruit. Isn't it the same with us as humans? When we are in flow, in an environment that allows for our gifting to grow and be refined, this is when we truly bloom. Flow can be defined as the sensation that we feel when we are in 'the zone' or when time passes with ease, as we partake in something that comes relatively easy for us. It is less about the task at hand and more about how the world seems to disappear as you fully engage in an activity. It is often in flow that we find purpose and meaning, as we are likely using our unique gifts.

Take note of the environment that you find yourself in, and when it is that you feel most in flow. Find your flow as you find your habitat.

Jesus, help me to understand the concept of flow better. May my times spent in flow, be honouring to You. Amen

23rd May

Faith & the promise

> "Without weakening in his faith, he faced the fact that his body was as good as dead -since he was about a hundred years old - and that Sarah's womb was also dead. Yet he did not waver through unbelief regarding the promise of God, but was strengthened in his faith and gave glory to God."
> - Romans 4:19-20

We can learn a great deal from studying the life of Abraham. In Genesis Chapter 15 verse 5, God promises Abraham that he will be a father of nations. Abraham, and his wife Sarah, were already far beyond their childbearing years (Abraham being close to 100 years old), but Abraham's faith was not based on the limitations of his earthly body. Abraham believed God for who God was and God was faithful to him. The faith of Abraham was so extraordinary that Paul goes on to recall Abraham's faith in the New Testament.

Whilst we live fully as humans and thus know our human limitations, this does not give us a right to place these same limitations on God. God is all powerful, He is outside of time and He is faithful to His promises; despite whether we feel they are possible or not.

The greatest responsibility that we have is whether we have the courage to respond with faith, to the tests in our path, that we may overcome and see God's promises fulfilled.

Father give me courage to trust You and Your word above anything or anyone on earth. Amen

Faith to follow

"Whoever wants to be my disciple must deny themselves and take up their cross and follow me. For whoever wants to save their life will lose it, but whoever loses their life for me and for the gospel will save it."
- *Mark 8:34-35*

'Your faith will cost you.' I remember a friend saying this to me a few years ago and thinking, no I would make this work without experiencing any significant cost. Surely, I could do that. This selfish notion lasted until I was bed-ridden with a chronic condition and my self-reliance was stripped from me. The combination of God meeting me where I was at, and the people He brought into my life through this struggle, brought me to my knees in humility and tears.

I have since realised that little good ever comes with no cost attached. It's the cost, the giving up of something, that makes the prize so much more valuable. A life with Christ is the greatest gift we're given but the cost means not always fitting in on earth. We do not get excluded from suffering, but we're called in our suffering to still praise and to allow God to be glorified despite our earthly state.

You've got this, Beautiful. God will always provide you with the grace to face what lies ahead, and behind you. Trust Him as you count the cost.

Jesus, You paid the greatest cost of all, I am saved because of Your goodness. Thank You that my hope is found in You. Amen

He keeps His promises

"Blessed is she who has believed that the Lord would fulfil His promises to her!"
- Luke 1:45

One of the most beautiful parts of writing this devotional has been looking back at old journals I have written over the years, and unbeknownst to me, seeing how God has so specifically led me to this point right now. God makes us promises, some general, like that He loves us deeply, and others that are more specific to us personally but just as meaningful.

Whilst it is not encouraged to cling to prophecies or words of God from others, it is wise to write these all down. By acknowledging what you feel that God is saying to you in the present, especially in the written or typed word, is a beautiful way of being able to track God's faithfulness. I've always been an avid journaler and I am grateful beyond measure for past journals that now form testimonies of God's answered promises.

I encourage you to explore ways in which you can remember God's promises to you, and thus be encouraged in your faith journey.

Father, reveal to me Your promises, that I may walk with faith in Your wisdom. Amen

Profess His name

"Through Jesus, therefore, let us continually offer to God a sacrifice of praise - the fruit of lips that openly profess His name."
- Hebrews 13:15

I went through a stage in my mid-twenties when I thought it better to keep my faith hidden under a rock. I felt if I kept it hidden, it would remain mine, but I wouldn't feel the need to challenge the world with it. How wrong this mentality proved to be. It took me hitting an all-time career goal only to land in a pool of tears to realize that I had kicked the ball into the wrong goal post, so to speak. I was chasing what the world thought to be the answer, but it never was and never will be. God is the only true God, and He calls us His children.

Our time on earth is miniscule compared to the eternity that we will spend with Him in Heaven; and it is with this in mind on which we should build our lives.

Know that no matter where you find yourself today, God is there with you. He never leaves you, despite your unbelief, and to those who are currently strengthened by their faith, He calls you deeper still.

Jesus, take me deeper. Give me a fresh perspective on eternity and how fleeting my life on earth is. You are my true home. Amen

What if's

What if everything you're facing at the moment turns out to be a springboard off which your future bounces? What if all your heartache teaches you compassion? What if all your pain teaches you the power of healing? What if facing your deep fears gives you the freedom to fly? What if everything that you are going through is preparing you for what you asked for?

What if's can limit us and feed our fears and deepest concerns OR they can be a source of hope. Thinking in 'what ifs' feels natural, but how we frame them, that is up to us. We can approach what ifs out of fear and allow our minds to doubt and feed negative cycles, or we can produce what ifs out of faith. The choice is ours.

Today be encouraged by framing your 'what if's' in the positive. God promises to use all things for our good and He will use the tough seasons of life too.

Jesus, teach me to trust You as I live out today and to rely on You to turn my tears into joy. Amen

Faith like a mustard seed

"The kingdom of heaven is like a mustard seed, which a man took and planted in his field. Though it is the smallest of all seeds, yet when it grows, it is the largest of garden plants and becomes a tree, so that the birds come and perch in its branches."
- Matthew 13:31-32

In today's parable, Jesus compares faith to that of a mustard seed. A mustard seed is minute in size and yet if cared for and watered correctly, will bloom into a great tree.

What a beautiful picture to compare our faith to. Our faith doesn't have to be grand or declared as noteworthy in the eyes of the public; Jesus requires a tiny amount of faith with the right intentions for tending to it, for it to bloom into something beautiful. I love how Jesus goes as far as saying that the tree later becomes a safe place for birds to perch on. Our faith, however small, has the potential to touch others' lives.

Be encouraged today to take any tiny amount of faith that you have and place it in Jesus. And watch as He nurtures your faith tree.

Jesus, I place my faith in You. Help me to nurture it and allow You more access to my life, so that with time I can stand firm and offer support to others. Amen

Your faith is a shield

"In addition to this, take up the shield of faith, with which you can extinguish all the flaming arrows of the evil one."
- Ephesians 6:16

Have you ever shot from a bow and arrow?

I remember having the opportunity to try archery on a school camp; gracious, I was humbled – it was far tougher than I had anticipated. I have watched expert archery on TV too and been amazed by the power of an arrow aimed at a target.

In Ephesians 6, Paul encourages us to wear our faith as a shield. An arrow is always set for a target and a shield's primary purpose is to protect its owner. Our faith has the same quality. Our faith is the shield that is used to protect us from doubt, from fear, to fight off temptation and to conquer. But our faith only offers us protection, as we wash ourselves in the word of God, and know how powerful our shield of faith really is and thus pick it up.

As you approach this day, ask God for His guidance in building your faith, and using it as a shield of protection.

Father, this world is a battlefield and my faith in You is my armour. Help me to stand firm on Your word and to use my faith for what it is intended. Amen

Jesus didn't crave comfort

"Now my soul is deeply troubled. Should I pray, 'Father, Save me from this hour?' But this is the very reason I came Father, to bring glory to Your name."
- John 12:27-28

Jesus knew the mission that He was on. He knew His purpose on Earth was to glorify God and He chose to not pursue comfort at the cost of His faith. Jesus's faith was built on the foundation of who God is, and He constantly watered His faith by drawing closer to God.

Jesus shares in today's scripture that His soul was deeply troubled prior to His crucifixion. He was experiencing true human anguish, yet He refused to ask God to remove His discomfort as His focus was ahead on the purposes of God, not on His earthly comfort. I find this scripture deeply challenging as it encourages us to move through discomfort with our eyes on God, and not always trying to remove the discomfort.

Is God calling you to push through discomfort today? What has God laid on your heart that can help you move through this or an uncomfortable season?

———

Father give me strength to focus on the goal of pleasing You and bringing You glory! Amen

My soul thirsts

"You, God, are my God, earnestly I seek You; I thirst for You, my whole being longs for You, in a dry and parched land where there is no water."
- Psalm 63:1

Have you ever experienced cracked lips, or skin so dry that you can write on it? I love the healing sensation of lotion on my sun-kissed body after a day on the beach, or on my dry, flaky skin when in the mountains. There is something healing about giving our bodies what they need and watching as they replenish and rebuild. Our faith is alike. Our souls' thirst for meaning on earth, for a God who cares, for living water, and yet so often we deny Jesus the opportunity to meet us where we're at.

It takes deep courage and vulnerability to break down the barriers we may have formed around us, and to call out to God. But in doing this, we take the first, and greatest step in establishing faith and finding true hope on earth.

Wherever you find yourself today, know that God is near. God is crazy about you, and longs to fill you with living water, with the only true hope.

Jesus, meet me in my brokenness today. Come and heal my heart as I surrender it before You. You are my true hope. Amen

JUNE

He is in the storm with you

"Then He got up and rebuked the winds and
the waves, and it was completely calm."
- Matthew 8:26

The storm

"Suddenly a furious storm came up on the lake, so that the waves swept over the boat. But Jesus was sleeping. The disciples went and woke Him, saying, "Lord, save us! We're going to drown!" He replied, "You of little faith, why are you so afraid?" Then He got up and rebuked the winds and the waves, and it was completely calm."
- Matthew 8:24-26

We need to stand on a beach in the middle of a storm and witness the power of the raging seas to know the fear that Jesus's disciples must have experienced in this situation.

We read in the Gospels that Jesus slept through this raging storm. The very storm that had the disciples doubting their mortality did not produce an ounce of fear in Jesus. Wow! We can only but believe that it was Jesus's deep knowledge of who He was as God Himself, that gave Him the confidence to rebuke roaring seas. Just as the storm still appeared, despite Jesus's presence on the boat, storms will surface in our lives. But take heart, He is with you in the storm and has the power to calm even the most life-threatening storms that we will face.

Whatever storms you are facing, He is there in the storm with you. Waves can roar and storms destroy but Jesus remains the one that we can always trust despite our circumstances.

Thank you Jesus that You are with me in the storms that I face. Amen

A good God

"And we know that in all things God works for the good of those who love Him, who have been called according to His purpose."
- *Romans 8:28*

Our perception of good isn't always the same as God's perception of good.

I was told a story in my youth that has remained with me for years. The storyline went 'A child asked God every night if He could please make all of her teeth fall out so that she could make people laugh, like her grandpa did with his false teeth. God didn't answer her prayer. Years later she couldn't have been more grateful that her immaturity had not moved the hand of God.' Life can, at times, feel incredibly difficult and the burdens of life too heavy to bear; but it is in these moments or seasons of life that God often reveals Himself and His goodness to us, in ways that would have gone unnoticed in everyday life.

I encourage you to ask God today to show you His goodness, despite what you are facing. God is good, and our limited perspective can often limit us from receiving all that God has for us, in every situation.

Jesus, thank You for Your goodness and that despite my limited perspective, You work all things for my good. Amen

Don't write-off yesterday

*"You armed me with strength for battle;
You humbled my adversaries before me."
- Psalm 18:39*

Yesterday may not have been your day, it happens.

We have some really rough days that feel long and hard and by 4pm we can think of nothing better than crawling into bed. But, despite what yesterday held, you got through it. You are here, awakening to a new day, a fresh start. There will come a day, in months or even years to come, when the difficulties of yesterday are but a distant memory. Much like yesterday, you will likely experience similarly trying days again. You'll be emotional, ratty and at your wits end. And it will be on that very day that you'll remember yesterday. You'll remember your resilience to get through that day or that season of life. And just like that, the tired, emotional you of yesterday will become the hero of this story.

Know today, that you've got this! This season will pass, and your great and glorious Father will carry you and energize you when you feel you've got nothing left to give.

Jesus, thank You for the newness of each day. Thank You for fresh beginnings, for hope and for resilience. Amen

You're not alone

"When you pass through deep waters, I will be with you."
- Isaiah 43:2

Loneliness has the potential to be exacerbated during suffering or hardship. We can feel so alone with our thoughts, feelings and of course, time. As you walk through periods of life, time even, becomes blurred. Days roll into each other, and our outlook can become limited.

One reassurance that I always turn to when facing trials or intense hardship, is to look to the skies. I often sense God's presence when out in nature and so I force myself to put a blanket on the lawn and lie down to look at the clouds and soak up some vitamin D, or wrap myself in a blanket at night and watch the stars. It helps me to feel connected and to regain perspective. We all wake to the same sun and sleep under the same stars. Let that sink in for a moment. Despite your distance from those close or far away, the heavens cover us all.

May you feel safe and connected under the Heavens today, in the palm of the hand of your Father.

Jesus, thank You that I am not alone. You placed every star in it's exact spot and You care for every detail in my life too. Amen

Surrender in thanksgiving

"There is no one Holy like the Lord; there is no one besides You; there is no rock like our God."
- 1 Samuel 2:2

A beautiful example of thanksgiving in the Bible is that of the life of Hannah. Hannah waited a long time for God to answer her prayer and bless her with a child of her own. When she did receive her son, Samuel, she remained faithful and dedicated him to God and to the work of the temple.

Like Hannah, you have, no doubt, at some point in your life been forced to wait a long time for an answer to prayer. I personally will never forget the difficulty of, too, desperately wanting to fall pregnant but it taking longer than I had hoped. Whilst I can totally relate to Hannah's praise to God as she received the incredible JOY that came with the blessing of a son, personally, I cannot imagine handing this blessing back over to God.

Today may we be encouraged to hold our blessings with gratitude but also with surrender to the work of God.

———

Jesus, thank You for my many blessings and the goodness in my life. May I always put You first. Amen

Faith shared

"For where two or three gather in
My name, there am I with them."
- Matthew 18:20

Faith isn't easy, life in fact isn't easy.

A faith journey can include all sorts of extremes, from renewal
to doubt, recommitment and questioning to absolute suffering.
What I do know for certain, though, is that praising God alongside
others has made my faith journey that much easier. We have
spoken before in this devotional about the power of community.
Today I want to mention Christian community. This may be one
close friend, a group of girls, a church community or your spouse;
there is no 'one size fits all' for where or with whom you choose to
praise God, but there is indeed power in numbers. The saying goes
'a problem shared, is a problem halved', and also 'joy shared is
joy doubled'.

*I encourage you to reach out, perhaps within your own home, perhaps
finding a Church or life group or perhaps merely having an honest, faith-
filled conversation with a friend. Open yourself up to Christian community
in whatever way you believe suits you best, and watch as God moves in
and around you.*

———

Jesus, thank You for those around me who love You too. Amen

Darkness into light

"You, Lord, keep my lamp burning; my God turns my darkness into light. With Your help I can advance against a troop; with my God I can scale a wall."
- Psalm 18:28-29

Sometimes life simply doesn't seem to make sense and we can even go as far as feeling as if we're stuck in the boot of the car (or our own life) and we're being forced to go places and do things that we never imagined we'd be doing. Things like; going into debt, or hating our jobs, things like considering emigrating or moving from our dream home into something smaller but safer or having only one child due to financial constraints. It can feel as if someone else is dictating our future, our happiness, our stability, driving "our car". But despite this feeling, God remains God and if we open our eyes and invite Him in, He will reveal light in the darkness.

You have the power to choose right now, to connect again with your Saviour and with yourself; and in turn to jump back into the driver's seat of your life!!

Jesus, thank You that You shine light into the darkest places within us, and empower us with hope. Amen

8th June

Clearer perspective

"Trust in the Lord with all your heart and lean not on your own understanding; in all your ways submit to Him, and He will make your paths straight."
- Proverbs 3:5-6

I so clearly remember walking through a Shopping Centre in Stellenbosch the night after I got engaged and asking my brother if he noticed how everyone was looking at my engagement ring. (You're allowed to chuckle at my ignorance).

Fast forward five years and I was walking along the promenade with my baby in her pram, and I mentioned to my mum how many mums were pushing their babies in prams on the promenade. My mum pointed out how mums and babies had always been on the promenade; I just hadn't been looking out for them.

Isn't it crazy how when we focus on one thing, we seem to block out everything else? This couldn't be more applicable in everyday life. Our brains are often more tuned into what is wrong in our lives (and in ourselves) than what is going right.

Today, even amidst the hardness of the season or situation you are currently in, may you find a fresh sense of clarity as you change your perspective and shift your thoughts to happier times.

Jesus, thank You that You understand my pain but too that You gave me a powerful brain that can in seconds trigger a fresh release of dopamine, my happy hormone, just by shifting my thoughts to happier times. Amen

Today is a new day

"Is anyone among you in trouble? Let them pray. Is anyone happy? Let them sing songs of praise."
- James 5:13

Whatever the situation that you are currently facing, be reminded that today is a new day, a fresh start. Today, there is only a future and a present. Today, you get to remember the past, but you do not have to travel there. Today, you get to start a new journey, one that leads you forward.

It's easy to get stuck in the past; I know I did this for years. On numerous occasions, I would find myself introducing myself to people by referring to my past, be it failures, life lessons, achievements, where I went to school, you get the gist. Now-adays, I find that I rely less on my past but still bring up yesterday all too often.

Yesterday was a day lived, BUT whether you did well or could have done better is a thing of the past. Today is your day: a new day to live as the daughter of your High King.

Jesus, thank You for this new day. Help me to not let yesterday rob from all that You have for me today. Amen

A detailed God

"I waited patiently for the Lord; He turned to me and heard my cry. He lifted me out of the slimy pit, out of the mud and mire; He set my feet on a rock and gave me a firm place to stand."
- Psalm 40:1-2

Whilst this scripture certainly suggests our salvation in Christ, I can't but resonate with its message of one being pulled from a miry bog.

I recently lived through a hardship of my own, in a physical nature, one that robbed my joy, my freedom of movement and even my family life. Whilst God did not heal me in the time that I so desperately hoped; through other wondrous ways He revealed Himself to me, amidst my hardship. A moment marked in my memory was when I'd completed one particular week of spending a great deal of money on seeing specialists, only to be told no further progress had been made. It was on this very day that I was presented with a new work opportunity. It was a speaking gig and the budgeted amount was outrageous, but when I looked into the detail it was exactly R30 more than what I'd spent on specialists that past week.

God is into the detail. He will reveal Himself and He will pull you from the miry bog and set your feet upon a rock.

———

Jesus, thank You that You are my rock and that You will, always, make my steps secure. Amen

Another in the fire

"And these three men, firmly tied, fell into the blazing furnace. Then King Nebuchadnezzar leaped to his feet... 'Weren't there three men that we tied up and threw into the fire?'...'Look! I see four men walking around in the fire, unbound and unharmed, and the fourth looks like a son of the gods.'"
- *Daniel 3:23-25*

A story that I love reading for my children is that of Shadrach, Meshach and Abednego, and more specifically their encounter with God in the fire. These three men were obedient to God in not bowing down to the standards of their times and the result was that they were thrown into a fire.

Does this sound familiar?

How often do we feel that by living out our lives as followers of Jesus that we just don't fit in? I know that I for one have even considered that it may be easier to forsake my faith, or water it down, in an attempt to fit in more. And yet here, in scripture, we see one of the most powerful messages of God when it comes to hardship. There is another in the fire. He is with you.

Whatever it is that you are facing, Beautiful, know that there is another in the fire. Ask God this week to show Himself to you amidst the fire that you may be walking through.

Jesus, what a joy and privilege to know that You are with me, even as I walk through what feels like a fire. Amen

Pockets of joy

"The Lord is close to the brokenhearted and saves those who are crushed in spirit."
- Psalm 34:18

"And maybe that was how it was supposed to be...joy and sadness were part of the package; the trick, perhaps, was to let yourself feel all of it, but to hold on to the joy just a little more tightly." These words by Kristin Hannah could not be more applicable today.

Sadness we may be facing, hardship we may be experiencing or suffering we may be undergoing, but there are still moments of joy, even in hardship.

As we go through seasons of sadness in our lives, may we too, pocket moments of joy, and later, like children empty out their pockets before bath time, may we empty out our pocketed joy at the end of the day. May we be reminded that there are moments of joy within sadness or a hard season of life.

I encourage you to repeat to yourself today, 'I will walk through and with sadness but I will pocket joy too.'

Jesus, thank You that even in the hardest of days, moments of joy still remain. Help me to not 'beat myself up' for allowing joyful moments despite my sadness. Amen

Trust your journey

"So do not fear, for I am with you; do not be dismayed, for I am your God. I will strengthen you and help you; I will uphold you with my righteous right hand."
- Isaiah 41:10

I lived through a season in my own life in 2018, where something had to give in order for me to smile again. It was whilst in this season for me, that I remember Christmas Day; a day that was normally an absolute favourite of mine, but this particular one was incredibly hard for me. I sobbed and couldn't get out of bed.

There was a lot going on in my life, and a serious lack of sleep in that season of life, but I did eventually see light at the end of a long tunnel. It's tough to relay what brought a positive shift for me, as we're all so different and what works for one won't work for another, BUT, if this is you, I can tell you that there is HOPE. You will get through this.

Just for today, trust your journey and keep your eyes on Jesus - your true HOPE. Keep hope alive until such time as it simply is alive.

Jesus, thank You that I can trust You despite my pain and that I will see the light again. Amen

You are safe

"When you pass through the rivers, they will not sweep over you."
- Isaiah 43:2

There is a lagoon that borders the main beach in the town where we have a beach house. Every December, following the KwaZulu-Natal spring rains, the lagoon breaks open into the sea. What starts as a trickle soon becomes a raging river, and this can continue for weeks on end. Being a busy beach, the lifeguards usually put a rope across the lagoon, aiding the beach goers in reaching the beach and not being swept out to sea by the strong flow of water.

I find this picture so appropriate to compare to life too. At times my life has felt so hard that I was convinced I would be swept away, and yet somehow I've always come out on the other end, shattered but okay.

Today, take stock of the rivers you've crossed over the years, and how despite the strong currents, God has got you through what you may have, at the time, described as impossible.

Jesus, thank You for Your grace in getting me through my struggles unharmed, but changed nonetheless. Amen

Renewal everyday

"Therefore, we do not lose heart. Though outwardly we are wasting away, yet inwardly we are being renewed day by day... So we fix our eyes not on what is seen, but on what is unseen, since what is seen is temporary, but what is unseen is eternal."
- 2 Corinthians 4:16-18

In a season of my life when I personally lived with chronic pain, it seemed to consume me. I was so focused on my physical healing, which just wasn't happening at the rate I had hoped, that my spirit and mind began to crumble.

From being a genuinely positive person, I moved into a dark space within myself. It was only on reaching rock bottom whilst on bed-rest, that I finally welcomed God into my chaos. To me, physical healing seemed the goal, but God quickly opened my eyes to a bigger picture at play. He began renewing my faith and trust in Him. He reignited a flame of passion for His Kingdom, and with that came a passion for life again.

Today, despite your earthly pain or struggles, may you place your eyes on Jesus? He will renew you, day by day, and as your spirit comes alive, so will your passion for life.

Jesus, thank You that my earthly body cannot be compared to all that awaits me in Heaven. Help me to fix my eyes on You, to not try to understand the workings of the world, but to be transformed and renewed by You. Amen

Keep on rejoicing

"Dear friends, do not be surprised at the fiery ordeal that has come on you to test you, as though something strange were happening to you. But rejoice inasmuch as you participate in the sufferings of Christ, so that you may be overjoyed when His glory is revealed."
- *1 Peter 4:12-13*

Trials and suffering are something that are referred to often in the Bible, and yet still we find ourselves shocked when we are experiencing them ourselves. Our faith does not disqualify us from suffering, at least not on earth. When you're in the midst of facing loss, suffering, pain or hardship, it can be difficult to keep on rejoicing, especially as we know that God can and does heal.

Others, who have experienced loss, have told me that their greatest consolation was rejoicing in the fact that their loved one was now with Jesus. Finding hope, in our suffering, is often the catalyst for rejoicing. It is hope that we cling to, not pretending to understand the ways of God, but keeping Him as our God regardless.

As you journey through today, may you find peace in the hope that is Jesus? And as you find hope, may you find a space within to rejoice, despite your current struggles.

Jesus, thank You that You are our reason to rejoice. Alight within us a new strength to rejoice even when experiencing hardship. Amen

Diamond in the rough

"But He knows the way that I take; when He has tested me, I will come forth as gold."
- Job 23:10

The heat of all that you are facing, or have faced, is creating in you a beauty that will last long after this world will stand. I love to think of the mining industry when I read scriptures like today's one. Miners chip away everyday, only to seek out that which is worthy. But when gold is mined, it does not resemble the pieces of gold that we find in jewelry stores, instead it is merely a raw lump, but still hugely valuable. The jeweler then transforms this lump of gold, into something truly beautiful.

God does the same with us.

He may not intend our suffering, His word is clear on this, but He is committed to always refining us into better, more beautiful versions of ourselves.

I encourage you to take a moment now to think back over your life, and especially the tougher parts of it. Try to recognize one trait or strength that God grew in you during a rough period of life. Isn't it powerful to see trials in this way?

———

Jesus, You are the potter and I am the clay. Thank You for chipping away at me, even when I've resisted, so that I can come forth as gold. Amen

A plan in Jesus

"Who is like You, Lord God Almighty? You, Lord, are mighty, and Your faithfulness surrounds You. You rule over the surging sea; when its waves mount up, You still them."
- Psalm 89:8-9

Stress is intensified by the way that the brain perceives it. Studies have shown that those who perceive stress to be bad for them, often experience exacerbated stress, which then has long-term effects on them. Those who see stress as something more fleeting and approach stress with a plan, tend to be less affected by it.

Whatever we are facing, as followers of Jesus, we always have a plan: faith, hope and love. Faith is trusting Him with our lives despite the stormy seas we find ourselves being tossed around in. We hope in Him as He promises to bring good out of every situation. And we love because by loving our Father, we are empowered to receive His love, which is our living water.

Today, may faith, hope and love be your beacons of truth, as you face what lies ahead of you. God will still your surging seas.

Jesus, thank You that You meet me in the surging seas, and that You promise, that regardless of my limited perspective and feelings today, I will not be forsaken. Amen

The gift

"Thanks be to God for
His indescribable gift!"
- 2 Corinthians 9:15

In the words of my friend, who suffered a tough road of infertility and her own father's suicide, "God used the worst moment of my life to heal another moment that I had been burdened with for so many years."

I was truly humbled upon hearing my friend tell the story of how her incredibly tough road of infertility and miscarriage, led her to a sadness beyond her own understanding. In turn, however, it gave her an insight into the state in which her father lived prior to his suicide. This suffering of her own, helped her to heal this deep wound in her misunderstanding of depression, for the first time. Suffering is not something that any of us would wish on another. Whatever it is that we face, true hardship can feel as if your very soul is being strangled, and yet at the heart of suffering is Jesus. The giver of gifts.

Whilst you may not get the answers you seek in your suffering, Jesus will always provide you with gifts right where you are at. Open your eyes and heart to Him.

Jesus, help me to recognize gifts that I may not ask for, but gifts nonetheless, on days when hope is all that I need to keep on going. Amen

Sow in tears

"Those who sow with tears will reap with songs of joy."
- Psalm 126:5

For years society was fed the lie that tears were a sign of weakness. I have learnt, especially since becoming a mother, that tears often in fact show strength. It takes deep courage to face what we are feeling, to stop our natural pull to avoidance or numbing, and to journey to and through the pain. Whether it is tears over loss, pain, suffering, trauma, despair or being moved by compassion, God speaks directly into this space of tears.

David writes in the Psalms that what we sow in tears we will reap in joy. God encourages us to go there, to allow ourselves the space to cry, to weep. He promises to bring joy out of the pain, even if it was our own doing that caused the pain.

Today, allow yourself freedom to express your pain, to weep and to release the build up of emotion within you. God is holding you and will turn those tears into joy.

Jesus, thank You for the freedom to weep and express all that I am feeling, knowing that somewhere in this process, You will turn my tears to joy. Amen

21st June

God goes before you

"The Lord Himself goes before you and will be with you; He will never leave you nor forsake you. Do not be afraid; do not be discouraged."
- *Deuteronomy 31:8*

In reading today's scripture I am immediately transported back in my memory to a family crisis, of sorts, that we faced a few years ago. None of us knew what was about to hit us. What would have felt incredibly uncomfortable and potentially even threatened my faith, did not, merely because exactly one year prior to this event, God had begun preparing my heart and faith for this very crisis. I had no idea what lay ahead of us, but He did. And He does. He knows your life story, from start to finish. He walks ahead of us and prepares the way; not in smoothing all paths but rather in preparing our hearts, our souls and our spirits for what is to come.

He is our strength, our guide, our hope and our rescuer.

Today, bring to mind moments in your past where you feel that God really did go before you and prepare you, without your knowledge.

Jesus, today we celebrate Your goodness in knowing that we are never forsaken. Thank You for going ahead of us and preparing us, for all that awaits us both on earth and in Eternity. Amen

22nd June

Storms may rage

"He stilled the storm to a whisper;
the waves of the sea were hushed."
- Psalm 107:29

If you have ever had the privilege of going out by boat or ship in the ocean, you'll know the utter extremes of the seas. The ocean is often compared to the unpredictability of life. One day it is calm and provides peace, the very next it is stormy and raging, ready to swallow you up.

The ocean can make us feel so small in just an instant, it's depth beyond our grasp, and nothing can prepare us for what the next day at sea will hold. And then you get the still days, when the ocean is perfect and yet, amidst the calm, an experienced surfer will get dumped whilst riding waves of perfection. Life is so often the same. Even within the calm, there are waves that hit us out of nowhere and have the potential to produce deep fear, but one day will again settle.

Today, know that whether you are facing a big wave in a calm sea, or a roaring storm at sea, God is with you, and you will see the calm of the horizon again soon.

Jesus, thank You that as I ride the waves of life, You remain my stability. Amen

23rd June

Deep calls to deep

"Deep calls to deep in the roar of Your waterfalls; all Your waves and breakers have swept over me."
- Psalm 42:7

It is often believed that when at our worst, most broken selves, that God's voice is clearest. I too, have experienced this. But I have also experienced the hardness of pressing into God, when life isn't making sense and His presence feels far from my reality. It is in these states, that I rely on God to call me back to Him.

It is when my heart has become hardened, by disappointment, delayed healing or hurt, that I hope that God will draw me to Him, when I simply don't know how to journey back to Him myself. And again and again, He has done so. Deep calls to deep, comes to mind.

When you are broken, or sad, or feel lost, may the Spirit of God call out to your spirit, and re-waken your faith and trust in Him.

Jesus, draw me to You. May Your deep call me deeper. Amen

Keep faith alive

"For we live by faith, not by sight."
- 2 Corinthians 5:7

A friend of mine has recently been fighting the battle of cancer. She is a wife, with 3 young kids, and has faced months on end of horrendous chemotherapy. One of the many things that I have learnt from her and her husband as they've faced this enormous battle is that they live by faith and not by sight. Never has she asked, 'why me?' Instead she has taken her reality before God, her everyday battles before God and continued to praise Him as King and author of her life. This has been a beautiful, humbling lesson for me.

Life and struggles are less about who we blame and more about how we choose to show up, and who we continue to praise, when the battle begins.

Be encouraged by today's scripture to live by faith and not by sight. God is bigger than your current situation. He is stronger than any battle that lies ahead of you. Find hope in this truth.

Jesus, thank You for faith despite hardship. Thank You for hope even when situations feel hopeless. You are my rock. Amen

Come to Me

"Come to me, all who are weary and burdened and I will give you rest."
- Matthew 11:28

Whilst the term "rest" may seem simple to define, in writing this book I asked a few friends to comment on how they see rest. One friend said that her mind goes straight to a day spent on a secluded beach, another spoke of an afternoon nap and still another, a day off from running.

I love that we serve a personal God. He created us with different desires, dreams, and personalities and of course struggles. Many times in the Bible we are encouraged as followers of Jesus, to lay our burdens down at the Cross. I love that we have someone to turn to when burdened, but even more so in today's scripture, how Matthew takes it one-step further and says that all who are heavy laden will be given rest. There are no questions asked; take your burdens before God, and He will provide you with rest.

Be encouraged today – the fact that you carry heavy burdens was predicted in the Bible before you were born; as was the rest that God has for you.

Jesus, thank You that You know what I need. Please provide me with the rest I so desperately desire, as I lay my burdens before You. Amen

Build spiritual habits

"Because you are His sons, God sent the Spirit of His Son into our hearts, the Spirit who calls out, 'Abba, Father.'"
- *Galatians 4:6*

Life is full of both trials and joys, every day a part of the big picture unfolding. Rarely can we truly prepare for the future, as we do not know what awaits us. Our knowledge of the future is so limited. I have been so grateful, in past moments of utter despair or fear, when my faith has carried me, without any effort.

When my daughter was 3 months old she aspirated in the night and as we raced her to the emergency rooms, I remember both my husband and I crying out to God to save our little girl. We both prayed in tongues. It was so natural to turn to God. We didn't talk to each other or run the idea of prayer by each other; our spirits merely cried out to God, in our time of need.

I encourage you to use the seasons when life is going well to build spiritual habits that will carry you through the harder seasons of life.

Jesus, teach me to turn to You in both the good and tough times of my life, so that my spirit becomes comfortable with connecting with Your Spirit regardless of the circumstances that surround me. Amen

Raise a Hallelujah

"Though the fig tree does not bud and there are no grapes on the vines, though the olive crop fails and the fields produce no food… yet I will rejoice in the Lord, I will be joyful in God my Saviour. The Sovereign Lord is my strength; He makes my feet like the feet of a deer, He enables me to tread on the heights."
- Habakkuk 3:17-19

The words of a song by Bethel Music, "Raise a Hallelujah", come to mind when I think of what it takes to praise God as storms rage around us. Fear, disappointment, pain or suffering can cause our hearts to harden and in turn our hope to dissipate. As we praise God, we edify who He is, but also who we believe Him to be, amidst our suffering.

One beautiful truth that we can cling to, allowing us to praise as we face hardship, is that God remains unchanged. This may sound like common knowledge, but to the soul that is tired, certainty is a gift. And certainty can in-turn produce hope. And hope has the power to carry us through even the darkest of days.

May you raise a Hallelujah amidst the storms that you face today, knowing that your King remains unchanged, and your certainty rests in Him.

Jesus, thank You that You remain unchanged, despite what the world looks like or how uncertain circumstances may feel. Amen

The ultimate comforter

"Even though I walk through the darkest valley, I will fear no evil, for You are with me; Your rod and Your staff, they comfort me."
- *Psalm 23:4*

Whilst there are many views by various commentators on the meaning of today's scripture, the meaning that most resonates with me, is as follows: David, who wrote the Psalms, was a shepherd boy. Shepherds used rods or staffs to both guide and correct the behaviour of their sheep. The rod was also used to fight off robbers, in times of need. I love to imagine that David is saying, through this scripture, that he does not need to fear, even when facing the darkest valley, as God, his shepherd, will guide, direct, protect and comfort him.

And too, God promises to do the same for us today: to guide, direct, protect and comfort us in our time of need.

Be encouraged today to know that God is bigger than anything you are currently, or will ever, face.

Jesus, You are my comforter, my protector, my compass and my guide. Help me to trust in You always. Amen

The armour of God

"Finally, be strong in the Lord and in His mighty power. Put on the full armour of God, so that you can take your stand against the devil's schemes."
- Ephesians 6:10-11

How often do we wrestle with God, wondering what more we can do to escape the hardships of this world? And yet here, in this scripture, God gives us the very answer to this oh-so-common cry for help.

It is the armour of God that we are instructed to wear daily, that is our weapon in this world. We are instructed to put on this armour as it empowers us to stand strong, despite our circumstances. The belt of truth on our waist, the breastplate of righteousness, the gospel of peace on our feet, the shield of faith in our hand, the helmet of salvation on our head and the sword of the Spirit, which is the word of God. *(Ephesians 6:13-17)*

Today, ask God to deepen your understanding of this instruction and to convict you of one or more of the weapons that He longs for you to equip yourself with.

Jesus, empower me today to be fully prepared for battle in obedience to You. Amen

30th June

Your rainbow

"I have set my rainbow in the clouds, and it will be the sign of the covenant between Me and the earth."
- Genesis 9:13

"I can't change the direction of the wind but I can adjust my sails to always reach my destination". Jimmy Dean was spot on when he quoted these words. God is more powerful than the circumstances before us. He can use anything, and will use everything, to bring good out of all situations, in order to fulfill His perfect plan in you, and me.

You may be amidst a storm but may I encourage you not to believe that your life on this earth is ever on hold. There is purpose in everyday life - your life matters. You may be far from seeing your storm end, but I know that I for one am a better person for having walked through my storms. And that right there is a rainbow.

Rainbows are God's promise that the storm is over. Your rainbow will come but it may look very different to the one you'd thought up. God won't fail you now!

Jesus, open my eyes to the rainbows that You place amidst the storms that I face. Amen

JULY

dive deep into Jesus

"Jesus answered, 'I am the way and the truth and the life. No one comes to the Father except through me.'"
- John 14:6

Jesus is remarkable

"Truly I tell you, if anyone says to this mountain, 'Go, throw yourself into the sea,' and does not doubt in their heart but believes that what they say will happen, it will be done for them. Therefore I tell you, whatever you ask for in prayer, believe that you have received it, and it will be yours."
- Mark 11:23-24

It is Jesus's faith that He is most remembered for. The life of Jesus on earth was extraordinary. Jesus changed lives in both His time and generations to come, and brought a hope to the world that answered our deepest longings as human beings.

We are not qualified to enter Heaven. We are not holy enough to approach God. But Jesus, through His obedience to God, took our place and died the death of a criminal so that we might have access to God, personally possess His spirit within us, have access to eternity with God and live fullness of life on earth. Jesus's life was remarkable and we can learn so much from His character, behaviour and faith.

Open your heart, Beautiful, to the life of Jesus. Let us celebrate His life as we study who He is. I encourage you to do a self-study of the life of Jesus through one of the gospels as we too look at Jesus's character this month.

———

Jesus, teach me more about You, so that I can be changed into Your likeness. Amen

Discernment

> "Immediately Jesus knew in His spirit that this was what they were thinking in their hearts, and He said to them, 'Why are you thinking these things?'"
> - Mark 2:8

To discern is to have a strong sense of something, or to easily distinguish between right and wrong. Jesus had a deep discernment on both the calling of God on His life as well as on His sense of what was wrong or correct in this world.

To have spiritual discernment is to sense how God sees a situation or person. It is almost to see beyond what the natural allows for. Discernment is hugely empowering as it helps us to act on our gut feeling, which is led by the spirit of God within us. Have you ever felt as if you just knew something about someone or you knew you shouldn't attend a specific event, and just like that your intuition was fulfilled or something took place that you wouldn't have wanted to be a part of? This is discernment.

Trust God today to lead you as you say this prayer from Psalm 119: 125, "I am Your servant; give me discernment that I may understand Your statutes."

Lord, give me discernment that I may ask according to Your will. Amen

Humility like no other

"By myself I can do nothing; I judge only as I hear, and my judgment is just, for I seek not to please myself but Him who sent me."
- John 5:30

Jesus was born in a stable to a simple family. He did not arrive with a crown on His head, or leave this earth in robes of earthly splendor. Jesus is our ultimate model of true humility. Jesus was so sure of who He was as the Messiah, that He needed no earthly adoring to live out His mission on earth. Jesus knew that His purpose was to please God, and thus the things of this world were of lesser importance to Him, and rather His calling of great importance.

We can learn a beautiful lesson from this. Whilst only Jesus can be perfectly humble, we can learn from Him to find our identity in God, knowing that everything that we possess, our giftings, finances, assets and talents are from God. As we confess this, we open ourselves to deeper humility.

Thank God today for all that He has given you. Praise Him for His blessings in your life and be amazed as your praises produce in you, a deeper humility.

Lord, convict me today of my true purpose here on earth that I may approach today with a deeper humility knowing my true identity is in You. Amen

Obedience to God

"And being found in appearance as a man, He humbled Himself by becoming obedient to death - even death on a cross!"
- Phillippians 2:8

Our obedience to God is not about following rules or feeling pressure to conform to certain standards. Our highest call of obedience is to accept Jesus as the Son of God, to submit to God's guidance, and to accept the grace that is offered to us as children of God.

The Bible has often been confused as a book of instructions, and the Christian faith, a religion of rules. But I believe that we have this all wrong. The Bible is a book of love. Jesus, God's own Son, loved us so much, that He chose to be obedient to God's call to save us. Even obedient to carry His own Cross and die a death set for criminals. That is no religion of rules, but instead deep powerful love.

Our obedience to God is our pledge to come before Him and be transformed by Him, not in our strength but by His grace.

The love of God for you is so great. Find comfort in His kindness today, knowing that Jesus was obedient, so that you may have life.

Jesus, open my eyes, let me see the power of the Cross anew, that I might be challenged in obedience to submitting my life to You. Amen

Life with no pretenses

"He will yet fill your mouth with laughter and your lips with shouts of joy."
- Job 8:21

Have you ever skinny-dipped? *(Yes, you read that in your daily devotional)*. I'm a rule-abider by nature. I find joy in sticking to routine and what is expected of me; but as the years have gone by, I too, have come to realize that not all rules keep us safe. There are many societal rules that in fact do quite the opposite, instead of safety, they box us in. Trap us even.

Whilst you'll rarely find me breaking rules, one unspoken rule that I often break, is swims in the sea in my underwear. I find it totally exhilarating to go for a run or walk and then make my way onto the beach, usually a deserted one, and whip off my running top and dive into the ocean. There can be freedom in breaking the rules. Jesus was without sin, but often did things that broke societal rules. Today's scripture reminds us that God wants us to experience joy in life.

Ask God today to lift your pretenses, and to allow you the freedom to experience more joy, in your every day life.

Lord, You are joyful. Teach me to allow more joy into my life, as I live with freedom and conviction that I am Your daughter. Amen

Practice patience

"Therefore, as God's chosen people, holy and dearly loved, clothe yourselves with compassion, kindness, humility, gentleness and patience."
- Colossians 3:12

Patience is a virtue, and not one I'm renowned for. Perhaps, like me, you struggle to practice patience too? It is virtues like this one that I get wrong so often, that keeps me humble and aware of my great need for more of God.

Much like how we adopt the habits of friends when in their company; as we spend time in the presence of God, we begin to become like Him. We begin to speak like Him, act like Him and look like Him. If patience is a quality that you battle with, or need more of, fear not, God is the giver of all good gifts, and qualities alike. As we spend time studying the character of Jesus, we see again and again how He humbly practices patience as He deals with both His disciples and the public, and their lack of faith.

Jesus is our ultimate model for patience and too, has the ability to transform us into more patient women. Let us repeat the prayer found in Romans 15:5 (NKJV) today.

———

"Now may the God of patience and comfort grant you (me) to be like-minded toward one another, according to Christ Jesus." Amen

Stillness within

"Very early in the morning, while it was still dark, Jesus got up, left the house and went off to a solitary place, where He prayed. Simon and his companions went to look for Him."
- Mark 1:35-36

Again and again, we hear of Jesus retreating to a quiet, private place to be with His Father. What a beautiful picture.

When the noise of the world drives us to deep discomfort, it is God that we need to seek out. His goodness, His presence and His quiet voice. The temptation to busy ourselves or distract ourselves with our phones or schedules is all too pressing. To hear God's voice; we need to actively seek out calm within our lives.

Years before Jesus was born, Moses modeled going up a mountain to hear from God, but Jesus confessed that the Holy Spirit now lives in us, and thus we merely need to quiet our minds enough to hear Him.

When all is silent, may it be well with your soul. Seek out calm today, and press into God and His goodness.

Jesus, help me to practice being still in order to benefit from hearing Your voice and to find peace within. Amen

Trustworthy Jesus

"For even His own brothers did not believe in Him. Therefore Jesus told them, 'My time is not yet here; for you any time will do. The world cannot hate you, but it hates me because I testify that its works are evil. You go to the festival. I am not going up to this festival, because my time has not yet fully come.'"
- John 7:5-9

Jesus reveals His trustworthiness again and again on different accounts in the scriptures. He has integrity like no other as at the core of Jesus is a simple mission, and one that He allows no one and nothing to get in the way of Him accomplishing.

Jesus is trustworthy to the mission on which His father sent him. He does not waver. Jesus loved His family deeply but even when they doubted Him as the Messiah, He still did not waver from His mission on earth. The ultimate trustworthiness of Jesus is found in the very mission that Jesus remained trustworthy to accomplish, the reason that we get to approach Him today with full confidence. He came that we may have life, through accepting His sacrifice. We can trust Him with our lives as He trusted God all the way to being sacrificed on the Cross, for our sake.

Today, be encouraged knowing that Jesus is trustworthy because He remained true to the mission that God set out for Him to accomplish. And that mission was to rescue you, and me.

Jesus, You are trustworthy like no other. Teach me what it means to live a life where my integrity is founded in doing the will of God. Amen

Servant leadership

"So He took off his outer clothing, and wrapped a towel around His waist. After that, He poured water into a basin and began to wash His disciples' feet, drying them with the towel that was wrapped around Him."
- John 13:4-5

Our views on leadership these days are often tainted as many leaders consider their role to be one of significant power, and power is so frequently abused.

Jesus models the most extravagant form of leadership throughout His life. Whilst He admits to being the Messiah; after a shared meal with His closest friends and moments before His crucifixion, He gets down on the floor and washes the feet of His disciples. This is the ultimate act of servant leadership; to lead from the front but inspire with humility. Jesus is not afraid that by serving His disciples they will think less of Him or take advantage of His kindness; instead He gains their respect by making Himself one of them; and honours God in the process.

May we be encouraged today to research the topic of servant leadership and ask for God's guidance as we lead in our workplaces, homes, communities or churches, with a servant heart.

Jesus, what a beautiful model of servant leadership You taught. Teach me what it means to live with humility and to not allow fear to produce in me arrogance. Amen

Honest living

> "Jesus answered, 'I am the way and the truth and the life. No one comes to the Father except through me.'"
> - John 14:6

We all know the concept of something being 'watered down'. Faith can often be described in this way. 'To water down' is to reduce or make light of faith. A watered down faith often contains elements of faith or the Bible but not the full version.

If there is one thing that Jesus did not do on earth, it was conform to the times that He lived in. He was one of them, but He never allowed society or doubters or even His own family, to come between Him and His faith. He was fully committed to God and this meant that He upheld an honest message with His life. He did not change His story to fit in with those around Him. He felt compelled to be honest at all times, but also was not scared to be seen with those who were considered the worst of sinners. He did not fear that His faith would appear watered down if He were to spend time in the presence of prostitutes or taxpayers. He lived out His faith day by day, with deep integrity and love.

May we learn from the character of Jesus that a watered down faith will only lead to a watered down life.

God, teach me how to live with deeper integrity. Convict me where I may be watering down my faith to fit in. You give my life meaning. Amen

Fear or faith?

"There is no fear in love. But perfect love drives out fear, because fear has to do with punishment. The one who fears is not made perfect in love."
- 1 John 4:18

Everything we do in life is birthed from either faith or fear.

Every action taken, every thought entertained and every feeling felt, is led by faith or fear. Both faith and fear require us to believe in a future unseen. Fear cripples us, it produces anxiety and reduces our hope, whereas faith sets us free.

We cannot walk in faith and fear simultaneously.

We are either believing or we're doubting! Be encouraged to build into your faith, rather than your fears. It is often easier to doubt ourselves, a situation or even God, than it is to believe. But the reward of faith is eternal. Faith allows us to walk in truth, to believe God for who He says He is, and this produces true peace of mind.

A beautiful question that I love asking myself, and I encourage you to do the same today is: What do I have faith for today?

───────

Jesus, help me to walk in faith over fear. I trust in You, Father God. Amen

True gentleness

"Blessed are the peacemakers, for they will be called children of God."
- Matthew 5:9

Have you ever heard someone say that they're a much nicer person after spending time with Jesus?

As I've grown up, and had to face the many stresses that life throws at us, this lesson has become more real for me. The presence of Jesus changes us. Time spent with God is the perfect reset button; a time to practice self-awareness, to ask for forgiveness, to express emotion vulnerably and to be refilled afresh. Isn't this the very stuff that prevents breakdowns or burnout? Just reading these words brings me great peace. Jesus modeled gentleness in beautiful ways, and we too are called to be gentle; but can only live with true gentleness by the grace of God.

Be encouraged that regardless of your personality or natural go-to's, God has the power to bring out all the qualities of Jesus in you, as you submit your life to Him.

Father, draw me to Yourself, that I may be changed into Your likeness. Amen

Wisdom of Jesus

"And Jesus grew in wisdom and stature,
and in favor with God and man."
- Luke 2:52

Do you know anyone who is particularly wise? I have a friend who has been absolutely gifted with wisdom. She is bright, of course, but wisdom differs to intelligence. Wisdom knows when to speak and when to remain silent. Wisdom is having insight into situations or people. Wisdom draws people in, and wins their favour.

Today we read in Luke, that Jesus grew in wisdom. What a beautiful idea, that one can grow in wisdom. We know this to be true for maturity but wisdom often seems a little more innate; as if either you have it or you don't. But scripture is truth, and thus we know that each of us has the ability to grow in wisdom, to become wiser.

There is no time limit placed on gaining in wisdom, but we do know that Jesus modeled it, and we can thus only but follow in His footsteps to gain similarly.

Father, teach me to grow in wisdom that I may gain favour with You and with people. Amen

The long road

"Whoever has my commands and keeps them is the one who loves me. The one who loves me will be loved by my Father, and I too will love them and show myself to them."
- John 14:21

Do not be afraid to take the long road.

I'm a short-cuts-kind-of-girl. I've always been quick to action and if a short cut is offered, you'll find me on that path. But we learn from scriptures that Jesus never took shortcuts; in fact more often we see him taking longer roads and enjoying the journeys.

Faith is far from an easy journey, and there sure are no short cuts to Heaven. But God is full of surprises and it is often on the longer roads, amidst our journeys, that we see Him, grow in understanding of His character, hear from Him and find a clearer sense of direction. Jesus was never in a rush and we do not need to be either.

Do you, like me, tend to take short cuts, or perhaps are struggling mid-journey at the moment? Take heart, God is in the detail. He meets you right where you're at and He will transform you within your circumstances.

Jesus, open my eyes to see the wonderful mystery of You. Amen

15th July

The compassion of Jesus

"Jesus went through all the towns and villages, teaching in their synagogues, proclaiming the good news of the kingdom and healing every disease and sickness. When He saw the crowds, He had compassion on them, because they were harassed and helpless, like sheep without a shepherd."
- Matthew 9:35-36

Compassion is a conversation point that I often have with close friends. In the times that we find ourselves, the needs of society are rife and our efforts can feel hopeless.

A characteristic that I love about Jesus is His compassion for people. Jesus made every person feel noticed; a cripple, His own friends and even a woman who merely touches His coat. Jesus never overlooks a man or a woman, despite their faith or lifestyle, and in this, He shows that compassion is for all. God delights in showing mercy, this is no weakness. Whilst we see Jesus perform many physical miracles and showing earthy compassion; Jesus shows His greatest compassion on those that are spiritually lost. Today's scripture points to the deepest longing in the human heart, the need for a Saviour.

May we take on the challenge today, to be compassionate at all times, but mostly to offer compassion to the spiritually lost and to ask for God's guidance in bringing His children into His loving arms.

Lord, thank You for the ability and the call to live a life of compassion. You are my teacher, help me to show more compassion in my life today. Amen

Hold yourself in

"But the fruit of the Spirit is love, joy, peace, forbearance, kindness, goodness, faithfulness, gentleness and self-control. Against such things there is no law."
- Galatians 5:22 – 23

The Greek word for self-control, mentioned here, as a fruit of the Spirit, is 'egkrateia' which means literally 'holding oneself in'. I love that self-control is not fighting oneself, but rather holding oneself.

When Jesus modeled self-control, He was not being untrue to His nature. He merely stood His ground against the enemy. The very enemy that we face today. The enemy who approaches us with temptations that lead to sadness and brokenness. The enemy who robs from our joy by promising earthly pleasures, that never fulfill us like we think they will. Self-control is a contentious topic in the century we find ourselves in, but I find peace in understanding the Greek meaning of this term.

Jesus doesn't want you to be less of you, but rather to be more like Him, and in-turn live with abundance, not bound by rules but led with freedom.

Take this meaning of self-control to heart today and ask God to further lead you into the freedom that He has for you.

Jesus, help me to hold myself in, so that I can walk in the freedom that You have given me. Freedom to life in abundance. Amen

Practice forgiveness

"Jesus said, 'Father, forgive them, for they do not know what they are doing.' And they divided up His clothes by casting lots."
- *Luke 23:34*

One of the final pleads that Jesus utters before He dies, is to ask God for forgiveness for sinners. The power of forgiveness is the basis of our faith. We cannot access God as we are, sinful by nature, but by His blood shed for us on the Cross, we are forgiven. The fall of man is forgiven and we are redeemed.

There is enormous blessing that follows really grasping the message and power of forgiveness. Forgiveness has the power to strengthen relationships, release resentment or anger and improve our mental and physical health significantly. It is far easier to forgive others when we understand the depths to which we have been forgiven.

Ask God today to take you on a personal journey of understanding His forgiveness, and how this empowers you to forgive others too.

Jesus, thank You for the power of the Cross in my life. Thank You that nothing can separate me from Your love, because of Your forgiveness. Amen

Withdraw & pray

> "But Jesus often withdrew to lonely places and prayed."
> - Luke 5:16

Jesus placed enormous value on His prayer life. Whilst God is outside of time and thus knows our beginning and end, this did not stop Jesus from praying.

Jesus connected with God through prayer, and this is one of the greatest gifts of our faith, our connection to God. It is through prayer that we connect with the heart of God. Prayer and thanksgiving allow us to edify God and thus reaffirm our identity as children of God. Prayer activates our faith; it reminds us that God is in control and that He cares and as we pray, we bring God into our greatest needs. We call Him in, we ask for His discernment, His guidance and His help.

Be bold as you approach God in prayer. He longs to hear your prayers, to direct your prayers and to answer your prayers, in His perfect timing.

Father, teach me how to retreat and to pray about everything. You are the only one with all the answers to my life questions, draw me to You I pray. Amen

Great friend

"You are my friends if you do what I command. I no longer call you servants, because a servant does not know his master's business. Instead, I have called you friends, for everything that I learned from my Father I have made known to you."
- John 15:14-15

Have you ever wondered whether you're allowed to call Jesus your friend? Doesn't that rob from His role as King?

Jesus actually longs for us to be His friends. Jesus contains the very best characteristics of a great friend. Jesus is loyal, He is a great listener, He has our best interests at heart and He loves us deeply.

Just as I have learnt in my adult life, that my mum is no longer just my mum but my close friend too, Jesus too can play both roles. He can be your Saviour and your friend. Today's scripture reminds us that Jesus has given us everything He has learnt, making us His equals here on earth, empowered by God's grace.

We can both learn from what Jesus modeled a true friend really is, and accept the friendship of Jesus. We have full access to both privileges.

Jesus, help me to see You as my friend as well as my Saviour. I love You. Amen

Availability

"But the Pharisees and the teachers of the law were furious and began to discuss with one another what they might do to Jesus. One of those days Jesus went out to a mountainside to pray, and spent the night praying to God. When morning came, He called His disciples."
- Luke 6:11-13

Availability is being willing to adjust our own schedule, agenda, and plans to fit in God and others.

Whilst personal boundaries are vital in maintaining our mental health, Jesus rarely ran out of energy and became unavailable. This has been a deep challenge for me to wrestle with. I often find life to be exhausting and the responsibilities that I carry heavy, but Jesus modeled retreating when tired, being refreshed by God and then returning to the crowds.

Jesus lived fully human, and felt all the things that we feel, but He did not rely on His earthly body for refreshing; for that He went to God. It was Jesus's absolute certainty of where His hope lay, that drove Him back to God again and again to refuel.

Jesus's cup overflowed, as God continuously refilled it. Allow God to do the same for you today.

Father, draw me to You so that I may be refilled and in turn be available when You call me. Amen

21st July

Jesus is attentitive

"While Jesus was still speaking, some people came from the house of Jairus, the synagogue leader. 'Your daughter is dead,' they said. 'Why bother the teacher anymore?' Overhearing what they said, Jesus told him, 'Don't be afraid; just believe.'"
- Mark 5:35-36

Jesus modeled for us what it truly means to be attentive. How rare it is in our times, to be truly listened to!

The distractions that we have access to today often draw from our ability to connect and from our intimate relationships. How easy is it to pick up your phone even amidst a conversation with a friend or your partner? Distractions distance us and remove intimacy as they create barriers in communication and offer subliminal messages of neglect. Jesus being attentive to the needs and requests of His friends and followers led many to trust Him deeply, and to know they could rely on Him. What beautiful qualities to possess.

Take your life before God today and ask Him for guidance as you work to be more attentive to those around you, who you love or feel deserve your attention.

———————

Jesus, teach me how to shake off distractions and give my full attention to those I love; just like You modeled. Amen

Endurance

"Carrying His own cross, He
went out to place of the Skull."
- John 19:17

Have you ever watched someone face something that you feel would have knocked you off your feet, and yet they remain steadfast in their faith? This is endurance. Endurance is the inner strength to remain in Him, despite what our life or circumstances look like. Endurance is often connected to finishing strong, but endurance is actually more about the journey than it is the end goal. Enduring is to struggle but to keep going.

Jesus is our ultimate model of this. When I think of this term, I see Jesus carrying His own physically heavy Cross. Jesus, the sufferer. Endurance takes enormous willpower but is rarely possible without a goal in mind. You are and were Jesus's goal. He endured His mission to the Cross, despite the absolute agony which He faced, because of you and me, and the mission God had set before Him.

Be encouraged today as you endure certain elements of life, knowing that Jesus faced utmost anguish and rejection, but still chose to continue on His mission from God. You have the strength to do the same.

Jesus, as I turn to You, refill me today as You remind me of the inner strength that You placed within me. Amen

Jesus remembered God

"For we do not have a high priest who is unable to empathize with our weaknesses, but we have one who has been tempted in every way, just as we are - yet He did not sin."
- Hebrews 4:15

At the center of Jesus's life is God. God as Father is the foundation on which Jesus's life unfolded.

Whilst Jesus experienced sympathy and empathy, neither led His behaviour. He did not give or serve out of sympathy but rather by an overflowing of what God was doing in Him. What a beautiful concept to take in. We are not called to feel sorry for people, and thus give, but rather to be drawn to Jesus, saturated in His love, and to allow this to overflow into the lives of others. By merely giving-in to an emotion like pity, we satisfy the need for the release of this emotion, but with no lasting impact. Jesus can sympathize with our every need, as He was fully human, but he does not give-in to our longings, but rather gives us what our Father knows is best for us, in season.

Be encouraged that we too can be led by God as we serve those around us; not influenced by pity but rather by discernment from Jesus.

Father, thank You for the ability to experience deep sympathy for others, but the courage to turn to You to know how to approach any given situation. Amen

Intentional living

> "For it is God who works in you to will and to act in order to fulfill His good purpose."
> - Philippians 2:13

When people speak of morning routines and the power there in, my mind immediately travels to a long secluded beach in the south of Thailand. After backpacking for close to a month, my husband and I found ourselves on a beautiful island for a whole week of quiet bliss. Well, it started as bliss, but by day 3, I began to question my own sanity. You see I'd assumed that I'd be happy everyday, waking late, sitting on the beach, tanning and sipping on coconuts, but we were well past needing a vacation stage of this trip. I needed purpose.

I've since discovered that many others feel the same way. Whilst we hope to float around and find joy in everyday, we rarely do, without some intention. Jesus modeled intentional living. He knew why He was here on earth, and everyday was lived with this in mind. This brings me great peace. A morning routine can often set the tone for one's day. Knowing why I feel that I am alive today dictates my morning routine and in-turn how the day usually plays out.

Use a moment today to reflect on the power of your morning routine or lack there of. Ask God to speak into this space for you, as you redefine it for yourself.

———

Jesus, You lived with enormous intention. Help me to set the tone for each day so that I too can feel that every day is important. Amen

Self-acceptance

"Jesus knew that the Father had put all things under His power, and that He had come from God and was returning to God."
- John 13:3

Loving and accepting my postpartum body has been a journey for me, for sure. Whilst I totally understand the desire for mums to lose weight, I too know in the depths of my soul that whether I have a six-pack or a whole lot of loose skin, it holds little significance over who I am and what my value in this world is.

Self-acceptance is a thinking habit, not a body one. It's not an easy road to rewire our brains to look for good on a body they previously may have labeled wrong; but it is possible. Jesus never spoke of His physical body or stature, this seems mostly unimportant to Him. I love that Jesus was so sure of who He was, as the Son of God, that He felt little pull to fit into the times He lived in.

Today, be encouraged as a woman of God, to renew your mind to the likeness of Christ. Ask Him to empower you to make what is important to Him, important to you.

———————————

Jesus, break my heart for what breaks Yours and help me to separate myself from the vain battles of this world. Amen

Frame your world

"For we live by faith, not by sight."
- 2 Corinthians 5:7

Reality is changing by the day and with that our views on life, the world and faith. I find that one of my greatest challenges, as a parent, is how I choose to frame the world for my kids. Kids see the world as their parent/caregiver suggests that the world should be seen. This is both a gift and potentially a nerve-wracking reality.

In truth though, we see the world too, how we choose to frame the world for ourselves. We can see the world as the news depicts it. We can see our health as doctors report it. We can see our futures as economists predict them. Or we can see the world as God sees it. This is not a call to be unrealistic of how your world looks right now. We are flesh and blood and live very much in this world, but we are not of this world.

Be encouraged, this is not as good-as-it-gets, per se. What awaits you in Heaven is far beyond anything you can imagine. Take heed, He has overcome the world and He calls you to frame your world, as He sees it. Real but limited in length and scale.

Jesus, help me to see the world as You see it. Help me to know that my time on earth is meaningful but that what awaits me in Heaven is my true home. Amen

Conviction

"And I will ask the Father, and He will give you another advocate to help you and be with you forever - the Spirit of truth. The world cannot accept Him, because it neither sees Him nor knows Him. But you know Him, for He lives with you and will be in you."
- John 14:16-17

Jesus lived by His convictions. I read a funny anecdote recently, which suggested that when one has a tough decision to make, merely flip a coin. Because when the coin is in the air, you'll suddenly realize which option you're really hoping for. How true? So many of us doubt ourselves, our decisions, our purpose and even our peace; yet often when we watch another facing a traumatic situation, we are so sure of how we would handle that decision or circumstance.

Jesus was never indecisive because He knew His identity in God. He knew that He had the answers within Him and that He could trust Himself fully based on His convictions. When Jesus was preparing to leave earth, He told the disciples that the Holy Spirit would live in them and be with them. The voice or answer that we yearn for when we are seeking conviction lives within us. The Holy Spirit lives in you; guiding you, directing you and convicting you.

Today, quiet the world around you as you recognize the Spirit within you. The more practiced you are in listening to God's still small voice, the louder His voice will become.

———

Holy Spirit, direct me as I go about my life. Thank You for Your omnipresence. Amen

Rest in Him

> "Then, because so many people were coming and going that they did not even have a chance to eat, He said to them, 'Come with me by yourselves to a quiet place and get some rest.' So they went away by themselves in a boat to a solitary place."
> - Mark 6:31-32

Jesus rested. I wrote these words in a blog post a few months back, "When all of her hustling was forced to a stand still. She cried and then picked up the pieces of what looked like a broken life, only to realize that perhaps if she put them back together slightly differently, she may finally feel at home within herself!"

This was me, and perhaps you too. I lived for the rush. Adrenalin-fueled my blood and I rarely stopped for long enough to catch my breath. But life caught up with me. My body spoke up first, stopping me in my tracks and forcing me to embrace a far slower season of life. I realized that the hurried nature of the world may seem appealing but it is in fact suffocating, and so contrary to the way that Jesus lived. Jesus poured out His love on both His disciples and the public, but He always retreated when He felt the need to be refilled. Jesus placed value on resting His soul and body, and His spirit was refueled during these times of rest.

Today, give yourself space to explore yourself more deeply and to not just look in but to look up.

Jesus, teach me to go slow. Thank you that I am enough, and that striving adds nothing to my worth in Your eyes. Amen

Freedom in Christ

"It is for freedom that Christ has set us free. Stand firm, then, and do not let yourselves be burdened again by a yoke of slavery"
- Galatians 5:1

The concept of freedom is one that has always drawn me in. I've craved it for as long as I can remember. I believed freedom to be a reward of sorts, something I could work for. Until one day, I felt God saying to me that I had lived like a donkey pulling a heavy cart (burdened) for a long time. But even after that cart was removed (Jesus took over my burdens), I walked around oblivious of my freedom. I walked as if burdened, although I was in fact free.

If this resonates with you today, know that by the power of God, through belief in Jesus, you are FREE. It is His promise and you can claim it right now and hand over your burdens to Your Father.

What does freedom look like for you? Bring your life before God today and boldly proclaim that you're letting go and claiming the freedom He has given you.

Jesus, You have already set me free. Help me to grasp this so that I can walk in this promised freedom. Amen

God works in us

"For it is God who works in you to will and to act in order to fulfill His good purpose."
- Phillippians 2:13

Jesus lived to do the will of God, and we can too. Faith in God can be compared to that of a mighty river that begins in the mountains and travels all the way to the sea. Whilst one main river remains, it too will break into tributaries, smaller streams, with differing purposes. Some of these streams will full up dams, some will turn to smaller streams for crops, some will feed into other greater rivers, some will rejoin their source river whilst others will simply come to an end.

Each of us gets to live our own lives on our own terms. God gave us this privilege. Much like a tributary, we flow from the same source, but if we separate ourselves from this source we will simply dry up. God works in us, to do His will. It is not out of selfish ambition or running ahead of ourselves that we live out our calling, instead it is by staying connected to our source.

Take your vision and current dreams before God today, as you reconnect to the source that gives you life.

Father, help me to stay connected to You, my source of life, so that You can work in me to do Your will. Amen

Jesus is here

"I have been crucified with Christ and I no longer live, but Christ lives in me. The life I now live in the body, I live by faith in the Son of God, who loved me and gave Himself for me."
- *Galatians 2:20*

It's with salty hair, sandy feet and sun-kissed cheeks that I feel most alive. We all have these moments or places that make us feel most ourselves. When all is quiet, we sense an inner joy, something more meaningful than what everyday life offers; despite our circumstances. Can you go there in your head now? Find that quiet space to explore you in full bloom?

Jesus felt this way about doing the will of God. Jesus's ultimate calling was to love. Above all else, He loved. He loved His Father, and He loved us, enough to die on the Cross. This made Him feel most alive and fulfilled. His radical love has the power to absolutely transform us.

Jesus is love and He calls you to soak in His love. Not fluffy, self-seeking love, but rather deep, life-altering love; a love that will make you feel in full bloom.

Jesus, teach me to love and accept Your love, that I may live in full bloom. Amen

AUGUST

whet your appetite for God's purpose

" 'My food,' said Jesus, 'is to do the will of Him who sent me and to finish His work.' "
- John 4:34

Appetite for purpose

"He said to me, 'It is done. I am the Alpha and the Omega, the Beginning and the End. To the thirsty I will give water without cost from the spring of the water of life.'"
- Revelations 21:6

When life is happy and things are going well, it's easy to allow those moments to give our lives meaning, but when life slows down or forces us to introspect, it's then that the questions around purpose often surface. What does it mean to be alive? What is it that fuels me to wake up each day and live out that day? Do I live each day on purpose?

These are questions that all of us will wrestle with again and again in this lifetime. Fortunately as believers we have access to the "big man up there" who has all the answers. God is intentional by nature and your being here is no mistake on His part. May today be the beginning of a beautiful journey of bringing your tough, deep questions around your purpose before your loving Father, and seeking Him out for answers.

Let's use this month ahead to let go of 'busy' and to choose intentional living instead, as we wrestle with topics around our purpose here on earth.

Lord Jesus, You knew Your purpose on earth and You lived from that conviction. Help me in the days to come, to go deeper with You, as I explore my purpose and what I'm called to do here on earth too. Amen

Your true purpose

"Everyone who is called by My name, whom I created for My glory, whom I formed and made."
- *Isaiah 43:7*

Our highest purpose on this earth is to bring God glory. I love this. Praising God is our most natural purpose. We were created as worshippers. We all worship something, whether we realize it or not. Jesus is our ultimate model when it comes to knowing how to glorify the Father. Jesus brings God glory by making God's character known to the world as He bears His image.

Our greatest calling on this earth is to do just the same; to be changed, by God's grace, into His likeness. We praise God and bring Him glory as we spend time with Him, in praise, prayer, studying the Word and fellowship. And as we do these things, we become more like Him and, in turn, reveal His beautiful nature to a longing world.

Today, be encouraged that you do have a purpose here on earth, right now. Your purpose is to know God and, in turn, mirror God to the world.

Jesus, thank You for being my role model of how to live out my true purpose here on earth. Help me to be transformed into Your likeness and in so doing, to live out my purpose on earth. Amen

Make disciples

> "Therefore go and make disciples of all nations, baptizing them in the name of the Father and of the Son and of the Holy Spirit, and teaching them to obey everything I have commanded you. And surely I am with you always, to the very end of the age."
> - Matthew 28:19-20

Second to being put on earth to bring God glory, is our purpose to go out and make disciples. Whilst disciples are often defined as followers, most of us are quick to relate the term 'disciples' to that of Jesus's disciples. If I look at the life of Jesus and the characteristics of the 12 men whom Jesus called His disciples, these characteristics would stand out:

A disciple:
~ Is a close friend with whom you walk a journey
~ Is an ordinary person who watches as you live and speak, and seeks to model that behaviour
~ Is generally on a mission with a single purpose
~ Loves people wholeheartedly as you do
~ Is encouraged to live by faith, and rely on the Holy Spirit for guidance
~ Shares confidently, in their own way, about their faith in God
~ Is connected to other believers

Today, as you consider this list of characteristics of Jesus's disciples, may you discover how you can make disciples of Jesus.

———

Jesus, firstly I am Your disciple. Thank You that as I watch and learn from You, I too can be inspired to make disciples as I live my life, by faith. Amen

God's goodness in your life

> "I remain confident of this: I will see the goodness of the Lord in the land of the living."
> - Psalm 27:13

Don't you love how specific God was in creating each of us? We are collectively humans and yet no two humans are exactly alike. Whilst we know that our collective purpose on earth is to glorify God and make disciples, we know too that God prepared us, ahead of time, to do good works as individuals.

Before digging into our personal purpose, I believe it valuable to firstly recognise the goodness of God. God promises to bring good from everything that we experience here on earth. God created you, and me, with intention. We will not know the depth of that intention until we meet Him one day in Heaven and can ask about the purpose behind our personal physical attributes or personalities. But, the goodness of God confirms that He will use everything you were given, to mould you into a person who resembles Christ and brings glory to God.

Today, will you look upon yourself and others with grace and kindness? Will you step away from the internal war of self-hate that so many of us fight? And will you take your whole being before God and ask Him to grow you in character and into His likeness?

———

Jesus, thank You that despite my quirks and internal wars, You intend to use me for good. Change my heart today that I may begin to submit to Your higher purpose for me on this earth. Amen

What's in your hands?

"For we are God's handiwork, created in Christ Jesus to do good works, which God prepared in advance for us to do."
- *Ephesians 2:10*

A question we will all ask in our lifetime is "What is my purpose on earth?" Commentators will differ in their answers to this question.

I grew up believing that my purpose was going to be one big moment; where everything would come together and I could say THIS IS IT!! I've since deviated from this viewpoint. I once heard a sermon that spoke of another view on the subject of purpose. In the book of Exodus, God appeared to Moses as he was heading for the red sea, and asked him what he had in his hand. Moses replied "a staff". God then encouraged him to use what was 'in his hands' when he reached the Red Sea. The staff's role grew and changed with the narrative, and Moses used this very staff as God performed a number of miracles. I love this idea of the same physical thing being used in so many different ways to fulfill purpose.

Today, may you consider that your life may fulfill numerous purposes on earth, in different seasons of life? Reflect today on what you have in your hands and how God can use that to fulfill your, and His, purpose in the season that you're in.

Jesus, thank You for placing different talents, people and opportunities in my hands in the various seasons of my life. Help me to find purpose as I use what is in my hands today. Amen

Define your season

"A person finds joy in giving an apt answer, and how good is a timely word."
- Proverbs 15:23

I've personally found so much freedom, and have watched others do the same, when they define life in seasons and not just as one big picture. Life is changing all the time and what is required of us is changing all the time too. The more we're aware of this, the more we can live in sync with who and where we are right now. Continuing on yesterday's theme of what is in your hands, I'd like to add in one more nugget of wisdom. Your purpose right now will be found where what you have in your hands and what you have access to in this season, meet the world's aching and brings you joy.

For some this may be a season of early motherhood and what you have in your hands is a precious life to pour love into; for others this may be a season with access to finances that allow you to impact lives outside of your immediate needs.

I encourage you today to be honest with yourself as you evaluate your current reality. Take note of what you have in your hands, what you have access to and how this combination meets the world's aching and brings you joy.

Jesus, I acknowledge right now that this is not an off-season of my life; it is a season with purpose and I can make my current reality work, with Your guidance. Amen

Surrender your will

"Then Jesus said to His disciples, 'Whoever wants to be my disciple must deny themselves and take up their cross and follow me. For whoever wants to save their life will lose it, but whoever loses their life for me will find it.'"
- *Matthew 16:24-25*

God created you with talents that we He longs to use, for His glory. I am reminded of a time in my life when I was convinced that I was living in flow. I had created a business that I loved, and that I felt I was good at. I convinced myself that this must be the will of God, as I was using my talents. It took my being on the cover of a magazine, my ultimate career dream, for me to realize that gaining attention in the world's eye would never fill me, as I believed it would.

I sobbed my eyes out the day that the magazine came out. I felt so proud to have been acknowledged but so empty too. I had been using my talents, but perhaps had run ahead of what God had for me. This began a hard process of surrender. God has since taken me full circle. I don't believe I am free of the need for personal recognition, but I know now, that by surrendering my plans at His Cross, I receive a joy, a peace and a purpose that is immeasurably more than what I can do on my own.

Use this day to re-surrender your will, your plans and your future before your King. He longs to see your talents multiplied, but in His timing.

———————

Jesus, use me as You see fit. You deserve all the glory. Amen

Find Him at the altar

"The Lord descended to the top of Mount Sinai and called Moses to the top of the mountain."
- *Exodus 19:20*

A close friend of mine, who is a pastor, wrote recently of the significance of many prominent people in the Bible returning to the same place to worship and hear from God. She referred to this as an altar. Moses, for example, frequently returned to and heard from God, on a mountaintop. I know I personally have a spot on the rocks below our beach house, overlooking the sea, where again and again God has redirected my life path: His presence has been tangible.

After understanding this concept of altars, I now journey to this very spot when I need direction, hope, or merely refreshing or refueling. And God has never failed to do just that!

Have you discovered a space or place that could represent an altar for you? I encourage you to think this through, and if it isn't a space or place, perhaps it's a season of life when you hear clearest from the Lord.

Jesus, thank You that we are Your children and You care enough to direct our paths. Help us to learn to listen. Amen

The purpose of Jesus

> "'My food,' said Jesus, 'is to do the will of Him who sent me and to finish His work.'"
> - John 4:34

To set the context for today, our scripture for today is taken from John 4, not long after Jesus was speaking to the Samaritan woman at the well. Jesus radically impacts the Samaritan woman's life as He tells her that He is the true Messiah. He returns to the disciples, who suggest that He eats something: He responds with today's scripture.

Merely minutes after making His newest follower, Jesus feels fueled and alive, much the same effect that food would have on the body. What is pivotal here is how He compares food to doing the will of God. When we live in sync with the Holy Spirit, moved by Him and allowing Him to direct our lives, our spirits and souls will be sustained, just as food does for the body.

Today is as good as any, to ask the Holy Spirit to be your guide, to direct your feet and to feed your Spirit.

Jesus, teach me how to be fueled by doing the will of God, modeling Your example. Amen

Seasons of life

> "There is a time for everything, and a season for every activity under the heavens."
> - Ecclesiastes 3:1

In this day and age, we can do a two minute online test and discover our personality, we can pick up our cell phone and get lost in an online world for hours on end and the demands of work call on us to fill our time to a point of exhaustion.

Within the hurry, and chaos, of our lives, it's important to know that God refers often to life happening in seasons: segments of time that are often marked by something new, or by change. It can often be daunting when change takes place: when we lose a job, or friend, when we move house or country, when we sustain a sports injury or health problem – but what we can know for certain, even with change and uncertainty, is that God is in each of these seasons. He is present and that is a certainty within itself. In the scripture for today, the author of Ecclesiastes, writes how there is a time for everything, each has its season.

Rather than fight the season you're in now, even if it is one of uncertainty, ask God what He has planned within this season. Perhaps it is a season of deep growth, deep giving or deep rest.

———

Jesus, thank You that You remain my certainty, even within life's uncertainty. Help me to celebrate the different seasons of my life and what You may have in store for me. Amen

Your Esther moment

"And who knows but that you have come to your royal position for such a time as this?"
- Esther 4:14

The story of Esther is a well-known one. We often hear quoted the words 'for such a time as this' and this inspiration comes from the chapter we're reading from today. Esther is Queen but her purpose as Queen is unknown, until in Esther 4, her authority as Queen has the power to massively impact God's people. Esther is challenged to make a decision that may threaten her life, but one that could have a radical effect on the lives of the Jews.

Today, you may not know the purpose behind why you live where you do, or why you are pursing the career that you are or why you're married to who you are, but God has a plan. Trust God as He directs you in every avenue of your life, and your life will bring Him glory.

I encourage you to go and read the whole of Esther 4 today. Allow God to birth an excitement in you for the big moments in your life.

———

Jesus, Your timing is always perfect. Help me to find peace in knowing that You have gone before me, and yet are right here with me. Amen

12th August

Showers of blessing

"I will make them and the places surrounding my hill a blessing. I will send down showers in season; there will be showers of blessing."
- Ezekiel 34:26

I've always found something totally rejuvenating about running in the rain. I'll never forget a day in my University years, when on a casual trail run with a friend, a massive rainstorm suddenly engulfed us.

Being out in the open, there was nothing to hide beneath and so instead, we stopped, and we laughed and danced and jumped in puddles. We spun around and around like children until eventually falling over: muddy and exhilarated! Life is like this too. We may get hit by unexpected showers, but take heart; these are not only scary storms that we have to face, but also showers of blessing. God will always meet you right where you are, and provide you with blessings that match the season of life you're in.

Right now, take heart; your shower of blessing will come. He is Your faithful Father.

———

Lord, thank You for Your faithfulness in my life. May I always look and find pleasure in Your showers of blessing in the right season. Amen

13th August

Obedience to God's call

"'Go to the great city of Nineveh and preach against it, because its wickedness has come up before me.' But Jonah ran away from the Lord and headed for Tarshish. He found a ship bound for that port. After paying the fare, he went aboard and sailed for Tarshish to flee from the Lord."
- Jonah 1:2-3

The story of Jonah and the whale is a favourite in our home.

God spoke to Jonah and gave him direction for his future. Jonah was terrified, and out of fear, chose to follow a different life path. As you well know, this didn't end up well for him and he was tossed overboard during a great storm at sea, and swallowed by a whale. During his 3 days and 3 nights inside the whale, Jonah called out to God in his despair and eventually the whale spat him out onto dry land. Jonah was then quick to listen to the instruction of God.

How often does this happen in our lives? We feel convicted to do something, and we choose not to out of fear. God is always gracious though, and gives us time to grow in faith and maturity and ultimately, to be ready when He calls us again.

Be encouraged today; submit your will before God and ask Him for the courage to be obedient to His call.

Jesus, You have a plan for my life that glorifies You. Help me to be obedient when You call. Amen

God is not in hiding

"You make known to me the path of life;
You will fill me with joy in Your presence,
with eternal pleasures at Your right hand."
- Psalm 16:11

There are times in life when we just feel stuck. I will always remember the smog that hung over Beijing, when we travelled there. It was ever-present. I remember never seeing a blue sky, and yet becoming somewhat okay with that as our week there went by.

Life can sometimes feel this way too. We know that we are stuck, or that the light feels far from us, but we do not know a way out: we simply dwell there. In scriptures, we see that David wrestled so often with God. David too, felt stuck at times, but instead of getting comfortable in that state, he always searched for God amidst each season of life.

Be encouraged by today's scripture; God wants to make known to you your life path. He will fill you with joy again. Bring it all before Him now.

Jesus, please help me to learn to move through this stage of feeling stuck and to walk with more surety, as You promise to direct my path. Amen

Choose your battles

"In the spring, at the time when kings go off to war, David sent Joab out with the king's men and the whole Israelite army... But David remained in Jerusalem. One evening David got up from his bed and walked around on the roof of the palace. From the roof he saw a woman bathing. The woman was very beautiful, and David sent someone to find out about her."
- *2 Samuel 11:1-3*

I once heard a commentator suggest that it was possible that David ended up having an affair with Bathsheba because he abandoned the purpose marked out for him (battle) and stayed at home instead.

I have at times felt like David. I have felt compelled to live by faith but I've rejected that call, only to find myself fighting other less significant battles. When I went through a period of my life when I questioned my faith, I quickly developed a pattern of disordered eating. Coincidence? I think not. When I abandoned my purpose to build God's Kingdom, I had to find another battle to fight and so I choose that of physical acceptance and the desire for attention.

Can you think of a time when you've felt a lack of purpose and so instead of turning to God for answers, you've found purpose in something that didn't bear positive fruit? Bring that before your loving Father today.

Lord, You know my heart. Thank You for forgiving me when I've chosen to fight battles that were never meant for me to fight. Amen

Set a vision before you

"Then the Lord replied: 'Write down the revelation and make it plain on tablets so that a herald may run with it.'"
- Habakkuk 2:2

Vision is the picture that we see in our minds, before we take action. It's the thinking time we give to ideas – the daydreaming. To visualize is to imagine where you want to be and what it will look like. There is so much power in having vision.

The whole of the Old Testament prepares the way for Jesus's coming in the New Testament. Vision does this; it brings to mind that which is to come, and helps us prepare the way for just that. Today's scripture in The English Standard Version Bible reads "Write the vision; make it plain on tablets, so he may run who reads it." (Habakkuk 2:2) I love this. As we recognize our vision, and make it visible, we can then run in the direction of where we are wanting, or feel led to go.

Use a few moments this week to create a vision board for the remainder of your year. This picture in your mind and perhaps a physical copy, will thoughtfully guide your behaviour in the months to come.

———

Lord, may my vision be inspired by You and be my guide as I live each day. Amen

God-given gifts

"For whoever has will be given more, and they will have an abundance. Whoever does not have, even what they have will be taken from them."
- *Matthew 25:29*

The parable of the talents is one that many of us may know. This scripture talks of a master leaving his servants with bags of gold. Each servant had the choice as to what to do with his or her gold; much like each of us does with our God-given talents. When the master returned, he praised those who had used and grown their quantity of gold, some even with great risk. He rebuked the servant who had merely hidden his gold due to fear.

God has given each of us varied talents and we are encouraged to step out in faith and to use these. As scary as it may be, God is far wiser than we are, and He knows why He gave you the specific talents that He did.

Find courage today, knowing that you bring God glory when you use what you have been given.

God, give me strength as I find ways to grow and use my talents, that You have so graciously given me. Amen

Nothing more, nothing less

"And be found in Him, not having a
righteousness of my own that comes
from the law, but that which is through
faith in Christ - the righteousness that
comes from God on the basis of faith."
- *Phillippians 3:9*

God loves you because of who He is, not who you are. Nothing
that you can do, whether in line with His perfect will or outside of
that, will change the way that He feels about you. You are saved by
grace, by the blood of Christ: nothing more or nothing less.

On the days when purpose or calling feels heavy, or when
uncertainty makes you feel lesser than, remind yourself that God
has fully accepted you as you are, right now, in this moment. Your
purpose on this earth is less about you, and more about the YOU
that brings Him glory.

*Live out today from the safest place that you know: in the arms of your
Father.*

Jesus, thank You that my calling has nothing to do with my worth. I am
worthy, because You say that I am. Amen

Content in prison or plenty

"I am not saying this because I am in need, for I have learned to be content whatever the circumstances. I know what it is to be in need, and I know what it is to have plenty. I have learned the secret of being content in any and every situation, whether well fed or hungry, whether living in plenty or in want. I can do all this through Him who gives me strength."
- Phillippians 4:11-13

Have you ever wondered if it's genuinely possible to live content, despite what your circumstances look like? Many of us have had this thought and have read of Paul's great statement that he'd learnt to be content with much and with little; but it sounds a bit too watered down, right? I mean how can one genuinely be happy in prison and happy when in plenty?

I believe this all comes down to our personal view of the term 'content'. If we limit our view on contentment to a place, or feeling evoked from having our "ducks in a row", then certainly this is not possible in all circumstances. But if we take contentment as another way of saying 'I have deep peace within', perhaps it is more do-able.

Be encouraged today that contentment is not saying that you're okay with the circumstances that you're facing, but rather that circumstances cannot rob from the peace of God which guards your heart and mind.

Lord, thank You for Your peace and empowering me with strength to face anything that comes my way in this world. Amen

Despite your feelings

"Keep your lives free from the love of money and be content with what you have, because God has said, 'Never will I leave you; never will I forsake you.'"
- Hebrews 13:5

Chin up Beautiful, you're not frazzled; you're simply mid conquer. Frazzled you may feel. I do too. Often. But the beauty in life is that seldom do we ever 'make it'. Living for 'make it' moments, is truly limiting. There is no single purpose on earth that will fulfill your every need: not money, or a new car, or a new husband, or a magnificent holiday. Nothing but God can bring true contentment. We cannot 'make it' here on earth. Instead, life is not a quest for one goal, but instead it is a journey, a journey that includes both highs and lows, both purpose-filled seasons and seasons that lack in all things purpose... joys and sorrows.

Perspective has a Latin root, translated as "look through". I love this.

I encourage you to pursue perspective in every season of your life. Look through and beyond the obvious, and seek out where God is moving right now. You are a part of His plan, despite your feelings, and recognizing this could bring you great contentment.

Lord, help me to learn to truly look through and beyond what is obvious, and to see Your hand at work in this world, and my life. And may this bring me deep contentment. Amen

21st August

"Guess what?" moments

"He split the rocks in the wilderness and gave them water as abundant as the seas; He brought streams out of a rocky crag and made water flow down like rivers."
- Psalm 78:15-16

Don't you love hearing the things that little kids say?

Just the other day, my son (aged 3) said, "Mom, guess what? Ice makes water!" I love the innocence of this statement. He felt that the fact that ice became water, deserved to be a 'guess what' moment. How often does this in fact happen to us, even as adults, too? Things that have made sense to others for years, can hit us in a moment, and just like that, suddenly make perfect sense for the first time. In those moments, it's as if God whispers GUESS WHAT, and whilst the world may not feel the excitement behind this insight, you do. And you have every right to.

Today, may God provide you with loads of 'guess what' moments, as He opens your eyes to all that He is and the beauty that surrounds you.

Jesus, help me to be amazed as You open my eyes to see things for what they truly are, perhaps for the first time. Amen

Let go of regrets

"Let your eyes look straight ahead;
fix your gaze directly before you."
- Proverbs 4:25-27

Whether it's regretting the top that you put on this morning, what you chose to study after school, who you married (or didn't) or eating a cupcake at teatime today…whatever it is, regrets are real. And we know this all too well.

Although I've always been someone who keeps moving forward, seldom giving the past any rights over my current circumstances, I can still honestly say that I haven't always felt that each season of my life (experience, job, choice) was beneficial. Yes, I've moved on anyway, but it was only recently that I realized the importance of counting every season of life, as valuable.

Every experience that you go through further creates your story; a story well worth telling. The mistakes I've made have humbled me; the studying I've done enriches others even though it didn't always seem worthwhile at the time; the clients I've seen have taught me acceptance and, the hardships my family have faced make me real. It didn't all make sense then. But it does now.

Your story matters too my friend. Every part of it is and has shaped you into the remarkable being that you are today. God longs to use you and your story. Yes, all of it.

—————

Jesus, thank You that despite what felt like mistakes in my past, You can use it all to bring You glory and to shape me into a mighty woman of God. Amen

Lessons from the ocean

"Let us not become weary in doing good, for at the proper time we will reap a harvest if we do not give up."
- Galatians 6:9

I was fortunate to grow up on the coast. Nippers (pre life-saving) was my favourite Primary School sport and I spent hours on end in the ocean on weekdays and all weekends. One of the first lessons that you are taught in life-saving or nippers is the power of the ocean, how to spot a rip and how to make your way out of a rip when it's pull is strong.

A rip often looks calmer than the sea around it, but is simply a narrow current of water that pulls out to sea. The simple rule of thumb is to never fight a rip. Either swim diagonally out of the current or, if too fatigued, allow it to take you out to sea, it will eventually release you and you will wash back to shore. All rips lead out to sea, but ultimately lead you back in too.

What I've learnt from rips is that life can do just the same. It can take us out to no-man's land, only to spit us out back where we belong.

When you feel that your life is taking a direction that you're not convinced is you at your best, but you're actively pressing into God; just go with it. Moments or seasons don't always make sense but we always land up where we're meant to be, when we're surrendered under God's guidance.

───────

Jesus, thank You that whilst life may not make perfect sense now, I would have missed these life lessons had I not plunged in in the first place. Amen

Cling to the light

"The path of the righteous is like the morning sun, shining ever brighter till the full light of day."
- Proverbs 4:18

Success should look different for all of us. I recently read Shoe Dog, by the founder of Nike, and was so humbled at how the author spoke of how money changed his life for a short while, but then everything went back to normal. Purpose should never feel like a chase after things of this world. If it does feel that way, you are not abnormal in your thinking, but God wants to take you deeper.

There is strength within you; a real, deep inner strength that you may only know when the going gets tough. Embrace it as you wrestle with God on the topic of purpose. Dig deep. Ask Him those hard burning questions in your mind and heart. Surrender. But keep moving forwards as you live your life on purpose, right now.

Cling to the light today. The pulls of this world always lead to darkness. Let God lead you into the light as He illuminates the path before you.
In His time.

———————

Lord, illuminate the darkness with me and in my thinking and help me to celebrate the light. Amen

You will flourish

"The righteous will flourish
like a palm tree."
- Psalm 92:12

Just the word palm tree transports me to a secluded tropical island. Peace and quiet, perhaps a book in hand.

Back in reality though, I love this scripture. Palm trees flourish in tropical settings; they are evergreen and grow where rain is common and soil rich. In ancient Greece, a palm tree was a symbol of victory, peace and eternal life. In today's scripture, David says that 'the righteous will be like a flourishing palm tree'. The joy in this is that nothing that we can do can make us more righteous. We are righteous because of who Christ is. By simply accepting Him, we are made righteous. This means that we will flourish, just in knowing our identity in Christ.

Recognize the potential within yourself to flourish even amidst uncertainty. Your certainty comes from who you are. Righteous. Not by anything you do, but because He says so. You won't lose your way, Darling - look in, look forward and mostly look up.

———

Jesus, I am righteous because of who You are. I am found in You. Amen

Your legacy

"Love the Lord your God with all your heart and with all your soul and with all your strength. These commandments that I give you today are to be on your hearts. Impress them on your children. Talk about them when you sit at home and when you walk along the road, when you lie down and when you get up."
- Deuteronomy 6:5-7

A legacy is an extraordinary concept: for some of us, a concept we think of often and for others, something that never crosses our minds. Your legacy is simply what you leave behind; be it money, a message, a life impacted. I understand the drive to want to make our mark on this world, but I find peace in knowing that as I choose rather to live with eternity in mind, my earthly impact will be just as God had planned it to be.

Our purpose is not to be remembered on earth because we set out building altars for ourselves, but rather that we lived with a longer-term perspective, building God's kingdom.

Today's scripture is taken from the Old Testament, and is a beautiful reminder that our legacy will stand in generations to come. May we find purpose in how we praise and honour God, in our lives and speech and beings.

Be encouraged today that your legacy is at play, whether you know it or not. Do not work to get known, but rather to get people to know God, and you too will be honoured for this.

———

Jesus, teach me what it means to think long-term, to build into Your Kingdom and not for my own glory. Amen

Pour out & God pours in

"Give, and it will be given to you. A good measure, pressed down, shaken together and running over, will be poured into your lap. For with the measure you use, it will be measured to you."
- Luke 6:38

The culture we live in today is all about a person investing in oneself. Self-preservation comes before all else.

Whilst this movement is powerful, and acknowledgement of the self is paramount to growth; we are taught in scripture, that God calls us to live outward lives too. Your skill-set, talents and even characteristics were designed, when used correctly, to bring you great joy, to honour God and also to build others up. It is easy to get so introspective that we in fact limit God moving through us, as we overthink our every move. The beauty of pouring love into others is that God always pours this love back into us, as long as we return to Him for refilling.

God wants to use you, right now, despite how you're feeling. Let Him fill you, so that your cup can overflow and you can intentionally pour love into those around you.

God, You fill my love tank so that I can pour out love into others. Show me opportunities to be Your hands and feet in my world today. Amen

More than a goldfish

"Teach me knowledge and good judgement, for I trust Your commands."
- Psalm 119:66

Have you ever heard the myth that goldfish are limited in size by the dimensions of their home or fish bowl? If you let goldfish swim in a lake, they'll grow 100 times larger than the usual-sized goldfish. I've researched this topic and whilst it has truth in it, the real catalyst for growth of a goldfish is the container in which it is kept and the quality of the water. Fish bowls are rarely home to high quality water, hence the little goldfish. This concept can so easily be a metaphor for our lives. How many of us are limiting our potential by the size of our comfort zones, environment or quality of substance around us?

Here are 3 questions we can ask ourselves as we commit to growth:
~ Is the environment I find myself in challenging me, enriching me and making me a better person?
~ Am I currently in a comfort zone that is preventing me from growing, or is my comfort zone the place where I am growing?
~ What is God telling me about my environment right now?

You contain more potential than you know. Trust God to bring light to areas within you that He longs to speak life into.

God, today I open my heart and mind to Your teachings. Show me how or in what ways my environment is affecting my growth, and direct my path. Amen

September is knocking

"Your beginnings will seem humble, so prosperous will your future be."
- Job 8:7

Gosh, how is September merely days away? Do you ever feel as if every year goes faster than the last?

I've reflected on this notion. I do not believe that the years go faster, but rather that as life gets busier, the days pull us in and roll onto one another, and this makes them feel so fast moving. In light of this, I've heard a recent buzz term "Start Something September". To start something might sound exciting for you. It may bring with it connotations of dreams forgotten, making things happen. For others, the very last thing that they feel like doing this upcoming month is starting anything; they merely need to maintain. My encouragement is to take some time over the next few days to slow down, to look in and to look up. Pause the racing year, and ask God what it is that He has for you in this coming month.

Starting is powerful, so be open to what God has for you. It may be to start a new hobby, it may be to start slowing down, or may it be to start allowing Him to fill you up when you're feeling exhausted. He will direct you, as you press into Him.

Lord Jesus, help me to slow down enough to hear Your voice in this season of my life. Direct my "now" as I begin habits or practices that You have on Your heart for me. Amen

Patient with His process

"See how the farmer waits for the land to yield its valuable crop, patiently waiting for the autumn and spring rains. You too, be patient and stand firm, because the Lord's coming is near."
- James 5:7-8

If you have a garden of your own, you'll know all too well the expectancy that builds as the seasons change and you wait for rain. For crops, or plants, rain is the fuel that ultimately leads to life.

But it happens in season. How appropriate is this for each of us too? Whilst we expect results or answers in the moment, God's timing is far grander than our own. God is into the detail and He promises to bring rains in season. He will grow and prepare you in months or moments when you're not even aware and have you ready for your moment of springing to life. And life in abundance.

Trust in Him and His timing, as you wait patiently for answers or direction. He is listening.

Father God, teach me patience as I wait on Your perfect timing. Thank You that I can trust You for rains in season that set me up for life in abundance. Amen

Heaven is home

"But our citizenship is in Heaven.
And we eagerly await a Saviour
from there, the Lord Jesus Christ."
- *Philippians 3:20*

One of the beautiful things about growing up, is being faced with a body that changes every year. I always thought aging was for one day when my kids had kids, and I was contentedly sitting in my rocking chair with a flabby tummy, but I was so wrong. Aging isn't a thing that suddenly happens. It's gradual. And it starts early. How often do we hear women, or even ourselves, saying to younger girls 'Stop complaining about your body; you have nothing to worry about. I wish I was your age'? What we forget to realize is that this girl is thinking the same thing, about someone half her age.

Body image and aging will follow us all of our lives, but how we choose to embrace it, will form part of our legacy. Each new mark, wrinkle or crease tells a story of its own. Our ageing can too, be a beautiful reminder, that we were not made for earth, but rather that Heaven is home.

As you face your physical body today, be reminded that this body was created to grow and change and age, but that your spirit will live on for eternity.

———

Jesus, teach me to keep my focus on eternity and invest more in my Spirit than I do my physical body, here on earth. Amen

SEPTEMBER

beside quiet waters

"With joy you will draw water from
the wells of salvation."
- *Isaiah 12:3*

Streams of living water

"Let the peace of Christ rule in your hearts, since as members of one body you were called to peace."
- Colossians 3:15

The concept of peace has always made me think of water.

Peace elicits images in my mind of flowing rivers, rolling waves and steady slow streams. I see reflections of palm trees on still turquoise seas and streams alongside gardens of green. I love that today's scripture says that we are called to peace. It is our calling: designed in our very being. Peace should feel right, safe and purpose-filled. To live at peace is not to exclude emotions or deep uncomfortable feelings, but rather it is to be at ease, despite our feelings or circumstances. This is what has been given to us, by the grace of God.

Are you experiencing peace in this season of life? Remember that God promises a peace, which surpasses human understanding, and thus, our circumstances cannot stand in the way of His peace.

———

Jesus, thank You that as a child of God, peace is my birthright. I embrace the peace that only You can give, peace that surpasses understanding. Amen

He is the giver of peace

"I have told you these things, so that in Me you may have peace. In this world you will have trouble. But take heart! I have overcome the world."
- John 16:33

Jesus never sinned, yet still He wrestled with unspeakable discomfort in His lifetime.

We read of Jesus wrestling with Satan in the wilderness; we read of Jesus mourning the death of a close friend, and most importantly we read of Jesus agonizing whilst on the Cross. Jesus did not sin, but still wrestled with uncomfortable feelings. Peace is not the absence of uncomfortable feelings; instead it is the state of mind that we occupy when experiencing both the ups and downs of life. We can experience deep despair but still recognize the peace of God in our hearts and minds.

Be encouraged, God provides us with a peace that the world cannot offer. It is a peace that surpasses human understanding. As you experience the range of emotions that any normal woman experiences each day, trust God to lead you in peace, despite your feelings.

Jesus, You are our perfect model. Thank You for showing us that even as You wrestled with uncomfortable feelings, You remained at peace. Teach me to do the same. Amen

Trickles of peace

"Now may the God of hope fill you with all joy and peace in believing, that you may abound in hope by the power of the Holy Spirit."
- Romans 15:13

Have you ever stood under a showerhead that merely trickles out water? I find little as frustrating as dancing under a showerhead trying to catch every drop. We may eventually get clean or wash out our shampoo, but it takes longer than we hoped and often produces frustration. I find life and faith can feel this way too. It's easy to feel relatively certain that we're on the right path in our lives, but the abundance we think that God promises, only appears in trickles. Do you ever feel as if you have to jump to the left or to the right to receive His blessings? You are not alone.

We need to remember, that much like with a shower, the water source may be healthy, but the showerhead faulty. God too does not hold back on blessing His children but our immaturity to receive it, may stand in the way and thus feel as if we only receive trickles of blessings.

Instead of longing for more or doubting ourselves or worse, doubt God, let us instead draw near to Him and allow Him to mature us, so that we can walk in the fullness of what He has for each of us.

———

Lord, draw me closer still, that I may mature in You and find pleasure in doing what You have in store for me, my life and Your glory. Amen

4th September

Hope in His faithfulness

"But those who hope in the Lord will renew their strength. They will soar on wings like eagles; they will run and not grow weary, they will walk and not be faint."
- Isaiah 40:31

Have you ever faced a situation that was so dire, that the only way for you to see each day through was to cling to hope? I have too, many a time. Hope fuels us. Hope is rarely a wish, but rather provides us with trust and confident expectancy of good things. We can have hope in the world, hope in doctors, our government or hope in mankind; but mostly this leads to disappointment. People can, and do, come through for us all the time, but they also let us down, leading to hope deferred.

The only true hope that we should have in this world is hope in God. Hope in His faithfulness to make all things work for our good, just as He promised. This can empower us to appear to have hope in doctors, or circumstances or mankind, but in fact to not hold them solely accountable, but rather to hold tight to God's faithfulness and His promises.

Bring to mind today a situation that requires hope in your life. Give this over to God, knowing that He, and only He, has your best interests at heart.

Jesus, thank You that You are my hope. You alone know what is best for me, and so I place my hope in You. Amen

Hope deferred

"Hope deferred makes the heart sick,
but a longing fulfilled is a tree of life."
- Proverbs 13:12

The topic of hope deferred is something that I have personally experienced. When dealing with a chronic condition, I saw 14 specialists, had 3 MRI's, 2 x-rays and 2 ultra-sounds in the period of 1 year. Each time I was due to see a new specialist, I would build myself up on the hope that this would be my moment of breakthrough, only to leave each appointment devastated and consequently burst into tears in my car.

Today's scripture mentions that the heart can indeed become sick, following hope deferred BUT that longing fulfilled is a tree of life. When our hopes are indeed fulfilled, then we are refreshed, encouraged and rejuvenated.

As you approach today, know that you will experience both extremes when it comes to hope. You will feel let down by hope and you will feel renewed when your hopes are fulfilled. Regardless of which surfaces when, know that ultimately your life is in the palm of God's hand and that is the greatest hope that you have on earth.

Jesus, awaken in me a new and fresh longing for more of You. You are my hope. Amen

Lessons from rock pools

"I keep my eyes always on the Lord. With Him at my right hand, I will not be shaken. Therefore my heart is glad and my tongue rejoices; my body also will rest secure."
- Psalm 16:8-9

I have recently had the joy of seeing the beach through my children's eyes. One of my favourite things to bear witness to, is to watch them as they explore rock pools. They leave no rock unturned, no snail unlatched and no starfish untouched. They can spend hours on end splashing in crystal clear water, finding hidden treasures, collecting shells and chasing tiny fish.

Rock pools fascinate me. With the changing of the tides, twice a day, the average rock pool will be washed of its previous contents and filled afresh, with living and non-living matter. And yet, when you approach a rock pool, the water is generally dead still and conveys tranquility.

While change happens within and around you, may it be God who remains your anchor of hope and may you rest secure.

———

Jesus, help me to keep my eyes on You so that I will not be shaken by change, but can rest secure in You. Amen

Full of joy

> "These things have I spoken to you, that My joy may remain in you, and that your joy may be full."
> - John 15:11

As I wipe the sleep out of my eyes and put on my woolly slippers and gown at my pre-4am work wake up call, a smile spreads across my face, one, which I know, will not easily be removed. There is joy found in living our lives with purpose.

For some of us, we will find joy through work, for others through a hobby, others a church responsibility and still others friendship or motherhood. God wants us to experience joy. Jesus speaks of His joy, and His hope, declaring that they will remain in us. Our greatest joy will be experienced when we live with conviction on the path we feel that God has us on.

Be encouraged today, joy is God's idea and He wants you to experience it. Turn to Him and allow Him to reveal more of Himself in you, and in turn produce more joy in you.

God, help me to remember that joy is Your idea. Fill me with joy as I search Your heart for meaning and peace in my life. Amen

8th September

Pursue peace courageously

"Have I not commanded you? Be strong and courageous. Do not be afraid; do not be discouraged, for the Lord your God will be with you wherever you go."
- Joshua 1:9

Part of living a life of peace, especially peace which surpasses human understanding, takes courage. It is often easier to give in to the worries of the world: to fear, to envy, to stress or to become restless.

Joshua speaks of being strong and courageous because God is with you wherever you go. I've often thought of how wonderful it would be to have a little mini Jesus in my pocket, who could pop out and remind me that He is always in control. But truth be told we have an even better option at our disposal, the Holy Spirit, who resides in us and guides us from within; all we need to do is to learn to listen, to trust and to have the courage to embrace peace, despite our circumstances.

What burden can you hand over to Jesus today? What is robbing from your peace in this season of life? Remember, nothing is too big for our God.

Jesus, please take these burdens from me and make Your peace tangible to me, despite my worrying mind. Amen

Draw from the well

"With joy you will draw water
from the wells of salvation."
- Isaiah 12:3

A few years back, I lost my way.

As a strong Enneagram Type-3, setting and achieving goals comes very naturally for me. But sometimes life just doesn't allow for that. Whilst I love and thrive off working towards goals, sometimes life throws curve balls our way and despite our willingness to succeed, we simply cannot. How do you regroup when something you've worked so hard for, simply doesn't go as planned? What happens when life throws you a curved ball that knocks you off balance?

Today's scripture reminds us that our true hope is not here on earth, but in our certainty of our eternity with Jesus.

As you face circumstances that make you feel alone or defeated, may you draw joy from the wells of your salvation, and your true hope and joy of eternity in Heaven.

Jesus, help me to remember that life on earth won't always be easy or make sense, but that my true hope and joy is founded in knowing You. Amen

10th September

Make space for peace

"Peace I leave with you; my peace I give you. I do not give to you as the world gives. Do not let your hearts be troubled and do not be afraid."
- John 14:27

Stillness comes in many forms; we need to give ourselves permission and forgiveness to go there. For peace to be present in our lives, we need to first approach God with vulnerability. It is difficult to experience peace when holding onto opposing thoughts and feelings. Many of us, in our busy lives, may struggle to find peace in the chaos. This is not uncommon.

At times, I have found great value in seeking out stillness in order to regain peace. I find that when I actively seek stillness, I gain control of my nervous system and adrenal glands. As I consciously focus on slowing down my breathing, I not only bring calm to my mind and body, but I also make space to allow God and the presence of His peace back in.

Do not be afraid to seek out stillness amidst the chaos that may surround you. It is in the stillness that you may find space to welcome God and His peace back into your life.

Jesus, thank You that You promised to leave me with peace and not a fleeting peace but a lasting one. Give me courage to seek out stillness that I may receive Your peace again. Amen

Contentment

"I know what it is to be in need, and I know what it is to have plenty. I have learned the secret of being content in any and every situation, whether well fed or hungry, whether living in plenty or in want."
- Phillippians 4:12

I love today's scripture for many reasons, but I think the greatest reason is my constant striving for contentment, being sure I've found it, only to be awakened to the fact that I have not. There is no mistake in Paul referring to his contentment as a secret. The nature of a secret is that of something that others do not know.

It is often our pride that gets in the way of our contentment. As we leave the shores of safety and find belonging or acceptance through our talents, or gifting or comforts, we drift away from the lighthouse, which is our identity in Christ. Paul faced numerous challenges that humbled him, again and again. He was forced to reassess his comforts, his belonging on earth and his faith, constantly. And this, his discomfort, brought him to the knowledge of the secret of contentment; to stop looking elsewhere for fulfillment and to truly rest in God.

May each of us be open to the tests that we face today, knowing that God is developing in us character that is ready for His revelation of secrets, whispered to our hearts.

Father, teach me what it means to stop looking to the world to answer my life questions and instead to find my full identity in You. Amen

12ᵗʰ September

The dress-up box

> "So then, just as you received Christ Jesus as Lord, continue to live your lives in Him, rooted and built up in Him, strengthened in the faith as you were taught, and overflowing with thankfulness."
> - Colossians 2:6-7

Did you ever play dress-up as a child? I can remember hours on end, of fun with my brothers as we explored our dress-up box. Life can sometimes feel as if we're playing dress-up: as if we wake up each morning, put on our happy face, get dressed, do our make-up (or don't) , all with the single intention of fitting into the mould we feel would be appropriate for that which we have planned for the day.

We can feel pressurized to fit certain moulds or to change ourselves in order to succeed. We can follow trends and become exhausted by simply being unable to keep up. One month it's high-waisted pants, the next full costumes and the next bikinis that barely cover anything at all.

Today, as you prepare for the day ahead, do so with absolute certainty that despite the fast-moving, peer-pressured society you find yourself in, you are rooted in Christ. Your identity does not change. Your value does not change.

Jesus, help me today to find stability in You. Help me to let go of feeling external pressure from the world, and rather to find my safe place, my peace, in You. Amen

Peace over happiness

"The fruit of that righteousness
will be peace; its effect will be
quietness and confidence forever."
- Isaiah 32:17

Search for peace above happiness.

The pursuit of happiness is all too appealing, especially for the 21st century wired-mind, but it will always have an expiry date. Happiness will always be a momentary feeling; something fleeting that does not last. Peace is different. Peace is a state of mind, not a goal. Peace is waking each day, despite our circumstances, and feeling at ease. Peace is choosing to lay our burdens at the Cross every day, and to hold lightly to the little control that we do have over our lives and circumstances. Peace quiets a busy, stressed mind and gives us confidence to face the day. Peace is given to us freely by our Saviour, but is a state of mind that we get to choose everyday.

Today be encouraged to choose peace above chaos. Embrace the quiet confidence that comes from living a life surrendered at the Cross.

Jesus, thank You for peace, that it is my birthright, because of who You are and help me to walk in peace every day. Amen

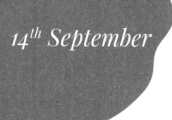

14th September

The door is wide open

"The thief comes only to steal and kill and destroy; I have come that they may have life, and have it to the full."
- John 10:10

Why do you stay in prison, when the door is ajar? Wow, this concept hits me so hard every time I read it.

Prisons not only lock us in but also lock out blessings. God promises us an abundant life, and while this may differ from the abundance that we imagine, abundance it is nonetheless. Abundance includes deep peace despite our circumstances, freedom from the hold of unhealthy habits and unwavering faith in our Father. Many of us live in prisons of our own, often self created. Prisons can give us the illusion of safety, they offer the bare essentials; but they also prevent us from experiencing life to its fullest.

Take some time today to reflect on the prison walls that you have perhaps built around you. These may be physical boundaries that you have in place, resentment, addiction or even an unhealthy relationship. Take these acknowledgements before your loving Father and watch as He empowers you to break down these walls, with wisdom, and regain the abundance that He has for you.

————

Jesus, give me strength today to take that, which has me feeling trapped, before You. Amen

Sunrise or sunset?

"…because of the tender mercy of our God, by which the rising sun will come to us from heaven to shine on those living in darkness and in the shadow of death, to guide our feet into the path of peace."
- Luke 1:78-79

Sunrise or sunset, which is your favourite?

I find this one tough to answer but being a morning person I think I lean more towards sunrises. Both though, hold within them a measure of beauty that is hard to put into words. Like me, I'm sure just bringing your awareness to the rising or setting sun, will bring to mind occasions when you've experienced this wonder. In today's scripture, the sun is described as a guide for our feet, in our pursuit of peace. What a beautiful picture.

The sun brings light, and light often has connotations of freedom, awakening or faith.

May God bring light to your path today, so that you may walk in His perfect peace.

———

Jesus, You are the light that leads me, I place my trust in You, today. Amen

He is the Wonder

"Peace I leave with you; My peace I give you. I do not give to you as the world gives. Do not let your hearts be troubled and do not be afraid."
- John 14:27

I recently watched the animated movie, Wonder Park, with my daughter and gracious, what a gorgeous movie it is! The theme song repeats the words 'you are the wonder in our wonderland.' It is beautiful and a song that replays in my head often. I know that I personally find my deepest peace, though, when I turn my focus from myself, instead to Jesus.

He is the wonder in wonderland. When we look for Him in our daily lives, we suddenly see Him in everything, everywhere. He is in the smile of your child, the beauty in the butterfly that flutters in your garden; He is in your neighbours' act of kindness and in the rain that waters your plants.

Today, may your eyes see what they often miss, the wonders of our Creator in Creation, and may this bring you peace.

Jesus, thank You that You truly are a wonder. Open my eyes to see You more. Amen

Happiness magnets

"Therefore, since we have been justified through faith, we have peace with God through our Lord Jesus Christ, through whom we have gained access by faith into this grace in which we now stand. And we boast in the hope of the glory of God."
- Romans 5:1-2

Happiness magnets may be robbing from your joy and peace right now.

We all have a happiness magnet; some of us have a few of them. I refer to a happiness magnet as the thing that others have, that we so desperately want. We often go as far as believing that if we had this very thing, it would provide us with a degree of happiness we're yet to experience. We believe this, usually, until we actually get there or acquire the happiness magnet. And unbeknown to us, instead of reveling in that predicted happy space, the happiness passes within hours and we move the goal posts; we choose a new happiness magnet.

What would it take for us to say goodbye to happiness magnets? What if we chose a "happy now" mentality over a "happy then" one? What would change?

What would you pursue today if you knew that happiness wasn't in fact a goal but rather a thing that happened as you lived in peace with God?

Jesus, remind me of the peace that I have in You, so that I can confidently let go of that which is convincing me that happiness is always just out of my reach. Amen

Fighting for freedom

> "Were you a slave when you were called? Don't let it trouble you - although if you can gain your freedom, do so."
> - 1 Corinthians 7:21

I will never forget in my early 20's, having recently overcome an eating disorder and the impending December holidays upon us, I muttered to a close friend that I hated this time of year, as now I had to get in shape for the holidays. She replied with, 'But Kit, Jesus thinks you're beautiful.' I laughed and said 'I know HE does, but when I walk across the beach no-one else knows that.' Oh, the irony.

If you're feeling the pressure right now to hit the gym, or perhaps you've deemed it too late and you're simply giving up and heading into the holiday season with what you feel is a deserving level of body hate, then listen up. Darling, YOU are REMARKABLE: so remarkable that Jesus would walk that long road carrying the cross, all over again, just FOR YOU. It's a crazy story. I know. And hard to live with this reality everyday when the world shouts otherwise. But the truth is, that self-acceptance is ALL founded in your headspace; the same place where faith is birthed and takes flight.

You matter. You're beautiful. You're so worth fighting for. JUST AS YOU ARE. Take this message in today.

Jesus, thank You for a peace which passes human understanding. Thank You that I can find my full security and identity in You. Amen

Peace over dissatisfaction

*"Now the Lord is the Spirit,
and where the Spirit of the
Lord is, there is freedom."*
- 2 Corinthians 3:17

Is the nearness of the end of the year bringing on a feeling of dissatisfaction in you?

This time of year is often the start of many of us running around like headless chickens. It is also very common to notice the presence of dissatisfaction creeping up inside of you. A common question that often surfaces at this time of year is: 'What have I even accomplished this year? ' We utter statements like 'Next year will be better. I'll be better.' And the underlying tone of 'Am I good enough?' is always at the core of this inner debate.

Let me start with this: without you this world would have missed an essential element in it's functioning. You with your all quirks, character and strengths have added enormous value to this earth this year. You've touched lives (I know for sure). You've grown. You've been challenged and … you've made it through. And that, my Darling, means that you have every right to celebrate the closure of the year with triumph and not as a victim.

Today, as you begin reflecting on the year past, don't be afraid to cut down limiting beliefs just as they begin, with higher truths found in scripture. You are enough.

———

Jesus, thank You that I am enough. Thank You for your acceptance of me and for all that You've taught me this year already. Amen

Your break will come

"I wait for the Lord, my whole being waits, and in His Word I put my hope."
- Psalm 130:5

Any avid surfer, body-boarder or body-surfer will know the art of perfecting 'waiting for the break'. If you know the ocean, you'll know that waves always come in sets. They roll in one after the next. Six is a common number to go by, but they can come in sets of even ten. Waves are caused by wind, and sets are merely groupings of waves that come in one after the other, often with the middle one in the set, being the biggest of them all. But, after the set, comes a lull. A lull is the calm that follows a set, a break in the waves, and it lasts until the next set appears. No matter how rough the sea is, lulls will come.

Life is much the same. No matter how rough life may feel, a lull will come. A break in the pain, or the despair or perhaps even just a glimpse of hope.

Cling to the lulls when they appear. Lulls can easily be missed if you're so focused on the crashing of the waves around you, so be encouraged to look for lulls today. For moments of pause. Moments of stillness. Moments of hope.

———————

Jesus, thank You that despite the feeling of wave after wave hitting me, I can trust You for a lull, a moment of peace and clarity. Amen

His grace is sufficient

"Lord, You alone are my portion and my cup; You make my lot secure."
- Psalm 16:5

One morning, while engaged in the process of writing this devotional, I had a morning that looked like this.

I made four different breakfasts for the four members of my family. Wow, you're so committed, you may say? Nope. It was more my avoidance and utter inability to cope with meltdowns that prompted that. After school drop off, I washed the dishes, hung up two loads of washing and then found myself gravitating towards the floor. My cup had run dry. I lay on the floor for a full 30 minutes. I had worship music playing but I wasn't singing, I simply lay there. I had a crazy looming deadline but I knew that I couldn't move from that spot until my cup had been refilled! You cannot run a fulfilling, abundant life from an empty cup. It simply isn't possible. You will burnout, or fall apart, or create an internal war, where there are no victors, only casualties.

Right now, let Jesus fill your cup. Allow Him to refresh your soul. He is living water!

Jesus, come right now and refill me. You are living water and I thirst for something that this world cannot offer. Fill me up so that I can go into this day and my cup, and life, can overflow and impact those around me in positive ways. Amen

Embrace the quiet

> "And to make it your ambition
> to lead a quiet life."
> - 1 Thessalonians 4:11

"When did I become so scared of quiet?" This is a question I asked myself just one year ago when I noticed my need, my craving, for constant distraction. The need for a phone, for noise, is ever pressing!

Rarely do we just sit, with no device close by, and listen to the birds, or sip hot tea or notice the quiet around us. I have personally journeyed to a quieter space within myself, and gracious was I surprised to find that when I stopped and intentionally choose moments of quiet, the reward was peace! It is so often only in the quiet that we calm our adrenal glands enough for us to truly experience peace and calm, both in our hearts and minds.

Ask God to lead you on a journey to a quieter place within yourself, where you feel at rest.

Lord Jesus, thank You that quiet is not quite as scary as my mind may have made it out to be. Walk with me as I embrace a quieter place within myself, to hear You and walk in peace. Amen

Diligent in pursuing peace

"The plans of the diligent lead to profit as surely as haste leads to poverty."
- *Proverbs 21:5*

Be diligent as you pursue peace. Other Bible translations refer to the plans of the diligent as leading to abundance.

Despite my impulsive nature, I have learnt that planning and diligence are key precursors for abundant life. The Bible also tells us that abundance on earth is less about fancy cars or a big home, and more about the state of our hearts and heads; the home to peace. We are encouraged in this scripture to plan wisely how we live our lives, and with whom: peace will be our reward. I thus see this scripture as a way of encouraging us to plan wisely how we live our lives, what we fill our lives with and whom, as it is in the planning that we profit.

Find peace today in knowing that Your Father meets you right where you're at, and is ready and eager to help us reassess our planning in pursuit of abundance.

———

Jesus, You are the Prince of Peace. Teach me to slow down and approach even my pursuit of abundance, with planning. Amen

24th September

Unfathomable peace

"And the peace of God which transcends understanding, will guard your hearts and your minds in Christ Jesus."
- Philippians 4:7

Have you ever experienced something that had the ability to totally derail you, and yet somehow you remained at peace? That is the peace of God. It makes no sense to the human mind and yet still exists in every sense.

My Gogo has always been an example to me of what peace from God looks like. Though she's walked through many trials of her own, her faith remains unscathed. She trusts God wholeheartedly and, in turn, is a woman whose presence alone is peaceful. She has so graciously carried the weight of others' burdens over the years, mine at times too.

I cannot but be humbled knowing that it was, and is, God's peace that her heart finds comfort in when life hasn't made sense.

Today, may we be reminded that we have the privilege of taking our burdens to Jesus, and receiving from Him a peace, which surpasses our human understanding?

Lord God, today help me to walk in the peace that you so freely give, despite what my day looks like. Amen

Face your fears

"Have faith in God and He
will bring you success."
- 2 Chronicles 20:20

Coral reefs of turquoise, azure and indigo: fish of every colour and shape. An olive-green turtle. A baby shark. These are a few of the sightings I've had the privilege of seeing while scuba diving.

A big part of learning to scuba diving is facing one's fears. As you leave the comforts of naturally oxygenated air and head down into the depths of the ocean, it takes deeper courage to trust the process as you dive deep. It's easy to panic, but the deeper you get, the slower you need to approach your ascent to avoid decompression sickness. This is scary, as you simply cannot become unnerved and quickly return to the water's surface.

Steps in faith can often feel this way too. It takes courage to leave our comfort zones and to dive deep into what and where we feel called by God. When we feel convicted and at peace with a prompting from the Lord, it is more important than ever to trust God's process, and not to allow fear or doubt to prompt us towards making mistakes.

Bring your vision before God today and ask for His guidance in the steps that you need to take, as you follow His call.

Jesus, please fill me with perfect peace as I remain in You. May peace be my guide in truly knowing that I am on the path that You have for me. Amen

Patient in the process

"Do not be afraid, for God goes with you to give you victory."
- Deuteronomy 20:3-5

Did you know that an octopus's tentacles regrow if damaged? If an octopus damages or even loses part of a tentacle, with time and patience, that tentacle will regrow. I learnt this recently whilst watching a documentary and it reminded me of how our hurts or deep emotional pain as humans, can, with patience and time, heal.

God is ready and always available. He longs for us to bring our hurts to Him. He finds pleasure in our vulnerability and He promises to comfort those who mourn. Mourning is not limited to loss of life but to emotional hurt too. We cannot rush the process of healing, but we can place our trust in the One who knows us best and has our best interests at heart.

Whatever it is you've faced in your past, know that God is your safe place for healing. God restores things to us in ways that no human can do.

Lord God, thank You for Your deep love for me, and that You hold all my concerns and hurts with care. Help me to allow You to heal my wounds as I practice patience with myself. Amen

Refresh & refill

*"I will refresh the weary
and satisfy the faint."
- Jeremiah 31:25*

Have you experienced the thrill of a swim in a mountain pool or a river? I've always been naturally drawn to water and rarely pass up the opportunity to take a dip, regardless of the season or temperature of the water. I love how a mountain pool swim literally takes my breath away, but also refreshes me with an energy that is hard to replicate.

God's presence can, and should, have this same effect on us. Time in God's presence has the power to refresh us on a deep level that the world cannot offer. This is much like standing at the edge of a chilly mountain pool and hesitating as you prepare to jump, knowing it will refresh you but may be uncomfortable. This reflects our wavering in turning to God for refreshment.

God is our greatest source of refreshment and yet so often we look to the world for an easy fix, but deep down we do know that with discomfort can come great refreshment.

Take your burdens and joys before your loving Father today. As you find Him in the stillness, a stillness that you may need to create, allow Him to refresh you and refill you.

Jesus, thank You that You empower me to create still moments to turn to You to refresh me in a way that only You can do. Amen

28th September

Materialistic vs. Realistic

"Keep your lives free from the love of money and be content with what you have, because God has said, 'Never will I leave you; never will I forsake you.'"
- Hebrews 13:5

Have you ever been surrounded by wealth or materialism and yet felt empty inside? And, on the contrary, have you ever been surrounded by nature or raw beauty and felt totally at peace? It often takes moments of reflection to take note of the difference between these experiences.

It's so easy to conform to what society deems as normal and to chase things of this world and yet, peace is rarely found in things. Our hearts often feel safest when surrounded by close friends, family or in simple settings. It is often when in nature that we feel our hearts have more capacity to love, our lungs more space to breathe and our heads more clarity to discern.

Walk outside onto the grass, root your bare feet into the ground and be encouraged today to free from your heart, the chase for things of this world. You have the courage, the strength and the experience to back your choice to quit the chase and to live powerfully in the now.

Jesus, awaken me and my heart to the beauty around me and the peace that comes from deep friendship, intimate relationships, nature and of course, time in Your presence. Amen

Courage before giants

"All those gathered here will know that it is not by sword or spear that the Lord saves; for the battle is the Lord's, and He will give all of you into our hands. As the Philistine moved closer to attack him, David ran quickly toward the battle line to meet him. Reaching into his bag and taking out a stone, he slung it and struck the Philistine on the forehead. The stone sank into his forehead, and he fell facedown on the ground."
- 1 Samuel 17:47–49

I've often heard, and even experienced the doubt that can come when reading the Bible and considering the times in which it was written. Could a book written so long ago, really be significant in my life right now?

In the century in which we find ourselves, one of the greatest giants we will face is that of unbelief. In previous centuries it may have been fear or mortality but for us- never before has belief in oneself and atheism been so alive and even encouraged. Whilst the Bible was written a long time ago, giants are no new topic for our God. Giants were present in Bible times, and giants of differing statures are ever-present. There will always be opposition to our faith but our weapon is Jesus.

I encourage you today to take to heart this message. Jesus is no current craze or trend; He is alive and lives in you. He is your weapon.

Jesus, please give me courage today to face the giant of unbelief and fill me afresh with peace that surpasses human understanding. Amen

Peace is within reach

> "'Everything is possible for one who believes.' Immediately the boy's father exclaimed, 'I do believe; help me overcome my unbelief!'"
> - Mark 9:23-24

Unbelief alone does not limit us from walking in God's peace; the combination of our unbelief and pride does. To walk and live and dwell in God's peace, is to believe firstly that He is who He says He is. Unbelief is a very normal human condition, but it is in acknowledging our unbelief and doubts amidst our belief, that give us the freedom to approach Jesus with confidence.

In today's scripture we read that merely by acknowledging this man's own unbelief, his son was healed by Jesus. Jesus is not threatened by our unbelief, but He asks that we admit it, and ask for His help in overcoming it. He is quick to provide peace and healing and fullness of life to those who approach Him with faith.

Peace is within reach, Beautiful, and your receiving it is not limited by your actions, but simply by your not asking for it. Jesus wants to love on you; He wants to provide you with perfect peace. Ask Him.

Jesus, today I bring my life before you. I acknowledge my unbelief and I ask that You fill me with peace as I journey through life seeking Your face and Your will everyday. Amen

OCTOBER

walk out on the water

"'Lord, if it's You,' Peter replied, 'tell me
to come to You on the water.'"
- Matthew 14:28

Walk out on the Water

"'Lord, if it's You,' Peter replied, 'tell me to come to You on the water.'"
- Matthew 14:28

Jesus speaks of child-like faith in scriptures, but nothing quite hits home as much as a personal experience does.

I will never forget a particular day when I sat on the rocks above the ocean below our beach house with my youngest brother. In my High School years, I'd often retreat to this spot over weekends, to pray, listen to worship and contemplate my teenage life; and being 6 years my junior, my brother would often ask to join me. On this particular day we were chatting about the gift of tongues. He was 8 years old, and I explained, in my very newly-saved-Christian-state that if my brother had faith to walk on water, then he could get the gift of tongues at any age. We closed our eyes and prayed, but instead of speaking in tongues, he then stood up and declared 'I'm ready. I'll try walk on the water now, Kit.' I was terrified and told him he simply could not. Gracious was I humbled.

Today, as we begin this month of courage, may God plant in you a new longing for a courage that calls you out onto the water.

———

Jesus, today I take Your hand. Help me to gain the courage to walk out to You on the water, when You call me. Amen

2nd October

Courage to believe

"Immediately He spoke to them and said, 'Take courage! It is I. Don't be afraid.'"
- Mark 6:50

Faith, the very ability to believe in something unseen, may be one of the greatest steps in courage we'll ever take. Doubt is the enemy of faith, it's admitting to being unsure. I've always loved the common comparison made, of faith to that of the wind. We may not see wind, but if we expose ourselves to its elements, we cannot deny its presence or existence. God or faith is much the same. We may not see Him, but if we open ourselves to experiencing Him, if we seek Him, we will find Him.

Whether wind or God, we need to step outside to know for sure. We need courage.

Ask God this week to give you the courage to know when it is Him who is speaking to you.

Jesus, thank You for the courage to step out of the boat, out of my comfort zone, and into a world where faith is a journey and Your voice my guide. Amen

Strength in God

"Then Samson prayed to the Lord, 'Sovereign Lord, remember me. Please, God, strengthen me just once more.'"
- Judges 16:28

Many of us build walls around ourselves to self protect, and even as we intentionally address our past hurts and let God into those spaces, there are indeed times, when those walls silently re-erect themselves around us. It is courage that we need to consciously make an effort to acknowledge them, to forgive, to breathe, and to let them fall once again. This process of living vulnerable is no easy task, but it does mean that we never fear being alone or so guarded that we miss out on the abundant life that we have in Christ.

Samson had lost his strength after having his hair cut, but still managed to push down towers at the time when it was needed. Sometimes, we feel that the walls around us are our strength. They are the very things that keep us safe, strong and capable, much like Samson's hair. But truth be told, the moment that those walls crumble, is the very moment when we realize our strength lies elsewhere.

Ask God today to give you the strength to cope in life, without walls around you. You have the grace to treat others with respect, even when it hurts. You have the courage to stand alone, even when it's scary. And you have the confidence to walk with your head held high, even when your life looks messy.

———

Jesus, thank You that Your strength makes me strong. Help me to let the walls around me crumble as I rely on You to hold me up. Amen

4th October

Know your source

"For with You is the fountain of life."
- Psalm 36:9

We're on the search at the moment for our first fountain. I thought I had found the perfect spot for it in our garden. I showed my mum where I thought the fountain should go and she laughed at my ignorance. I had placed it far from any water source, forgetting that the very thing that brought it to life was water. I feel that this applies to many of our lives too. We build businesses, pursue relationships, raise children or wrestle through struggles, feeling alone and defeated, but far from the source that brings us life.

Jesus is the fountain of life giving water; the only source that never runs dry.

Use this week, or day, to look inwards and to humbly ask yourself where your source of energy or life comes from. If it is outside of God, it is likely to run dry, and will continue a pattern of you chasing the next best thing.

─────────

Jesus, give me courage today to acknowledge what source I've been relying on and to shift my focus and my identity back to You. Amen

Fear limits us

"For the Spirit God gave us, does not make us timid, but gives us power, love and self-discipline."
- 2 Timothy 1:7

I was once chatting to a friend and she shared how she just wasn't getting around to putting her ideas into action. I challenged her by asking, "What's stopping you?" She thought for a while and then simply added; "I guess I'm scared it won't work out".

Fear is almost always the catalyst that keeps us frozen in the now. Fear is usually created when we experience something unpleasant and our unconscious minds then decide to label this so called experience as a "NO GO" area. This innate process that we go through is there to protect us; however, scripture shows us that life is about giving things a second chance, it's about taking risks and exploring avenues that may be scary but may yield beautiful results.

So often our fears go un-noticed, even by ourselves. Today ask God to open your eyes and bring your awareness to un-acknowledged fears that may be holding you back.

———

Jesus, open my eyes today to where fear is limiting me and give me the courage to admit this to myself. Amen

6th October

You make me brave

"Have I not commanded you? Be strong and courageous. Do not be afraid; do not be discouraged, for the Lord your God will be with you wherever you go."
- Joshua 1:9

Our fears are usually in line with that which we value the most; and of course often our calling in life or promptings from God, are in this same space. A little anxiety can be a good thing, but fear is different to anxiety. Where anxiety brings on fight or flight responses, fear or perceived danger, causes us to freeze.

When we experience fear, our frontal lobe in our brain becomes paralyzed which means that our problem solving ability disappears. This naturally feeds a cycle, more fear, more freezing, less problem solving and ultimately avoidance.

If, and when, God calls you towards or into a season or space that scares you, know that your fear is overcome by simply knowing what makes you brave. Jesus makes us brave, brave enough to face our fears with confidence and assurance.

Jesus, You make me brave. You are my courage, my rock and my strength. Amen

Faith over fear

"Be strong, do not fear; your God will come, He will come with vengeance; with divine retribution He will come to save you."
- Isaiah 35:4

For the most part, we were not born with fears...they are learnt through a process of trial and error. When we fail at something or feel an unpleasant emotion whilst doing something, we label it, and from then on, we usually fear it! At first, fear has a tiny voice, only heard on certain occasions, but give it time and you'll be checking in with fear before you make any big life decisions.

Fear is that convincing!

The scripture for today is taken from Isaiah and reminds us that God is coming to our rescue. Imagine living a life from that standpoint, from a foundation of strength and keeping trust in God, rather than off a wobbly foundation of fear.

Today, challenge your fears with faith. A simple rebuking of a fear-filled thought and replacing it with a faith-filled one, can teach our brains to rewire this process and begin building a foundation of faith over fear.

Jesus, thank You that You are coming to my rescue. Thank You that I have everything I need to stand strong and to live from a place of faith over fear. Amen

8th October

Fear of failure

"Do not be afraid; you will not be put to shame. Do not fear disgrace; you will not be humiliated."
- Isaiah 54:4

For years, my deep fear of failure prevented me from doing or starting anything that I wasn't convinced I'd be good at.

In Grade 6, my family went water skiing. It was my first attempt at skiing and I failed, miserably. From the ripe age of 11, until almost my 22nd Birthday, I avoided water-skiing altogether. At age 22, I finally decided that the moment had come to test if my fears had any right "at all" in dictating my life. And guess what? I failed to stand the first time but on my second attempt, I skied across the entire bay. How often does a fear of failure hold us back from living the abundant life that Christ promised?

Today, let's begin by acknowledging where you experience a fear of failure; perhaps it's at work, motherhood, a hobby, relationship, big dream or daily activity. Once you've acknowledged it, allow yourself the freedom to explore this a little deeper — this could be through a conversation with someone or simply thinking it through.

———

Jesus, give me courage today to address that which is holding me back from the life and freedom that You promised. Amen

"I prayed to the Lord, and He answered me. He freed me from all my fears."
- Psalm 34:4

Has God ever called you out of your comfort zone? Have you ever felt led to do something, talk to someone or to take a mighty step in faith that felt totally out of your realm of capability or wisdom?

It takes true courage and deep conviction to act on dreams that God has placed in our hearts, especially if those are outside the box of what would be expected of us, by others. It may be hard to believe but God knows you better than you know yourself. He knows exactly what you need in this season of life. If you bring yourself before Him, humbly and open to His promptings – He will direct your next move. And if that move requires courage to step out of a comfort zone, then courage He will provide.

Today, as you are led by God's spirit, in your daily life, remember that it is His living water that will sustain you. When you doubt your next move or even a past move, return to Him in prayer and ask Him to refill your cup.

———

Jesus, thank You that You call me out of my comfort zone, not to experience harm, but rather to grow in likeness of You. Give me the strength today to act in obedience when You call. Amen

10th October

All things are possible

"Jesus looked at them and said,
'With man this is impossible, but
with God all things are possible.'"
- Matthew 19:26

Do you have a distant dream, perhaps something that has been at the back of your mind for years?

I certainly did. For years, I worked on writing my first book; I'd get into the process of writing and then would lose interest. I knew it was a book that I was due to write, but I never felt the freedom to complete it. Until one day in late August 2020, when in a particularly difficult season of life, God redefined this dream and clearly re-positioned my view on this book. Today, this book that you are reading, was once a dream for me that felt very out of reach. With God all things are possible, but rarely do they look the way that we had envisioned.

Trust God today with your big dreams, and allow Him to refine and redirect your path, as you bring glory to His name.

Jesus, thank You that You are into the detail of my life. Thank You that I can trust You with directing my dreams and bringing them to life. Amen

11th October

Courage for breakthrough

"I will lead the blind by ways they have not known, along unfamiliar paths I will guide them; I will turn the darkness into light before them and make the rough places smooth. These are the things I will do; I will not forsake them."
- Isaiah 42:16

We started our daughter at swimming lessons at 6 months old. She progressed normally in her swimming ability but around age 2 we began to notice her deep-set fear of pushing the boundaries and stepping out into the unknown.

For at least a year, she had the ability to swim on her own, but instead of venturing out, she chose to rather be held, screamed at swimming lessons and perfected her stroke...on the step. It drove me mad, to tears even, a few times. Then, one day, at age 3 her very patient swimming teacher asked if she was ready to try to swim on her own. And just like that, she swam. A whole 5 meters and then 10 times more. As I drove home from the lesson, a full face of mummy tears, it hit me. How often does this happen in adult life too?!

So often, others can often see the potential in us but we don't have the courage to go there, to leave our comfort zones...until one day, we do, and we can't believe that we didn't venture out earlier. Today is your beginning, Beautiful.

Jesus, thank You for meeting me where I am at today. Thank You that You know my potential. Help me to take little courageous steps towards that one-day big dream. Amen

Consistency

"Therefore dear brothers and sisters, stand firm. Let nothing move you. Always give yourselves fully to the work of the Lord, because you know that your labour in the Lord is not in vain."
- 1 Corinthians 15:58

A friend told me about a ted talk she'd recently listened to that said if you brush your teeth for 2 minutes, as a once off, it would do nothing for your teeth. But repeat this behaviour twice a day for 20 years and the effect is mind-blowing.

Isn't it so true with life and faith too?

Consistency is where we see results. Prayer may still be a struggle for you, or perhaps reading the Word, or attending Church. Whatever it is that you feel is part of your faith-walk but still feels tough to repeat, remember that it is through consistency that we see progress.

My encouragement today is to challenge yourself to recognize which spiritual habits you know are beneficial but remain tough, and then to ask God for strength to continue to remain consistent with these habits, in the months to come.

Thank You Jesus, for the strength to repeat positive spiritual habits, everyday, until one day they form my new normal. Amen

Persistence

"I can do all this through Him who gives me strength."
- Phillippians 4:13

I will never forget night two of a multi-stage trail running race that my husband and I did together in my early 20's. We had run 65km's in two days, over grueling mountain tops, across rivers, through beautiful forests and amidst a mighty rain storm. There we lay in our two separate single-man tents, absolutely shattered, but unable to sleep, whispering to each other in the darkness. Our team was called FROG (Fully Reliant On God) and gracious, never in my wildest dreams did I realize just how much I would have to rely on God.

We woke at 5am on day 3, having slept very little and my husband had to pick me up out of my tent, as my legs were too stiff to lift me. That day we ran a further 26km's of single track, with the final 9km's on a beach that had a dreadful angle. Finishing that race was one of the greatest achievements and moments of my life. I sobbed.

Persisting isn't always comfortable but the reward of persistence is not easily forgotten. It goes deeper than the moment itself, and rather is marked on your soul: survivor, conqueror, brave. And that you are!

———

Jesus, thank You that as we rely on You for strength in our weakness, that You too remind us how strong we are, in You. Amen

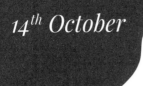

Perserverance & patience

"Consider it pure joy, my brothers and sisters, whenever you face trials of many kinds, because you know that the testing of your faith produces perseverance."
- James 1:2-3

Life is so fast-moving that we are more than just used-to things happening quickly, we expect them to. We expect speedy answers to questions, we expect immediate healing when sick, we expect relief when tired and we expect possible escape when uncomfortable.

But God is not into this game of rushing.

God falls outside of time; and He has not, and will never, conform to our generation of hurry. God is more concerned about developing our character, than He is in meeting our goalposts for happiness. One such characteristic is that of patience. It is only in the waiting that we learn what it is to be patient. Whilst our prayers move the hand of God, He is also out of time, and thus is not hurried to answer them on our clock.

As you walk through today, ask God where it is that He is teaching you patience and be open to learn this lesson, as Jesus modeled when He was but a man.

Jesus, thank You for the courage to be patient when waiting on You, and Your perfect time. Amen

Your cake

> "Teach me and I will be quiet; show me where I have been wrong."
> - Job 6:24

I'm a firm believer that you can have your cake and eat it.
Yet in saying that, I think what is paramount is that you know the cake that you need, right now, and not just the craving. For every season in life, we require a different cake. When you're a child, it's all Disney and icing, and later may come an elaborate wedding cake. The size, shape and flavor of the cake differ with each season we pass through.

So it is with real life. Yes you can have your cake and eat it, absolutely! But it will take courage to step away from the noise of your life and surroundings and to ask God what your cake could and should look like right now.

What cake would be right for this season of your life? Don't assume a one-size-fits-all mentality about your happiness or purpose. Approach the throne with flexibility, realism and self-compassion.

Jesus, thank You for the courage to quiet my busy mind and world and to press into You to define my next move. Amen

Noble character

"When Abigail saw David, she quickly got off her donkey and bowed down before David with her face to the ground. She fell at his feet and said: 'Pardon your servant, my lord, and let me speak to you; hear what your servant has to say.'"
- 1 Samuel 25:23-24

The story of Abigail, reported in 1 Samuel, is a beautifully inspiring one when it comes to the theme of courage.

"Abigail was an intelligent and beautiful woman, but her husband was surly and mean in his dealings" (1 Samuel 23:3). When David approached Nabal, and he refused to be kind to David's men, David instructed 400 men to follow him back to Nabal to bring disaster on him and his family. Abigail heard of this, and with great wisdom, courage and implicit confidence in God, she rode ahead with her servants, unbeknown to her husband, and approached David in humility by falling at his feet. She provided his men with food and managed to calm David's anger with her wise words and in turn save her family's lives.

You, like Abigail, were made in the image of God. You possess wisdom to rely on implicit confidence in God to direct your path.

———

Jesus, thank You for the courage that You have placed within me to live as a noble woman, who brings honour to her family and to You. Amen

Do not fear

"For I am the Lord your God who takes hold of your right hand and says to you, do not fear; I will help you."
- Isaiah 41:13

I love how when out and about with my two young kids, they naturally gravitate towards holding my hands. My hands provide them with safety, protection and security. "If I've got mum's hand, I know nothing can go wrong."

What a beautiful privilege it is to be a mother and to offer myself for the protection of another. It wasn't until I had children that I truly began to understand the depth of God's love for me. How endearing to think that God feels the same desire to protect us as a mother or father would her or his child. God longs to take your hand and offer you His safety, protection and security.

Be encouraged today that God's hand is ready and waiting to be grabbed hold of. The power is in your hands today to reach out and find comfort and safety as you take His hand.

———————

Jesus, I take Your hand today. I will not fear because You are my safe place. Amen

Big decisions

"If any of you lacks wisdom, you should ask God, who gives generously to all without finding fault, and it will be given to you."
- James 1:5

We make decisions everyday, about what we will wear, say and do, but all of us will go through the process, at some point in our lives, when we're required to make big life decisions. Decision-making can totally unravel us. I will never forget my husband and I having to make a decision as to whether to come back to South Africa after living abroad. We'd weighed up pros and cons, and still, even with our combined decisive personalities, we were both as undecided as ever.

We then remembered a sermon we'd heard the year before by Andy Stanley. It was about decision-making. Revisiting his message on this topic, changed the way that we've approached big decisions ever since. The simple question he suggested one asks is, "What story do you want to tell?"

Today, know that by simply asking yourself the right questions, you will access answers you may not have found otherwise.

———

Jesus, give me courage today to value my story, and Your story, enough to make tough decisions when they present themselves. Amen

Abram's model

> "The Lord had said to Abram, 'Go from your country, your people and your father's household to the land I will show you'...The Lord appeared to Abram and said, 'To your offspring I will give this land.' So he built an altar there to the Lord, who had appeared to him."
> - Genesis 12:1&7

What I love reading about the life of Abram, is how often God tested him and he responded in faith and obedience. Some decisions in our life feel like tests of faith, and others of obedience. Today we read of Abram being called to leave his country and all that was his normal, merely to head to a land that God would show him. Imagine that! Imagine leaving all you know, and not being sure where exactly you were going. God does this same thing with us today. He redirects our paths, perhaps not by country, but by occupation or relationship or home and He doesn't always show us the end result. Making decisions by faith is incredibly powerful though. Genesis 12 speaks of Abram setting out on his journey, and when he reached the place that God had for him, God suddenly appeared to Him and confirmed that this was the spot of his inheritance.

We can sometimes feel convicted to make a change, but be unsure of where we are headed. Take heed, He will answer you in due time, and when He does, like Abram, take note to record that moment so that when He calls again, you remember His faithfulness.

Jesus, give me courage today to take steps that honour You, especially when it feels scary and uncertain. Amen

Tough decision-making

"I will instruct you and teach you in the way you should go; I will counsel you with my eye upon you."
- Psalm 32:8

I recently made a decision that I felt was contrary to how many others in my circle of friends would approach that specific situation. Instead of walking proudly in the direction of the choice that I had made, I found myself explaining my reasoning to everyone that I met. My dad pointed this out to me, and asked why I felt the need to explain myself to everyone; if I was so convinced that I had made the right decision.

This hit me hard. It's tough to make hard decisions and tougher to make decisions that others may not agree with or approve of; but make them we must. As we submit our decisions before God and rely on His voice, peace or presence to direct us, we can do so with self-assurance.

Today, may you take stock of decisions that you've made previously, or perhaps recently, that you find yourself justifying, and let these go once and for all.

Jesus, thank You that my assurance comes from You, not from this world. Help me to stand firm in Your truth and my convictions, as I live a life surrendered to You. Amen

Face your past

"And through Him to reconcile to Himself all things, whether things on earth or things in Heaven, by making peace through His blood, shed on the Cross."
- *Colossians 1:20*

I often sit on my kids' beds once they are asleep and stare at them in wonder. I try to think back to what it was that drew me to my husband, the one who had to be present for these two humans to be alive. What may not feel like a big deal back then, was the catalyst for life-altering consequences. I cannot but believe that these little humans were in every sense meant to be here, and that that required me falling in-love with my husband. We are faced with so many choices everyday, some that we can be proud of, and others which we may prefer to remain hidden. As I've looked back over my past, and it sure isn't all pretty, I have been overcome with emotion that despite my mistakes, actions and character-flaws, I still am where I am today.

God says that He goes before us. God says He works all things for our good. We need to trust Him that even despite our wandering and potential past regrets, by His grace, we are set free from allowing our pasts to rob from us.

God is peace and He longs for you to have peace too. Take your past before Him today and allow His living water to wash over you, to cleanse you and to make you new. He sees you only as He is. Believe it.

———————

Jesus, by Your blood I am sanctified, made new in every way. Fill me with Your peace as I surrender my past to You. Amen

Just believe

"Jesus told him, 'Don't be afraid; just believe.'"
- Mark 5:36

To 'just believe' sounds so easy, but we know that this isn't always the case. In seasons of doubt, a helpful tool that I have used is to see my 'coping' as in-fact thriving, right now. We all face battles of our own and I know that now, mid-October, more than ever, we're tired.

Don't allow your 'not-thriving' to deny you the power of coping, of just believing! Do what you need to, to cope; have longer showers, shave your legs in the garden whilst watching the kids play, pray more, sleep in when you get the chance, ask for help. But mostly, keep coping. There is little advice others can give when life feels heavier than usual and you can't quite pinpoint why, so lean further into God. Ask God to help you to find the courage to make sense of your current reality. Make time for you. You're more likely to make and take time for yourself if you ask for it than you ever are of someone granting it to you.

Remember that you matter and that your coping matters. One day your coping will turn to thriving. So for today, just believe, Beautiful.

Jesus, thank You for the courage to just believe, even when I'm tired beyond words. I love You. Lead me beside quiet waters today, You are my living water. Amen

Renew your mind

"Therefore, with minds that are alert and fully sober, set your hope on the grace to be brought to you when Jesus Christ is revealed at His coming."
- 1 Peter 1:13

In my Psychology lecturing years, I was introduced to the concept of flexibility. Not putting your leg behind your ear, although I wouldn't mind being able to do that, but rather the power of a flexible mind. Whilst we often believe the world to be one specific way, this is rarely the truth. Mostly, we have learnt to adopt a certain view of the world and it takes deep courage to challenge that view. The ability to look at situations from multiple perspectives opens up our minds to more effective problem solving, powerful decision making and reduces anxiety.

Worldviews do not have to be fixed, we can change the way that we see the world, whilst still knowing that only the Bible provides us with absolute truth.

A fun way to challenge your brain this week to grow in flexibility is to use your less dominant hand whenever you dial a number on your cellphone or brush your teeth. The idea is to strengthen the brain pathways you don't usually use, and stimulate the production of chemicals in your brain that are involved in the development of new brain cells, allowing you to grow in flexibility.

———

Jesus, thank You for the power of the mind, and that I never need to feel stuck, but rather empowered to make changes where change is due. Amen

24th October

Courage to be curious

"A person can do nothing better than to eat and drink and find satisfaction in their own toil. This too, I see, is from the hand of God."
- Ecclesiastes 2:24

Curiosity breathes life into us and teaches us to squeeze the absolute most out of life. An experience I will remember forever was after our wedding night of dancing, celebration and fairy lights, Hendrik and I jumped on a plane headed for Bali.

On the first day of our honeymoon, we wandered a local beach and ended up in a lush, green little rainforest that jotted out into the sea. Our casual stroll quickly turned into a mad dash as we realized that this was considered a 'holy' spot and that our minimal beach attire wasn't appropriate. Amidst the chaos, we balanced our camera on a branch and H placed a flower in my hair to take a quick photo. This, said photo, is one that I deeply treasure as it reminds me that when we let go a little and we choose to explore beyond what we know, we enter a space where joy can spontaneously sprout.

Let the remainder of this year be a season of your life when you open yourself to curiosity. This may come naturally to you, or perhaps not, but as you open yourself to more spontaneity, God's hand of blessing is often more easily noticeable.

Jesus, You are the wonder of it all. Breathe new life into me today as I explore the beautiful world that You created, with eyes wide open. Amen

25th October

Bravery rewarded

"May the Lord repay you for what you have done. May you be richly rewarded by the Lord, the God of Israel, under whose wings you have come to take refuge."
- Ruth 2:12

Ruth was a Moabite woman and her bravery humbles me to my core. Ruth was married to Naomi's son, but after Naomi's husband passes away and then later her two sons both die, she encourages her daughter-in-laws to return to their native lands, just as she plans to do. Ruth, however, chooses to remain by Naomi's side. Ruth was willing to give up her own future, to ensure the security and peace of another's.

What a truly beautifully brave gesture. On returning to Bethlehem, Ruth then, bravely, goes out to the fields to pick grains for Naomi and her to eat, and she meets Boaz. So begins a beautiful story of God fulfilling His purpose in Ruth. Ruth and Boaz marry and she births Jesse, who later has a son of his own, David. Yes, the King David we all know too well.

Just like Ruth, you may be called to act out of bravery. Know that your great King, who sits on the Throne, will reward you for your obedience.

Jesus, help me to be brave, and to act out of obedience to You, when You call me. Amen

26th October

Slow it all down

"But those who hope in the Lord will renew their strength. They will soar on wings like eagles; they will run and not grow weary, they will walk and not be faint."
- Isaiah 40:31

Have you ever felt convicted to just stop everything, and rethink your life? I have, and no doubt I will again. For some people life is but an enjoyable journey. For others, like me, life feels like one big bag of responsibility and as the year goes on, that bag feels heavier and heavier until such time as you're convinced that you can totally relate to Father Christmas trekking his heavy load around the world.

In 2013, my husband and I spent a year living in South Korea. The time away from the craziness of routine, responsibilities and comfort zones gave me time to not only reset, but to flourish. I will forever be thankful for this season that brought me so much perspective about life, faith, marriage, my dreams and reality. I have since learnt though that when the world feels heavy, I don't need a year abroad to reset, but instead the consciousness to slow down.

Today, before you make any big life decisions, simply breathe and slow everything down. Turn your gaze inwards and upwards.

Jesus, help me to slow down the pace of my life and to acknowledge the weight of the burdens I am carrying. Amen

Courage to flourish

"Trust in Him at all times, oh people; pour out your heart before Him; God is a refuge for us."
- Psalm 62:8

In continuing with yesterday's theme of slowing down and turning our gaze inwards and upwards, there is so much power in the word 'reset'. To reset is to set again or differently. It takes huge courage to know when you need to retreat from the world, to a place where you are able to truly reset; to get your life back on track, to feel refueled and different.

For me I have always found calm and restoration at the ocean. I merely need one swim in the sea, even on a rainy day, to wake up my senses and remind me of what is really important in life. Getting to the ocean is relatively easy, but only if I know what I need when those moments hit.

Ask God to help you to identify what it is that you need in order to reset before you show signs of burn out, so that you can act quickly and with wisdom.

––––––––––

Jesus, You are wise beyond words and You know me better than I know myself. Help me to find courage to figure out what it is I need when life feels heavier than usual and I need to reset in order to live with abundance, again. Amen

28th October

Keep perspective

"Lord, remind me how brief my time on earth will be. Remind me that my days are numbered - how fleeting my life is."
- Psalm 39:4

I love the saying 'Try not to compare your insides to other people's outsides.'

I often giggle watching mums in the car park at school pick-up; a quick application of lipstick, or a face wipe of messy mascara, a neatening of a mom bun or pulling their panties out from their bum. We all love to set a good impression. We naturally want others to think that we have it all together; and the best way we know how to do this is to appear that way in the physical. The truth though, is that few of us EVER have it all together. We have days of high-fiving ourselves for getting our ducks in a row but mostly, we have geese and they're all wild.

Scripture never suggests that we should have it all together. Instead it only points to Jesus, as the one who is perfect. Today be reminded that your insides are just as, if not far more, important than your outsides.

Jesus, You are perfect. I am not. Help me to draw my strength and courage from You and to feel safe enough to go out into the world as I truly am. Amen

29th October

Your trust in Him

> "When I am afraid, I
> put my trust in You."
> - Psalm 56:3

If you've ever bungee jumped, you'll know that the absolute scariest part is not the falling, but rather getting yourself to the edge of the cliff or platform and actively choosing to plunge over the edge. I personally love all things adrenalin and so have bungee jumped a few times. When my brother, headed for his first jump, asked how I find it in me to dive over the edge, I replied with the answer: 'I trust the system'. If the system has proven itself to be worthy of holding up thousands of other jumpers, then what are the chances it won't hold me?

Faith is much the same. At first, we trust in God merely for who He says He is, and how He has come through for others; but with time we grow our own experiences and we realize that He, too, has never failed us.

Approach today with courage, as you trust the only system in the world, which truly never fails: the love and faithfulness of God.

Jesus, You are always faithful. Today I put my trust in You. Amen

Take courage

"I have told you these things, so that in Me you may have peace. In this world you will have trouble. But take heart! I have overcome the world."
- John 16:33

God never committed to us, a life without hardship. For some reason whilst growing up, I believed that He had. That the goal to life was happiness, but growing up has woken me to realizing this isn't so.

As we read in John 16, 'In the world you will have trouble.'
I have personally lived through seasons of life when I have cried out to God in deep frustration of having to live in pain and not have the freedom to embrace hobbies and the lifestyle that I love. But what I love about finding the courage to take deep matters before the Lord is that He always turns our tears into gratitude and hope. He has overcome the world and a day will come when every battle we've faced will make sense.

As you face seasons of trouble, may you ask Him to help you to see more clearly. May your tears wash away the grit and may you see your King for who He is.

Jesus, thank You that as I experience rough seasons of life, I can know that it will pass and it too will leave me with beautiful lessons if I give You the chance to speak into this space. Amen

31st October

A compassionate God

"They will neither hunger nor thirst, nor will the desert heat or the sun beat down on them. He who has compassion on them will guide them and lead them beside springs of water."
- Isaiah 49:10

As we come to the end of this month of courage, may we be reminded that God, in all His glory, does not require courage to draw us to Himself.

God is near; He will not let His children hunger or thirst. Take courage that He has you in the very palm of His hand. He treasures you. As you find your feet and your comfort in His palm, be aware of the springs of water that will surface and that are surfacing. Springs of water always give new life, and the springs of water He will, and is, leading you beside will do the same.

Ask Jesus today to lead you beside springs of water and to open your eyes to the new life He is birthing within and around you.

Jesus, thank You that it is not my courage that makes me strong, but Your strength that gives me courage. Amen

NOVEMBER

may your cup overflow

"You prepare a table before me in the presence of my enemies. You anoint my head with oil; my cup overflows."
- Psalm 23:5

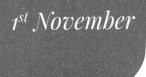

Reflecting on refilling

"You prepare a table before me in the presence of my enemies. You anoint my head with oil; my cup overflows."
- *Psalm 23:5*

'It's the most WONDERFUL time of the year, and I'm shattered' are words uttered by so many of us, at this time of year.

Along these lines (nope, not the ones on my face), and knowing the rush of the season, this month we'll be looking at reflecting on the year passed, de-cluttering our lives and space so that despite our exhaustion, our cups can still overflow. This time of year is often referred to as a time of giving, and yet we know that we can offer the world very little when pouring from an empty cup. Let's use the month ahead to collectively reflect and refill so that God can use us in this final part of the year.

Today, ask God to remind you what it is about time with Him that fills you up. It may be listening to worship music, praying with a friend or on your own, lying on the floor and just being still, reading your Bible or a number of other options.

———————

Lord Jesus, remind me today how best to approach You as I so desperately need my cup refilled. You are always good. Amen

A cheerful giver

"In everything I did, I showed you that by this kind of hard work we must help the weak, remembering the words the Lord Jesus Himself said: 'It is more blessed to give than to receive.'"
- Acts 20:35

Are you a cheerful giver?

By November, it's not uncommon to feel run-down and to lose the joy in giving. In saying this, Jesus was the one to utter the words of today's scripture. He didn't say that some days it was better to give; He merely stopped at 'it is more blessed to give than to receive'.

So why doesn't it always feel that way? We become run-down and lose the cheer in giving as we forget that our cups can dry and where to refill them. Giving should be an overflow. There is cheer in giving when we feel that it does not deplete us. Jesus is the only true source of living water. He is the hope that we have in refilling and refueling, despite our circumstances.

Be encouraged today to go back to your life source. Jesus. He has the power to refill you and re-ignite in you, the joy in giving.

Lord, by Your grace, please refill me, as I learn to put boundaries in place, so that I can find joy in giving, again. Amen

Greater things

"But You, Sovereign Lord, help me for Your name's sake; out of the goodness of Your love, deliver me."
- Psalm 109:21

Whilst I understand the natural pull at this time of year to get in shape for summer, I know that God longs for us to walk in freedom in this season. I personally feel my best when I'm fit and healthy, but that's not my only best. I'm also at my best when I'm investing time and energy into raising self-assured kids, when I'm working hard to build a company, and when I'm spending time in God's presence and that flows into me spending hours in local communities, mentoring, writing and loving others.

Whilst a fit, healthy body feels good, our lives, their impact and our vision cannot be limited to the shape of our bodies as we head into summer. It is mindsets like these that limit our impact on the world as they shrink our perspective.

Wherever you find yourself today, in this final quarter of the year, celebrate it. Don't enter a self-doubt mentality where you suddenly feel as if a body is the only source of achievement, it's not. You're on a far greater mission here on earth than to settle for a body-type as your source of happiness.

Jesus, thank You that my greatest call on earth is to love and know You. Help me to be reminded of this, and to live from a place of love, rather than seeking it out in the world in the form of acceptance. Amen

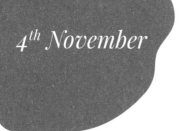

Grateful in the chaos

"The Lord has done it this very day;
let us rejoice today and be glad."
- *Psalm 118:24*

Does this time of year exhaust you?

I had a particularly exhausting day this time last year. My daughter screamed whilst we tried on her Mary outfit for the school play. The one my mum had sewed HERSELF. No thank you's, just screams. It was washing hair night and we incurred the usual run-down. Kicks, shouts, me eventually pouring water over her head, arguably a bit too forcefully. Then came drying hair. As my daughter wriggled in my arms, I suddenly glanced in the mirror and then the tears came. That was me. My life. A beautiful child in my arms. A tired mum looking back, with a heart so full it could burst. The reality I'd dreamed of for years prior. It took a pause amidst my chaos to notice that I truly had so much to be grateful for. Each of us does.

Let's not allow the exhaustion or busyness of this season of life to empty our cups. Let's be reminded of the good that we do have to celebrate and let's allow our brains to be truly grateful.

Jesus, I'm sorry for when I've focused so much on the negative, or the exhaustion that I've forgotten to be grateful. I am so grateful for all that You have gifted me with. Amen

Declutter & re-align

"And to be generous and willing to share. In this way they will lay up treasure for themselves as a firm foundation for the coming age, so that they may take hold of the life that is truly life."
- 1 Timothy 6:18-19

Clutter smothers. Simplicity breathes. It's amazing what a good declutter session can do for the mind and not just the home. Christmas time is the most beautiful time of the year to free you of unnecessary clutter and to embrace what it means to only keep that which we need and to bless others with that, which is excess.

You've got a lot of stuff. I hear you. But perhaps it's time to reclaim your inner peace by organising your external world. De-cluttering starts with an internal decision. A decision that less is more. Jesus modeled this for us and lived a life of true peace, and we can do the same. Clutter makes us feel like we're living in chaos so by simplifying your home, life and mind you're likely to feel happier, healthier, and freer.

Begin today by simply bringing before God your whole being; body, mind and spirit. Ask Him to empower you to acknowledge where your declutter process needs to begin.

Jesus, You modeled perfect peace and lived a simple, uncomplicated life. Teach me what it means to simplify my life, and things, and to get back to what truly is important in life. Amen

Time boundaries

"Above all else, guard your heart,
for everything you do flows from it."
- Proverbs 4:23

Do you ever feel like if you could just clone yourself, life would be so much easier? So many of us women feel that we are pulled in a million different directions all at once. Life can feel all consuming, and the desire to pass out on the couch every evening, engage in un-present social media scrolling or drinking another glass of wine, feels all too tempting.

Your calendar does not have to overwhelm you! Yes, your life is busy. But is it good busy or just busy for the sake of busy? The insight raised from this question can change our lives. Boundaries are healthy and are one beautiful tactic that Jesus used to protect His energy and to keep His cup from running dry.

Use some time today to rethink how many social activities you'd like to have in a week or weekend. Decide on the fullness of your schedule before the invites come. This is an empowering way to reinforce positive boundaries.

Jesus, thank you for your grace in helping me figure out what adds value and what robs from my energy levels. You knew how and when to retreat, teach me to do the same. Amen

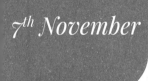

7th November

'No' is a powerful word

> "All you need to say is simply 'Yes' or 'No'; anything beyond this comes from the evil one."
> - Matthew 5:37

Many of us have trouble saying no; especially when we are more yes-people. No is a powerful word, but what if you were to change it to Yes? Is it not the same thing, to say no to a party invite but yes to a night in with our family?

A mere changing of how we word things can free us from the pressure we so often feel when reinforcing our own personal boundaries. This begins with intention. We need to be intentional about how we choose to use our energy, and how we conserve it so that our cup rarely empties. Self-assured women know their value and that their time is precious. Saying no doesn't come easily to many women, but those who know what they want for their lives, tend to find it easier to turn down invites, questions or demands that rob from this.

Let's begin our boundary-setting by simply bringing awareness to when we feel most pressure to say yes when in fact we mean no, or vice versa.

Lord, give me the courage to say YES to the decisions that I feel most convicted and at peace with, and NO to those that rob from my joy. Amen

The freedom of 'No'

"Like a city whose walls are broken through is a person who lacks self-control."
- Proverbs 25:28

Saying 'no' to certain events, or people may create a barrier of connection. But as long as we are living honest lives that feel true to God and ourselves then we need to let go of that pressure on us.

I remember a time in my mid 20's, when I was working ridiculous hours and had 2 young kids, whilst God's grace was sufficient, I had to be extra wise with how I chose to spend my 'free' time. My tank ran close to empty on most days, and so I simply could not commit to many social activities. There was grace in that period for me to juggle a lot, but I had to do so with wisdom if I wanted to keep my home stable; which of course I often got wrong.

Wherever you're at today; rather than focusing on the potential for your no's to create barriers; instead choose to focus on the stability that your 'yeses' will bring.

Jesus, You were so good at knowing when to say no and when to say yes, with such honest conviction. Teach me to do the same. Amen

Devices & the Kingdom

"If anyone loves the world, love for the Father is not in them. For everything in the world - the lust of the flesh, the lust of the eyes, and the pride of life - comes not from the Father but from the world."
- 1 John 2:15-16

A powerful message, we all would have heard before, is "Seeing is believing". As the year nears its end, many of us will be tired and thus turn to things like devices for escapism. This is of course not all bad; but we need to be aware that what we are seeing, our brains are taking in, whether it's a quick scroll or an hour-long series.

Who we follow on Instagram/social media platforms is thus super valuable in what message or internal narrative our brains are developing (with or without our knowledge). For example: If your feed is full of women in swimwear or fitness wear, regardless of whether you actively engage with these posts – your brain gets one message. This is the way a body looks. No questions asked. Rather than turn to extremes, which can at times to be helpful but not always, let's actively start investing in our headspaces and the way we are forming our current worldview.

Beat your internal algorithms, and start taking control of this area of your life today.

———

Jesus, thank You for the wisdom to discern and filter what I allow into my mind; ensuring that my faith remains in You and I am not distracted by things of this world. Amen

Love deeply

"Above all, love each other deeply, because love covers over a multitude of sins."
- 1 Peter 4:8

When it comes to learning to love, dating is one thing, marriage is a whole different ball game and by becoming a new parent, I took this one step further. To love is to risk, it's to put one's heart into the hands of another. It's to deeply trust and to demand nothing. It's to let go of selfishness and embrace sacrifice.

I have been on a number of mission trips into Africa and although I am often quick to say that my dream is to live with the poor in the poorest of places, my husband will quickly add "Caity, remember how much you cried the last time you were on a mission trip." I forget, you see, what it takes to love. Being amongst the poorest of poor, love teaches us what it means to give without wanting anything in return. Love truly is a sacrifice, it's real and it's raw.

Like many of us, there are things you may miss out on in life because you are too scared to try, to risk, and to embrace uncertainty. Don't allow love to be one of these things.

Jesus, You are the author of Love, teach me to love and to accept love. Amen

Impact through intention

"Do not dwell on the past. See, I am doing a new thing! Now it springs up; do you not perceive it? I am making a way in the wilderness and streams in the wasteland."
- Isaiah 43:18-19

The way that we impact others is often what we are most remembered for. Nelson Mandela is a beautiful example of what it means to live a life with integrity and deep conviction, and in turn impact lives for generations to come. How often do we hear people confess that when they are older they will re-look at the options, for exploring their purpose or the right career for them? Or it may not be others you're hearing; perhaps in this season of your life, this may feel even closer to home.

The impact that we have on the world, or our world, is not bound by a career, or lack thereof. It is not created in a day or an hour or at the so-called time in our lives when we feel "it would now make sense to stop messing around and make something of my life". Impact is achieved over a time period, of a life lived with intention!

You don't need to be famous to make a mark on the life of another; all it takes is a life lived with intention as God fills and refills your cup.

———

Lord, thank You that I get to make a mark on society, on people's lives, only as I bring my cup back to You to constantly be refilled so that I am refueled. Amen

Genuine faith

"I am reminded of your sincere faith...
For this reason I remind you to fan into
flame the gift of God, which is in you."
- 2 Timothy 1:5-6

There is genuine faith within you, a sincerity that goes beyond your actions and can only be defined by the state of your heart.

God finds joy in a sincere heart. Do not fear rejection from this world, or on the contrary search for acceptance in this world by your good deeds. God sees your heart and He knows your motives. God has placed remarkable gifts within you; the greatest of those being love, and He encourages us to fan those into flame. To fan into flame is to actively seek God out everyday so that our faith would be ignited, just as one would intentionally fan a flame in order for it to ignite or reignite. We have the power to ignite our faith and bring God glory as we live out who He created us to be.

We are called to do something with the love placed within us. Remember you have not been given a spirit of fear. Your God knows you and loves you deeply. Pursue sincerity.

Jesus, stir up a desire in me to actively pursue You and to fan into flame my faith, and thus giftings. Amen

What is God saying?

"My sheep listen to my voice; I know them, and they follow me."
- John 10:27

Are you feeling pulled in a million directions? What is God saying to you on this matter?

I remember as I teenager being taught what it meant to hear God's voice. The analogy that I was taught was this. Perhaps like me, in your childhood you phoned a friend on their home phone and as they answered, you said "Please can I speak to Jenny". Only for Jenny to giggle and say "It is me, Silly". But on the next phone call, or in the calls to come, you stopped making this mistake as you began to recognize her voice. So too is our recognition of the voice of God. It takes practice to discern what is or what isn't from God. We need to bring every thought, idea, decision, relationship or commitment, before God and ask Him to speak into this area of our lives. As we do this, we will become more familiar with God's promptings.

Remember that the more time you spend in God's presence, the more familiar you'll get with hearing His voice.

Jesus, I am your sheep and I do hear Your voice. Give me discernment to know when it is that You are speaking to me, and the courage to act on what You say. Amen

Always be kind

> "You must each decide in your heart how much to give. And don't give reluctantly or in response to pressure. 'For God loves a person who gives cheerfully.' "
> - 2 Corinthians 9:7

We have this little saying in our home; when I say, "Always", my daughter replies, "be kind". It's an encouragement to her to live her life from a place of love and it reminds us too to do the same. As children of God, compassion is within us all. Some of us feel moved to care for those who are in poverty, others for the elderly, others for animals in need, and others for those with special needs. We all have a compassion pocket within our hearts, made to full a need within this world, to be God's hands and feet here on earth – to love.

For many of us though, life may have damaged us and caused us to block out this part of our hearts. Protecting ourselves, I suppose, from the emotion that our compassion stirs up within us. But God is powerful to heal our wounds and He is powerful to use us in impacting others live, by His strength, not our own.

In what way were you created to offer compassion within your community? My encouragement to you today, is to find your thing, and then ask God to open your eyes to the opportunities before you.

Jesus, You know my heart and where my compassion falls. Help me to find opportunities to serve. Amen

15th November

On Jesus's team

"As the soldiers led Him away, they seized Simon from Cyrene, who was on his way in from the country, and put the cross on him and made him carry it behind Jesus."
- Luke 23:26

The scripture for today is awfully profound.

Whilst it appears in scripture that Simon was seized in order to help Jesus, the fact remains that in Jesus' greatest moments of suffering, even as the Son of God, He needed help. Jesus wants us to be part of His team, His mission. As they carried the cross together, Simon walked behind Jesus and this is a beautiful reminder for us. Even when we cannot escape hardship, or feel heavy-laden, Jesus walks ahead of us, always leading the way and willing to carry our burdens too.

Be encouraged this month to take your burdens before God. In a season that can bring with it exhaustion, let us be filled with hope in the one who has endured and overcome and chooses us to be part of His team in doing just the same.

Father, thank You that together we make a formidable team. Help me to turn to You in both my victories and suffering, as I continue on the path You've set before me. Amen

16th November

Give in secret

"But when you give to the needy, do not let your left hand know what your right hand is doing so that your giving may be in secret. Then your Father who sees what is done in secret, will reward you."
- Matthew 6:2-4

Of all the scriptures on giving, it is today's scripture that challenges me on the deepest level. God has placed in us a compassion for the world, a compassion for the lost and a compassion for the poor. God finds pleasure in our giving, but He too warns us of our reasoning behind giving.

In today's scripture we understand that if we give to receive glory from people, then our greatest reward for our kindness will be the approval of others. This reward is fleeting and pales in comparison to the approval of God. When we give in secret, or with the intention of pleasing God, not man, it is then that we truly honour God in our giving, and He promises to reward us.

Be encouraged today to continue to pour love into the world, as God pours love into your heart; but do so for the approval of God alone.

Father, You know my heart better than anyone. Help me to remain humble and to give in secret, that I may bring You glory and not crave it from man. Amen

Adventure of compassion

"The Spirit of the Sovereign Lord is on me, because the Lord has anointed me to proclaim good news to the poor. He has sent me to proclaim freedom for the prisoners and recovery of sight for the blind, to set the oppressed free, to proclaim the year of the Lord's favour."
- Isaiah 61:1-2

Walking with God is a sure adventure.

God longs to take us on an adventure of compassion too, one that is definitely embedded in our nature. I know this because in Genesis 1:27 it says "God created mankind in His image". Thus compassion, as Jesus modeled, lives in each of us. Today's scripture is the very one that Jesus refers to when He began His ministry. (Luke 4: 16 – 21). There is a call on each of our lives, as there was on the life of Jesus, to live with compassion. Compassionate people are concerned people. They serve others with humility, they are thoughtful and they are outwardly focused. As we remain connected to God and He fills our love tanks up, we can live lives of compassion without feeling heavy burdened by the yokes that others carry.

Bring your life before Jesus today and ask Him to stir up fresh compassion within you and direct your outpouring of this compassion.

Jesus, I bring my life and heart before You today. Show me ways in which I can model compassion to this world, as I live by the grace You give me. Amen

God's plan is at work

"And what does the Lord require of you? To act justly and to love mercy and to walk humbly with your God."
- Micah 6:8

Life can sometimes feel as if we're on this mission set from God. It can feel as if God is mission control, and we're His team on earth. This is true in part, but we need to remember that we are not doing something for God, but rather with God.

God has not put us on earth to do His work for Him, but to rather partner with Him as He does His work on earth. God's plan is already being rolled out; it has been for generations before us and will for generations to come. As we allow the Holy Spirit to guide us, we are better equipped to see what God is already doing and in turn can live bigger, more impactful lives.

Let us be encouraged today to live big lives, as we join what God is already doing here on earth.

Jesus, thank You that I am not alone, I do not work for my glory but instead I work with You, on what is close to Your heart. Amen

Longing after God

"As the deer pants for streams of water, so my soul pants for You, my God."
- Psalm 42:1

When you close your eyes, searching for peace, where do you go? When I crave peace or sleep, my mind drifts to a beach walk. I imagine walking with Jesus along a lengthy coastline. I visualize white sand squeaking under my bare feet, heat on my back from the summer sun, the smell of salt filling my lungs and the wind lightly touching the water's surface but not strong enough to blow up sand to sting my legs.

It is important to know where we personally find solace when we need to be refilled. In knowing this we empower ourselves to retreat either in our minds eye or physically, before we try to pour out of an empty cup.

If you need refilling or refueling today, ask God to awaken in you a safe place where you can retreat to, in your mind or physically, for Him to reach you.

Jesus, fill me up afresh today that I may stop trying to pour out love from an empty cup. Amen

Grace undeserved

> "We are made right with God by placing our faith in Jesus Christ. And this is true for everyone who believes, no matter who we are."
> - Romans 3:22

I love watching my kids' faith in Jesus grow, but too find their versions of grace before meals hysterical. They cover everything from family members to food, to chatting to us mid-prayer or having a bite of their meal and then back to God again.

Grace is one of the most beautiful words I know of in the English dictionary. Grace is simply 'receiving something undeserved'. To say grace is to utter our dependence on something external to ourselves. Grace, in worldly terms, is the exact opposite of karma. Where karma suggests that we are given what is due to us, grace suggests that we are given far more than we ever deserve. How truly beautiful is this notion? This is the God we serve, a God who loves us not because of what we've done but because of His loving nature.

Find comfort in the concept of grace today. It is yours and given freely.

Father God, thank You for a love undeserving that is the foundation of my life. Amen

21st November

Water from the sanctuary

"Fruit trees of all kinds will grow on both banks of the river. Their leaves will not wither, nor will their fruit fail. Every month they will bear fruit, because the water from the sanctuary flows to them. Their fruit will serve for food and their leaves for healing."
- Ezekiel 47:12

Today's scripture brings to mind a geography lesson in my Primary School years where we learnt of the great Nile River. I remember learning how this sizable river flowed through Egypt and provided irrigation for the crops in Ancient Egypt.

This picture of an expansive river, with banks of fruit trees, brings me joy. Where there is life and growth, there is water. Jesus is our source of life, He is the expansive river and we are the banks. As long as we remain rooted in Him, we will bear fruit, and it will impact the lives of those around us.

The question is, is He the water feeding our growth or are we looking elsewhere? As long as we search the world for meaning, we will only to be disappointed by the poor harvest or lack thereof.

Be encouraged today, Beautiful, Jesus longs to water the banks of your heart and produce lasting fresh fruit.

———————

Jesus, help me to remain connected to You so that I may bear fruit and that fruit will impact lives around me. Amen

Bird's-eye view

"Put your hope in the Lord.
Travel steadily along His path."
- *Psalm 37:34*

Have you ever watched birds fly above a shoal of fish? It's truly something magnificent to witness. The birds will circle the skies, high above the surface of water and then suddenly one by one, like rocket ships, shoot down breaking the surface of the ocean and come up with a fish in mouth. This perspective, high above the seas surface, guides their action and ensures their success.

It's incredible what perspective does for our goals or giving too. When we withdraw from the goal or even our busy lives, we regain perspective and in turn often return with a higher likelihood of success.

Do you need fresh perspective today? Ask God to inspire you with ways in which you can gain perspective for the goals, giving or situations you're facing at the moment.

Jesus, guide me in gaining perspective so that my giving and my goals are aligned with Your perspective. Amen

Lonely or alone

"And surely I am with you always,
to the very end of the age."
- Matthew 28:20

The worst type of loneliness is to not be content within oneself.

Have you ever experienced loneliness whilst physically surrounded by people, or been alone but not lonely? Loneliness is not the absence of people around us, but rather a feeling of sadness or isolation. To be alone is to physically not be surrounded by people. We can experience loneliness with people around us, or whilst alone. A beautiful lesson, or challenge, that we have in life, is to learn the art of contentment whilst alone. God wants us to be comfortable within ourselves, that we may find peace in retreating to be alone and not fear it. It is when alone, that God really has an opportunity to refill us, and when His voice is often most clear.

As God calls you to retreat, and find comfort in being alone; remember that you are never truly alone. God is always with you and your experience of loneliness can be fought with the truth of God's omnipresence.

Father, thank You that You are always with me. Help me to actively rebuke the feeling of loneliness and to find comfort in Your presence. Amen

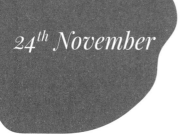

24th November

Less stress, more joy

"But let all who take refuge in You be glad; let them ever sing for joy. Spread Your protection over them, that those who love Your name may rejoice in You."
- Psalm 5:11

Have you ever wondered why we spend a year longing for our year-end break with the belief that then, and only then, can we do what we love? Yes holidays are for filling our tanks but imagine a life where we create time and opportunities in the now for more joy and less stress. It is possible to live with more joy in the now, and to feel less burdened by the end of each year, but it will take intention.

Use car-drives or bath times to brainstorm how you can enjoy more 'holiday habits' during the year, with the intention of adding more joy to your daily life and less stress. Perhaps it's more regular visits to the beach or saving for weekends away. Perhaps it's reading in the evenings instead of doing chores or being less hard on yourself. Perhaps it's pursuing a long lost hobby or starting up a new one.

The opportunity to reflect is within all of us, but it takes intention to process what is working and what isn't, before we make changes.

Jesus, help me to add more joy to my daily life that my energy remains more stable throughout the year. Amen

Slow down, Beautiful

"Do not run until your feet are
bare and your throat is dry."
- Jeremiah 2:25

Runs on the beach are one of my favourite pastimes. The Lord spoke to me once of a picture that I felt He wanted me to share with you today too. A woman was running on the beach and the faster she went, the closer her goal became but her weariness made it fuzzy and unclear. Then she tripped and landed on the beach sand. As she lifted her sand-soaked head, she laughed freely, as she saw for the first time, a beautiful clear picture of the future that lay ahead, waiting patiently for her.

I have found in my life that in my constant drive towards the future, I have often forgotten to breathe, to stop, to rest and to live. God calls us to slow down, to acknowledge the state of our hearts and to actively seek His face, just for today.

May our hearts resemble Jesus, as we slow down, and spend enough time being present with Him, to know Him and reflect Him.

_____

Jesus, teach me to slow down and to actively pursue You today. Amen

Noble character

"She sees that her trading is profitable, and her lamp does not go out at night... She opens her arms to the poor and extends her hands to the needy. When it snows, she has no fear for her household; for all of them are clothed in scarlet."
- *Proverbs 31:18-21*

The wife of noble character described in Proverbs 31 can be a little overwhelming to take in. Whilst many of us women, strive to juggle the many balls in our court, there are few of us who wouldn't be burnt out in the process of attaining all that the Proverbs 31 woman is supposed to manage.

The beauty of this passage though, is that perhaps it wasn't written about what a woman was to accomplish in a month or a day, but rather a lifetime. Over our lifespan as women, our responsibilities, dreams and actions change with each season of life. Perhaps later in life, we will reflect back and notice that we have displayed all of the characteristics of the Proverbs 31 woman, but rather than in a day, it will be in a lifetime.

What a relief. But a beautiful challenge too.

I urge you today to go and read the whole of Proverbs 31 and be encouraged by all that is said to make a woman noble. And then take pride in which noble characteristics you feel that you are displaying right now, in accordance with Proverbs 31.

Jesus, thank You that whilst I am called to many things, there is no urgency for me to run ahead of myself or You. Rather I am called to go about my life with humility, knowing that good character is built through a life spent with You. Amen

Faith changes us

"And have put on the new self, which
is being renewed in knowledge in the
image of its Creator."
- Colossians 3:10

To reach others requires action on our behalf. To reach is to put ourselves out there, to take action or move towards another. I have personally found that in the dryer seasons of my faith, my reach has been limited. As my faith has dwindled, so too has my impact, my kindness, my selflessness.

In society today we are often encouraged to turn our gaze inwards. This isn't all bad and in fact an idea that I support in the work that I do, but with our gaze only on ourselves, we may gain attention but rarely leave a lasting impact on others' lives. Today's scripture reminds us that faith itself changes us, it is less about our works and more about the power of God in us, that draws us to reach others.

Be encouraged today to build into your faith, and know that the result of this is a natural desire to reach out.

Father, draw me to Yourself that my faith might grow, and in turn my impact on others. Amen

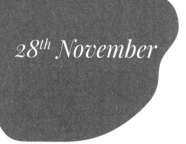

Ripples of kindness

"And God who generously provides all you need. Then you will always have everything you need and plenty left over to share with others."
- *2 Corinthians 9:8*

One of the great things about raising kids is how often their lives remind you of your own childhood memories. One of my son's favourite current pastimes is throwing stones into ponds. How powerful is the image of a still body of water suddenly broken by something as small as a stone? As the stone hits the water it creates ripples and what started at the spot of disruption suddenly becomes the new state of the entire pond.

Whilst the world and all its hurt may feel overwhelming and cause you to not know where or how to give; know that your kindness has the power to create ripples.

Where is God calling you to act in kindness? Be encouraged that no matter how big or small you feel that your next step of kindness is, it has potential to create ripples and change environments greatly.

Jesus, use my acts of kindness to grow Your Kingdom. Amen

Pour out & accept love

"As long as Moses held up his hands, the Israelites were winning, but whenever he lowered his hands, the Amalekites were winning. When Moses' hands grew tired... Aaron and Hur held his hands up - one on one side, one on the other - so that his hands remained steady till sunset. So Joshua overcame the Amalekite army with the sword."
- Exodus 17:11-13

When Moses could no longer stand strong, he called on his two closest friends to hold up his arms, and thus secured his victory.

I love this story and how God works. Little can be accomplished on our own. I have found great comfort in my life in leaning on those closest to me when I've needed them. Often this has been an old friend or family members but I love how God, too, brings specific people into our lives for certain seasons of our life. God, being out of time, has the perspective we often lack and knows exactly what we need before we even face our battles, or joys.

Let us find comfort today knowing that as we pour love into the world, we are allowed to ask for help, or support or love, ourselves too.

Jesus, thank You for the people in my life who hold me up when I need to conquer something that seems too big for me to do on my own. Amen

30th November

He is Love

"Each day the Lord pours His unfailing love upon me."
- Psalm 42:8

There is so much good in this world, despite the bad. There are so many people loving on others in beautiful, powerful ways. We show compassion, because God first showed us compassion. He is the source of all things kindness. He is the author of love. This may sound strange as love feels so natural, but that is only because we are made in the image of God.

It took me years of wrestling with Jesus on the concept of love before I began to understand it, be that still only in part. I always felt love should be earned or worked for, but each time I tried harder, I'd get caught in a pride cycle and then He'd humble me and remind me of my weakness. It is when we are weak, that He is strong. He is not strengthened by our weakness, but in our weakness we often allow His strength to become our own. That is the Jesus that we serve. The one who empowers us to love deeply, as we continue to return to Him to fill up our personal love tanks.

As you live out this final day of the month of November, know that you have the ability to love only because He first loved you.

Jesus, what a joy it is to know the author of love! Fill up my love tank as I turn to You, so that love can overflow from my life into the lives of others. Amen

DECEMBER

Reflections

"As water reflects the face,
so one's life reflects the heart."
- Proverbs 27:19

1ˢᵗ December

Reflections

"As water reflects the face, so one's life reflects the heart."
- Proverbs 27:19

One of my pet hates is a door, which isn't closed properly, and keeps banging every time the wind blows. I think this can be likened to many of our lives and the transition from one year to the next. In the mad rush at the end of the year, we often forget the importance of reflection. We go into the new year setting goals which in many ways resemble the past years goals and we forget to mark the progress we made the year prior. Much like closing the door behind you.

December, while being a month of celebration, friends, family and indulgence is also a time to reflect on a year passed. While there is so much joy, sometimes relief (and definitely benefit) in planning for the year to come; a powerful ending makes a new beginning even sweeter.

As you begin a simple reflection on your year, know that reflecting solidifies new learning, helps us face reality, allows us to let go and builds our trust in a faithful God.

———

Father, help me to find a space in my diary or head for reflection. Thank You for the year past and all that You have, and are, doing in me. Amen

2nd December

Your year & God

"Suppose one of you wants to build a tower. Won't you first sit down and estimate the cost to see if you have enough money to complete it?"
- Luke 14:28

Perhaps the past year was glorious, but perhaps not too. As you reflect on the year past, do not let your heart be troubled. Admitting where we're at, in life, relationships, your career, health, the works, may be a daunting task but it is also hugely empowering. Taking ownership of where we're at is the starting point of moving forward, and a great time to do just that is at the end of the year.

While the year may have held many successes, happiness, amazing insights and fond memories, there is likely to have been some ugly 'stuff' in amidst all that too. Ignoring negative experiences results in denial, and denial merely prolongs suffering. A simple acknowledgement of what took place and what we learnt about ourselves or life is a great way of closing doors, which could otherwise threaten to swing open every few months.

My encouragement to you is to bring your year before the Lord and find peace in the knowledge that He sees your life in totality. God will use everything for the good of those who love Him.

Jesus, I praise Your holy name. Thank You that You have been with me this year in the trials and You've been with me when I've stood on mountain tops. Amen

Your holiday plans

> "Come near to God and
> He will come near to you."
> - James 4:8

Whether you're jetting off to the Alps to ski or lying at home on your couch, nothing about your holiday plans determines your worth. You are loved and accepted and worthy just as you are.

Don't believe the lies that go on in your head, robbing you from walking in freedom just as you are. Whilst the world has a strong tendency to convince us that worldly pleasures, like wealth or appearance, make life far more pleasurable, this only ever lasts for a short while. Following this, we merely cling to the next best thing. Jesus is the only constant that provides lasting joy, peace beyond our understanding and hope, even when life doesn't make sense.

As you approach the holiday season, don't get caught up in the lies that the devil feeds, defining you on your plans. You are WORTHY. You are ENOUGH! Full stop.

————

Father, help me to find freedom in knowing my worth in You. Help me to not lower my standards and conform to the ways of this world whose promises only end in dissatisfaction. Amen

4ᵗʰ December

Forgiveness & ownership

"'Come now, let us settle the matter,' says the Lord. 'Though your sins are like scarlet, they shall be as white as snow; though they are red as crimson, they shall be like wool.'"
- Isaiah 1:18

As we reflect on this year may we practice forgiveness for both others, and ourselves just as Jesus modeled for us? It's so important to know your own story and to be proud of it. Each decision you've made this past year seemed right at the time. Forgive yourself now for those decisions that you made that, in retrospect, you would now do differently. Thank yourself for the decisions that you made this year, that benefit you today.

It's easier to blame your past then it is to grab your life with both hands and take ownership of it. I'm so sorry that life has happened to you, and it hasn't always been good. Life isn't always fair. But today you get to make a choice to not just embrace where you're at, but accept it too.

As you practice acceptance and forgiveness, it will not only give space to your 'lost in the past' mind, but will set you free to fly into what the future holds for you.

———————————

Father, You are the ultimate model of what forgiveness looks like. Help me to forgive myself for decisions that I've made that haven't served me, or honoured You. Amen

5th December

Rest in hope

"Therefore my heart is glad and my tongue rejoices; my body also will rest in hope."
- Acts 2:26

A healthy summer isn't about starving yourself or living on fruit alone. I've been there before and my mind was far from healthy. For me it's about putting more energy into doing what makes me come alive and less into indulging due to boredom or other uncomfortable emotions. It's about playing with my kids on the beach and choosing to turn my eyes away from body obsession or false standards of comparison that this world offers. It's about investing time into those I adore, having drinks together, laughter and consciously putting to bed the thoughts that linger after and challenge my status in the world. A healthy summer is about honouring God with my mind, body and spirit.

Health is so much more than pretending that cutting carbs or sugar was about a healthier you, when in fact it was an unhealthy mindset that triggered that. Been there, done that. No T-shirt worth showing.

Let us walk into summer this year, knowing our identity in Christ, and putting to bed thoughts that rob from who we are or how loved we are.

Father, refresh me with Your truth. You are the living God and I am Your daughter – there is no greater role that I get to play on this earth than that. Amen

6th December

Traditions & bonding

I grew up in a home where tradition was everything and I've since been very intentional with passing this (and lots of new ones) on to our kids. One such tradition is that we source and then set up a real Christmas tree at home late November. This tradition was birthed in my childhood when, yearly, my brothers and I piled into my mums VW-combi and drove along back roads until we found a Christmas tree to cut down and bring home. My mum would do the sawing and we'd watch in awe.

We've since extended this tradition and whilst we now buy our tree, we then decorate the tree while Christmas carols play in the background. Followed by making a Christmas bed (basically our big king sized mattress) in the lounge and all four of us sleep there that night, watching the tree lights and usually a Christmas-inspired movie.

Do you have any Christmas traditions? It's never too late to add traditions to your festive season. Traditions often bond us with those we share the festive season with and Jesus loves to see joy found in relationships.

Father, inspire me with ideas of how we can add a bit of fun and bonding time to our festive season this year. Amen

7ᵗʰ December

The countdown

"And we all, who with unveiled faces contemplate the Lord's glory, are being transformed into His image with ever-increasing glory, which comes from the Lord, who is the Spirit."
- 2 Corinthians 3:18

Christmas is fast approaching and that means that we're 25 sleeps until the New Year! Are you one who lives by the saying 'New Year New Me'? I used to conform to this idea, in fact I loved the hope that it held; but I've since seen too many new years to know that this notion merely sets us up to fail.

Jesus remains the same person although His ministry progresses with time. I love this clue of how our lives too can be lived. The world around us will change, our lives and responsibilities will change, but as we remain rooted in Christ, we stay the same apart from being changed into His likeness. Our goal becomes less about believing that the next best thing will answer our hearts longing, and more about dwelling in Christ every day, and continuing along the path we're already walking.

Let the countdown to the New Year begin. Not in pursuit of happiness or magical change but rather a continuation of the beautiful walk of faith, you're already on.

———————

Father, help me to live today with intention, knowing that each day spent with You, is another day being changed into Your likeness. The greatest goal I can have on earth. Amen

8ᵗʰ December

Hope renewed

"Yes, my soul, finds rest in God; my hope comes from Him. Truly He is my rock and my salvation; He is my fortress, I will not be shaken."
- Psalm 62:8

I'm all about living with intention, having goals and routines that serve us, and our faith too. But I too know that rigidity can limit our grasp on the enormity of God.

Past hurts, or a year we'd rather forget, can cause our hearts to become hardened and in-turn our perspective or hope for the future, diminished. But as we bring our hurts and disappointments before God, He is powerful to turn these adversities into victories. And as He does so, He too gives us a new hope and the ability to look beyond a past that may or may not have worked out, as we'd wanted.

Place your hope for the future back in Jesus today. He is all-powerful, and will turn your sorrow into dancing.

Jesus, thank You that You only want the best for me. Help me to trust You with my future and to not allow my heart to harden. Amen

Happiest when...

"Unfailing love and truth walk before You as attendants. Happy are those who hear the joyful call to worship, they will walk in the light of Your presence, Lord."
- Psalm 89:14-15

Fill in the blank. I am happiest when _____.
As much as I know that God is my only hope and constant joy; my happiness journey and figuring out what God designed for me to love about life, has been one I've immensely enjoyed. I love the idea of looking in with the intent of finding that which, uniquely, brings joy to my soul.

As you live out this final month of the year I encourage you to not get caught up in the pull to pretend to enjoy what others enjoy. Perhaps you love the ocean, or perhaps you're more of a mountains girl. Perhaps you love running, or perhaps it's dancing or piano playing. Perhaps you're happiest when at home on your own, or perhaps you come alive when in crowds. It's a great gift to know that God created us uniquely and thus that He finds pleasure in us getting to know ourselves well, and living from a space of self-awareness and peace.

Live your life like you meant to wake up today for this very day.

———

Jesus, thank You that despite my faith being the foundation of my life, I too am allowed to celebrate my uniqueness and find comfort living within a space that makes me happy. Amen

Beauty within

"God saw all that He had made, and it was very good."
- *Genesis 1:31*

Whales are magnificent creatures. Their enormity humbles me deeply. In certain parts of the world, if you make your way to the ocean and you time the seasons correctly, your chances of seeing a migrating whale are high.

I love this as it rings so true for life too. The potential for discovering beauty in the world, and within ourselves, is out there, but often we miss out merely because our timing was off or we failed to actively seek it out. God calls us to submit to His timing and not our own. This can at times mean that we may be on the right path but be running ahead of God, or on the contrary, be behind God due to fear. We too are called to live by faith, which means actively walking a road with Jesus. It is not in our luke-warmed-state that we walk in abundance but rather as we actively pursue our living God, that we come alive.

Be encouraged today to pursue God actively and to ask for His direction and timing, as you journey in faith and life.

Father, thank You for the beauty in and around me. Help me to walk beside You as You lead me on the beautiful journey of life. Amen

11th December

Grace over works

"And if by grace, then it cannot be based on works; if it were, grace would no longer be grace."
- Romans 11:6

As long as we're disconnected or running from ourselves, we partake in a life of performance. Every day feels like a show as we take on the role that we think we're meant to be playing, for today.

I know I lived this way for a long time, but by God's grace I was humbled to a point where I was forced to sit and face my discomfort. It is often our own headspaces that we fear the most. We fear what will surface if we quiet ourselves enough to listen. But be encouraged today my friend, the quiet is less scary than your mind has made it out to be. You may cry a little, or shout, or perhaps even throw something but after that will come a rest. And that rest will not be easily stolen again.

Remember that you are made in the image of God. Feel supported to face your reality and rest assured that God will meet you there with a peace that the world cannot give.

Father, by Your grace I am healed. Come and heal my mind today and help me to find rest in You again. Amen

12th December

Inner strength

> "May our Lord Jesus Christ Himself and God our Father, who loved us and by His grace gave us eternal encouragement and good hope, encourage your hearts and strengthen you in every good deed and word."
> - 2 Thessalonians 2:16-17

The feeling you get on summiting a mountain can be something quite surreal. I had the privilege of climbing Mount Kilimanjaro a number of years back and for a few reasons the summit climb for Kili is done at night. It remains one of the toughest nights of my life. I'm grateful that we did the climb at night though. With the steepness of the final summit, the unbearable effects of altitude and the pure exhaustion, if we did this climb during the light of day we may not have been mentally strong enough to accept the challenge that lay ahead of us. We were almost better equipped to conquer that great summit, not knowing what lay ahead of us than we would have if we did know.

Life is like this too. It's often only at the end of a year or grueling season of life that we revel in how far we've come and how resilient we in fact are.

As you reflect on this year be reminded of what you've overcome and of the strength you've found within when life required this of you.

———

Father, thank You for the gift of life and that with my eyes set on You, I can conquer anything that lies ahead of me. Amen

13th December

He intercedes

"Therefore He is able to save completely those who come to God through Him, because He lives to intercede for them."
- Hebrews 7:25

My Gogo is one of my greatest examples of a woman who lives by faith and to serve God alone. I have no doubt that her faith-filled prayers have drawn many of us back to God, in seasons of life when we were far from Him. The power of prayer is beyond our comprehension. But a further Biblical idea that I love, is knowing that Jesus Himself is interceding for us.

Jesus prays for you. That sounds crazy, I know, but it's true. As we give our lives to Jesus, He intercedes for us. He fights spiritual battles we cannot see on our behalf, especially when we feel too weak to face them ourselves. What a joy, and oh, what a privilege it is to be called a daughter of God.

Wherever you're at today, know that your prayers are powerful and are heard by God; and too that if you're too tired to pray or call out His name, He is interceding for you.

Jesus, thank You for your faithfulness in covering my soul and my spirit in both love, prayer and protection. Amen

Finish the race

"I have fought the good fight, I have finished the race, I have kept the faith."
- 2 Timothy 4:7

The smell of the ocean as I open my car door, crashing waves on giant rocks and the squawk of seagulls. It is on arriving at our beach cottage that I usually feel as if my 'work year' has ended. Do you have a place or a ritual that marks the end of your work year? I love that God, being outside of time, is not limited by the calendars that guide our plans and lives. God's purpose for us on earth runs from the moment of our birth until the day that we die; but He is still interested in our everyday lives.

For me personally I love the concept that Timothy refers to of 'fighting the good fight'. There are many battles that we can fight in our lifetime; battles for wealth, battles of self-esteem, battles in relationships but also battles to build God's Kingdom and bring Him glory. How has your year unfolded? Which battles found first place in your heart this year?

Be encouraged today to take your year before God and accept His love and grace afresh.

Father, thank You that I am called to the greatest battle of all, to establish Your Kingdom on earth. Help me to fix my eyes on You. Amen

A fresh vision

"In their hearts humans plan their course, but the Lord establishes their steps."
- Proverbs 16:9

A coaching client came to see me as she was seeking help and inspiration to create a life she loved, again. I say 'again', because she often spoke of how a few years back, she had been so happy, and longed to get back there. We chatted about what made her happy back then, and she was quick to try to recreate that now. But then it dawned on her that this was a different stage of life. Whilst she could rely on past experience to inspire her towards happiness, she needed to, MUST, create a new vision for this stage of life.

Realistically we need to approach God with humility, and assess what our best, in this stage of life, looks like and to run after that. You cannot have it all. And plus why should you? Or need to. Each stage of life requires something different from us and it's important that we keep our life goal as pleasing God and living a life that honours Him. By accepting our current reality, it is easier to shift our lifestyle to match our life stage rather than longing after something that falls in our past.

I encourage you not to make your life about living up to societal goals, that were never yours in the first place. Define your best life at this stage of your life, by asking for God's insight, and live it well.

———

Father, You have a plan for my life – direct my path and help me to walk with wisdom in the season that I am in. Amen

There's calm ahead

"God has told His people, 'This is a place of rest, let the weary rest here. This is a place of quiet rest.'"
- Isaiah 28:12

From a young age I was encouraged to swim out to backline, beyond the waves, with my dad. It was rarely an easy task. I'd swim as hard as I could and then grab my dad's hand as each big wave approached, and he'd pull me out on the other side. We'd do this again and again until we found our break and then we'd put our heads down, swim like mad and suddenly look up and know we'd made it. We were past the break. The sea was as calm as a lake out there and the horizon within sight.

In time I learnt to do this on my own and to read the sea, but even as an adult, the swim out to backline can be exhausting. I do it, though, with purpose, as I've experienced the joy and calm on the other side of the big surf. As you face whatever it is that's going on in your life at the moment, perhaps a rough past year, an uncomfortable personal experience or apprehension as you head into summer holidays and extended family time, know that there is calm on the other side. Trust your prior experience of coming out of rough seas, stronger.

God is with you. Take heed.

Father, help me to call on past experiences where You've brought me out of rough waters and into calm seas. Amen

The year past

"'I - yes, I alone, will blot out your sins for my own sake and will never think of them again. Let us review the situation together.'"
- Isaiah 43:25-26

Reflecting on the year past is a powerful activity.

For today, I felt it might be helpful to provide a few questions that I love working through every year. Grab a journal, a cup of tea and let's reflect together.

~ If you could sum up your year in one word what would it be?
~ What did you learn about yourself this year that you perhaps didn't know before?
~ What did you learn about God this year?
~ What was your absolute highlight of the year?
~ What are you happy to leave behind this year?
~ What has been the most meaningful learning from this year that you will take with you into the New Year?

I encourage you to approach this process of reflection with self-compassion and grace.

Father, guide me as I reflect on the year past. Help me to celebrate the victories and grow from the moments of learning. Amen

18th December

Are we there yet?

> "Submit to God and be at peace with Him; in this way prosperity will come to you. Accept instruction from His mouth and lay up His words in your heart."
> - Job 22:21-22

Are we there yet?

The dreaded words uttered by my toddler for the 15th time in our hour-long trip. How often do we as adults live this way too? We crave the end of the year or a specific goal, believing that following it will come ease, only to find it doesn't. The grass is rarely greener. I've spoken to many clients who admit that they believed they'd be a different person on emigrating or moving towns or changing jobs, only to find out that they couldn't escape themselves. We take ourselves with us wherever we go.

And thus peace within truly is a gift. It frees us from feeling the need to run away, from life, things, people or ourselves. Jesus is our only answer to true inner peace, to hope beyond understanding, and you have access to that today.

Find joy in knowing that you have been gifted peace. Inner peace is yours; you merely need to take hold of thoughts that threaten it and reclaim all that Jesus has done for you to walk in perfect peace.

———

Jesus, remind me today that peace is mine. I don't need to work for it or earn it. You have given this freely. Amen

19th December

Count your blessings

"Praise the Lord, my soul, and forget not all His benefits"
- *Psalm 103:2*

I'll never forget heading out for a run in my early twenties and saying to a friend how desperately I needed to clear my head. Knowing my planned running route, she replied with "on your way out name everything you're grateful for and on your way back name everything you're excited for." I thought this silly at the time; mostly due to the cloud I was living under that was blocking my view of what was good in my life.

But I've since found huge benefit in the practice of thanksgiving and positivity. It is less about lying to oneself and more about reinforcing the goodness in our lives. As we do this we teach our brains to rebuke the natural pull towards an 'always-needing-more-mentality' and we learn to embrace our present, our right now. We learn to find joy in the smaller things, in day-to-day living.

Jesus wants to meet you where you're at today. He's not waiting for your one day when you're ready. He is available and requires nothing of you, but a willing heart.

Jesus, I find it hard sometimes to let go of the pull towards trying to impress You. Help me to know that You do meet me where I'm at and that I have so much to be grateful for, right now. Amen

The three B's

"Therefore with minds that are alert and fully sober, set your hope on the grace to be brought to you."
- 1 Peter 1:13

A friend tells a funny story of his grandmother always saying that fruit, fish, friends and family go off after 4 days. I find this rather amusing, and there is truth in this statement. Whilst we may be excited for the prospect of extended family time at this time of year, it may also produce serious anxiety in some of us.

As I head into the festive season, I aim to apply what I call 'The Three B's':

~ *Boundaries* - Healthy boundaries can really help to constructively manage one's emotions and self and thus feeling less pressure to control situations.

~ *Breaks* - Taking breaks is essential when in the company of anyone for an extended period of time, yes, even family that we love.

~ *Be true to you* - When in the company of family that we grew up with, or the home we grew up in, we often become child-like and take on habits that served us then, but may not now. Be aware of these old habits creeping in and potentially stealing from who you are now.

All of these are easier done when thought through prior to the get together, so be intentional with the days leading up to family holidays or time together.

Be encouraged to look after yourself and in-turn be better equipped to honour God with your mind, body and actions, when in the company of others.

———————————

Father, help me to take the time to prepare myself prior to this festive season, that I may be equipped to honour You with my thoughts, feelings and actions. Amen

21st *December*

Chaos & joy

"The Spirit helps us in our weakness. We do not know what we ought to pray for, but the Spirit Himself intercedes for us."
- Romans 8:26

There was a Christmas Eve in my childhood, which stands out in my memories more than most. My cousins and I had decorated the table all afternoon as the mums prepared the Christmas meal and dads played cricket outside. That evening which started with carols, drinks and smart outfits, ended in the Christmas table catching alight and 80 year old Aunty May screaming at the top of her lungs as we all rallied around trying to stop the fire.

Amidst joys there can also be chaos. Neither has to exist within, or around, us without the other extreme. There are no musts or rights or wrongs. Each of us has been given a different family, a different set of traditions handed down to us and a different dynamic in our home. Don't allow the devil to play games with your headspace and plant seeds that make you doubt the beauty of your situation.

You have the ability right now to embrace your chaos, and your joy. You can bring both before the Lord and experience true happiness while the next minute balling your eyes out. He gets both extremes. He is there with you in it all.

Father, help me to keep perspective and to not compare my reality to that of others over these next few weeks.

"But He gives us more grace."
- James 4:6

My kids have a block puzzle that I suppose is much like a Rubik's cube. There are 9 pieces and if put together correctly, 9 animals, one on each side. The purpose is obviously to turn each piece until you have the correct animal together. It's possible to have 8 pieces right but if just 1 piece resembles the wrong animal, the picture looks hysterical and totally incorrect. My kids are still young and so they're prone to wanting to give up at this point, but are slowly realizing that whilst the puzzle still doesn't look complete, with only one piece to go, they're really close to completion and a goal reached.

This can so easily be compared to life. How often do we throw in the towel just minutes before achieving our goals, or for life to align as we'd always wished it would?

Be encouraged today that God continues to give us more grace, even when our grace stash feels low and we're simply 'over it'. He may still be at work.

_____

Father, help me to accept Your grace anew every morning, so that I'd have the courage and strength to not give up on dreams, goals or relationships that You are perhaps working on, with me. Amen

23rd December

Father of compassion

"Praise be to the God and Father of our Lord Jesus Christ, the Father of compassion and the God of all comfort."
- 2 Corinthians 1:3

Whilst the festive season is indeed festive for many, it is not for all.

During every celebration, there are those who are not celebrating. There are those who are mourning, those who are alone, those who have lost hope and those who are suffering.

Wherever you find yourself today, know that Jesus is there with you. Jesus knows the depths of loneliness and the hardness of sorrow. He knows the feelings brought on by mourning and the effects of personal suffering. He was fully human and He longs to offer comfort, not judgment, for whatever it is you're experiencing today.

Today let's take a moment to either pray for those who don't find this season of the year an easy one. Or if this is a tough season for you, find comfort in your Saviour's embrace.

Jesus, thank You for a love so deep it knows no end, and for Your comfort that provides me with peace for whatever this day holds. Amen

Intentions of Jesus

"But after he had considered this, an angel of the Lord appeared to him in a dream and said, 'Joseph son of David, do not be afraid to take Mary home as your wife, because what is conceived in her is from the Holy Spirit. She will give birth to a son, and you are to give Him the name Jesus, because He will save His people from their sins.'"
- Matthew 1:20-21

It's the day before Christmas and the excitement is building by the second in our home, and yours too I'm sure. While we excitedly put out cookies and milk for Santa and get merry, let us remember today the joy that we are preparing to celebrate. The birth of a King. Our King.

I love how intentional God was about the birth of Jesus. It was less about glamour or the detail of how's and where's and more about significance and purpose. How powerful is that really? To focus on the purpose of a birth over the how or the where. Jesus's birth was predestined, planned long before it happened, and the Star of David led many to the sight of His birth. You were on God's mind too, that day. He brought His Son into this world for your sake. For my sake.

Let's remember the significance of the build up to Christmas, as we enjoy the celebrations that full our homes or hearts.

Jesus, You were and are our gift. Thank You for being born a man, that I may know You and have access to You. Amen

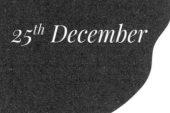

25th December

A Savior is born

"Today in the town of David a Saviour has been born to you; He is the Messiah, the Lord…You will find a baby wrapped in cloths and lying in a manger. Suddenly a great company of the heavenly host appeared with the angel, praising God and saying, 'Glory to God in the highest heaven, and on earth peace to those on whom His favour rests.'"
- Luke 2:11-14

Christmas is for tight squeezes, Christmas carols, brightly wrapped prezzies and feasts but it is also a beautiful birthday celebration. Today we celebrate the birth of our King.

A King who came to this world, not as one would have expected, but rather as a humble, down-to-earth man who befriended ordinary people, and loved even those who society rejected. Knowing the political state of many countries around the world, it is hard to imagine a ruler who meets their people truly on their level, not claiming any supremacy or recognition. What a King we serve. Today may we remember that it is the birth of Jesus that began the process of our redemption and our restoration.

Merry Christmas! Amidst the festivities, take a moment today to recognize the significance of this day in your faith walk and the magnificent Father that you get to call Dad.

Father, You are forever faithful. Thank You for the gift of Your Son. Amen

26th December

Thanksgiving

"Because of His righteousness;
I will sing the praises of the
name of the Lord most high."
- *Psalm 7:17*

It's the day after Christmas, a day on which many begin self-criticizing for overindulging.

My little's woke on this day last year, delighted that it was the day after Christmas and that we could reminisce about yesterday; the fun, the family, the food and the gifts. There was no mention of eating too much, family quarrels or disappointments due to comparison, or summer body pressures. There was only gratitude. They are my truest example of life to the full - they soak up every moment of family fun, memories being made, and engage in thanksgiving with no self-doubt.

What a beautiful gift we can each give ourselves today, to walk through the final days of this year with the gift of self-acceptance and thanksgiving.

Father, thank You that I have so much to be grateful for, despite it being different to others. Help me to live with self-acceptance and in thanksgiving. Amen

27th December

A word for the New Year

"There is surely a future hope for you, and your hope will not be cut off."
- Proverbs 23:18

A few years ago I came across the concept of choosing a word for the year that lay ahead.

This activity has become a comfort that I enjoy at the end of every year as it provides me with purpose behind my prayers for the year ahead. I ask God to give me a word, or a phrase, that I can take into the New Year. I've had a year of 'hope', a year of 'expectancy', a year of 'slow', a year of 'restoration' and a year when I simply couldn't come up with anything at all, only for the year to unfold as 'unexpected'. It's a fun, inspiring way to approach the New Year, and to bring the year that lies ahead, before God, before it even begins to unfold.

If this idea appeals to you, I encourage you to pray into it and decide on a word, phrase or even picture that most resonates with you for the year ahead.

Father, I bring the year ahead before You now. Thank You that I can walk in boldness knowing that You have gone before me. Amen

Celebrate the good

"'Leave her alone,' said Jesus. 'Why are you bothering her? She has done a beautiful thing.'"
- Mark 14:6

How often do we trip over our pasts?

A past thought, a past action, a past feeling – the past is rarely left where it belongs. Many of us will spend the last few days of the year thinking back over what we could have done differently to feel something different right now.

But I encourage you to stop that thought in its tracks.

There is so much about this past year that you have done well. Celebrate those victories. Jesus does! Whatever it is that keeps coming to mind bring it before God. Ask for His forgiveness or to teach you a lesson through your past, but be intentional to end your year on a happy, positive note. God has gone before you, and will guide your path from here.

Let us not continue to trip over something behind us. Let us move forward with confidence and hope in Jesus.

———

Father, help me to live in the present with You, not lost in my headspace in the past. Amen

29th December

Scenic destinations

"However, I consider my life worth nothing to me; my only aim is to finish the race and complete the task the Lord Jesus has given me - the task of testifying to the good news of God's grace."
- Acts 20:24

Challenging paths often lead to scenic destinations. As this year comes to an end, may we be reminded of the many biblical characters that forfeited their rights or an easier life, to follow Jesus.

Distractions are many at this time of the year. But it is in these busier times, that we have the opportunity to set the standards by which we'll live in the New Year, when again we're faced with busyness. To follow Jesus is to distance ourselves from the distractions that we face every day, and to choose to engage with Him, and build our faith. Much like getting fit, or starting a new hobby, it is the initial steps that are the hardest. Also, it is with building a stronger faith.

Today is the perfect opportunity for you to dig deeper in your faith. To ask God the harder questions and to begin habits that resonate with you and will serve your faith and future self.

Father, show me what I can begin today that will lead me on a path that my future self will thank me for. Amen

New year. New you

Do you set New Year's Resolutions?

I always love this time of year. It is often marked with families getting together, lots of beach-time (in SA at least) and just time-out from the busyness of normal life. It's also the time of year when we start planning, wishing and dreaming for the year ahead.

New Years' resolutions used to be the go-to's at this time of year. We'd all ask our friends what they were giving up, starting or becoming in the New Year and for the most part, we'd all jump on board with some crazy huge aspirations to be someone-else next year. The thing with New Years' resolutions is that it's always 'next year'. Year after year we repeat this cycle, hoping that things (or we) will change.

God is however outside of time, and he sees our life on a far greater timeline.

Let's be encouraged to not get caught up in the pull towards unrealistic expectations of ourselves and our lives. May we rather trust God with our futures, and embrace a more sustainable level of hope and happiness.

———————

Jesus, show me glimpses of Your perspective of my life and help me to stop conforming to the ways of this world and to rather embrace each day with integrity and intention. Amen

31st December

Hype of 'fresh starts'

"Why, you do not even know what will happen tomorrow. What is your life? … Instead, you ought to say, 'If it is the Lord's will, we will live and do this or that.'"
- James 4:14-15

I'm a total sucker for the build up to the New Year.

Whilst New Year's eves have definitely got quieter as the years have progressed, I love the energy today, on the 31st. I love the buzz in the air, the desire and realness of the FRESH start that will come with the sunrise.

But is it really a fresh start? I have thought long and hard over this, the reality that as much as we long for a fresh start, we often wake exactly the way we were the day before. I'm not here to destroy the excitement around fresh starts; I love them too (gracious I do) but let's be wise as we approach this New Year. Let's end today with self-compassion, not writing off the year as wasted; and look forward with anticipation and expectancy.

Let's celebrate the year past, our learning's, sorrows and joys. Let's take stock of all that we have to be grateful for right now. And let's place our trust and hope in Jesus for the year ahead.

———

Father, I have so much to be grateful for. Please go ahead of me and give me fresh hope and peace for all that the year ahead will bring. Amen

Acknowledgements

Hendrik de Beer
Thank you for holding the fort and giving me the space and time to write this book. Thank you for the hours spent proof-reading, too. I am beyond grateful for you.

Sarah and Noah
You have brought new meaning to my life like nothing else has. You are both the most remarkable people I know and I love you more than life itself.

Sue Keal
Mom, thank you for being my head editor and for never judging or critiquing my writing style. Thank you for working on such tight deadlines and for your love, friendship and support always.

Dave Keal
Dad, thank you for always believing in me and showing me what hard work looks like.

Mark, Greg, Dyl & Becs
I love you all and appreciate your support.

Kelly Lubbee
Your quiet, humble self-assurance is an absolute gift in my life. You designed this book on the tightest of deadlines and yet never complained. Thank you for trusting Jesus with guiding this process and for offering me your time and expertise over the past few months.

Darylle Iris Ziady
You have a talent like few others. Thank you for my beautiful book cover. Your artwork is outstanding.

Nikki Ducasse
Thank you for the late nights that you have poured into editing this book, and also for the hours shared over tea discussing it. You have added such depth to my life.

Colleen Coppin
Thank you for editing with such precision.

Caitlin Barnes
Thank you for writing my foreword and for the years of friendship that we've shared.

Meg Faure
Meg, you've been an icon in my life ever since I became a mum, and getting to know you personally has been a true gift. Thank you for your vulnerability shared and willingness to write my foreword.

Mari-Louise Candiotes
Thank you for writing my foreword and for always being an inspiration in my life.

And most importantly Jesus, thank you for calling me out on the water again!